"Scaffolding is a key component of [...] the right balance between challeng[e ...] tricky. All too often, teachers misj[udge ...] leaving students floundering and fru[strated ...]

Thankfully, Ball and Fairlamb have written a comprehensive, accessible guide to adaptive teaching in action. Informed by research yet highly practical in nature, *The Scaffolding Effect* offers teachers an expert guide on how to match the highest of expectations with the most helpful temporary support."

Mark Roberts, Director of Research and English Teacher, Carrickfergus Grammar School

"*The Scaffolding Effect* is an exceptional and timely contribution, offering a comprehensive, research-backed exploration of scaffolding strategies. Many teachers struggle with how to teach to the top and scaffold adequately and the clear explanations and practical case studies in this book demystify the complex nuances of adaptive teaching, making it accessible for teachers at all levels. This book empowers teachers to better support student learning, guiding them to implement scaffolding strategies effectively. Its reflective questions at the end of each chapter encourage deeper thinking, making it an invaluable resource for professional development. *The Scaffolding Effect* stands as a blueprint for teachers to raise expectations, bridge learning gaps and foster independent learners. A must-read for educators committed to honing their craft and enhancing student success."

Haili Hughes, Principal Lecturer in Mentoring and Professional Development, University of Sunderland and Director of Education, Iris Connect

"Teachers across the country understand the importance of guiding or supporting practice, before asking pupils to complete tasks independently. What we have been missing is an in-depth understanding of exactly how we can do this – until now! In *The Scaffolding Effect* Rachel and Alex provide us with a hugely comprehensive review of how we can scaffold every aspect of our teaching. Packed full of examples, research and case studies this is crucial reading for new and expert teachers of all subjects and Key Stages."

Jade Pearce, Trust Head of Education

"*The Scaffolding Effect* book is rich in thought, meticulously conceived and oozes moments of 'damn right!' What stands out is the balance of research, explanation of the core principles and carefully explored classroom application. Personally, I found the case studies especially useful as they prompted me to reflect on how I could use and apply this in the classroom and a school more widely."

Stuart Tiffany, Primary School Teacher, Subject Leader, Author and Consultant, and Visiting Lecturer

THE SCAFFOLDING EFFECT

Scaffolding is the support teachers provide students so they can successfully progress from novice to expert and is a crucial part of teaching and classroom management. This exciting book explores the research behind scaffolding and adaptive teaching whilst also debunking the myths and misconceptions behind this approach.

Drawing on evidence from cognitive science, it brings together best practice of tried and tested methods of effective scaffolding across different settings and disciplines. Featuring practical classroom examples, research evidence, and case studies, the chapters cover:

- The link between cognitive science and effective scaffolding strategies
- Using scaffolding to support literacy and oracy
- Scaffolding in practical subjects
- Ways to scaffold homework
- How to modify scaffolding for different ages and settings
- Pitfalls to avoid when implementing scaffolding

Part of the Teacher CPD Academy series from InnerDrive, this is essential reading for all teachers and school leaders that want evidence-based strategies which focus on impact in the classroom in sustainable and meaningful ways.

Rachel Ball is Coaching Development Lead at Steplab, former Senior Leader in charge of Teaching and Learning and CPD and an SLE, based in the North West, England.

Alex Fairlamb is Senior Leader in charge of Teaching and Learning and CPD, based in the North East, England. She is a Chartered Teacher of History, a Specialist Leader in Education and an Evidence Lead in Education.

The Teacher CPD Academy
Series editors: Bradley Busch and Edward Watson

The Homework Conundrum
How to Stop the Dog From Eating Homework
Jovita M. Castelino

Do I Have Your Attention?
Understanding Memory Constraints and Maximizing Learning
Blake Harvard

Creativity in Schools
A Cognitive Science Approach
Claire Badger and Jonathan Firth

The Scaffolding Effect
Supporting All Students to Succeed
Rachel Ball and Alex Fairlamb

THE SCAFFOLDING EFFECT

Supporting All Students to Succeed

Rachel Ball and Alex Fairlamb

LONDON AND NEW YORK

Cover Image: Courtesy of InnerDrive

First published 2026
by Routledge
4 Park Square, Milton Park, Abingdon, Oxon OX14 4RN

and by Routledge
605 Third Avenue, New York, NY 10158

Routledge is an imprint of the Taylor & Francis Group, an informa business

© 2026 Rachel Ball and Alex Fairlamb

The right of Rachel Ball and Alex Fairlamb to be identified as authors of this work has been asserted in accordance with sections 77 and 78 of the Copyright, Designs and Patents Act 1988.

All rights reserved. No part of this book may be reprinted or reproduced or utilised in any form or by any electronic, mechanical, or other means, now known or hereafter invented, including photocopying and recording, or in any information storage or retrieval system, without permission in writing from the publishers.

Trademark notice: Product or corporate names may be trademarks or registered trademarks, and are used only for identification and explanation without intent to infringe.

British Library Cataloguing-in-Publication Data
A catalogue record for this book is available from the British Library

Library of Congress Cataloging-in-Publication Data
Names: Ball, Rachel (Coaching development lead), author. | Fairlamb, Alex, author.
Title: The scaffolding effect : helping all students reach their potential / Rachel Ball and Alex Fairlamb.
Description: Abingdon, Oxon ; New York, NY : Routledge, 2025. | Series: The teacher CPD academy | Includes bibliographical references and index.
Identifiers: LCCN 2024057831 (print) | LCCN 2024057832 (ebook) | ISBN 9781032739861 (hardback) | ISBN 9781032739830 (paperback) | ISBN 9781003467069 (ebook)
Subjects: LCSH: Scaffolding (Education)–Great Britain. | Effective teaching–Great Britain. | Mixed ability grouping in education–Great Britain. | Active learning–Great Britain. | Inquiry-based learning–Great Britain.
Classification: LCC LB1029.S33 B35 2025 (print) | LCC LB1029.S33 (ebook)
LC record available at https://lccn.loc.gov/2024057831
LC ebook record available at https://lccn.loc.gov/2024057832

ISBN: 978-1-032-73986-1 (hbk)
ISBN: 978-1-032-73983-0 (pbk)
ISBN: 978-1-003-46706-9 (ebk)

DOI: 10.4324/9781003467069

Typeset in Interstate
by Apex CoVantage, LLC

Printed and bound in Great Britain by Bell & Bain Ltd, Glasgow

NP105822
For Product Safety Concerns and Information please contact our EU representative Taylor & Francis Verlag GmbH, Kaufingerstraße 24, 80331 München, Germany
GPSR@taylorandfrancis.com

CONTENTS

Acknowledgements ix
Foreword xi
Series Editors' Foreword xiv

Introduction 1

1 **Differentiation, adaptive teaching and scaffolding** 5

2 **Scaffolding of retrieval practice and verbal prompts** 27

3 **Scaffolding through modelling** 41

4 **Scaffolding of explanations** 58

5 **Scaffolding and reading** 76

6a **Scaffolding and writing** 117

6b **Scaffolding and writing: Primary case studies** 147

7a **Scaffolding and oracy** 170

7b **Scaffolding and oracy: Case studies** 199

8 **Scaffolding in practical subjects** 212

9 **Scaffolding at KS1/KS5** 254

10	**Scaffolding of homework**	288
11	**Potential pitfalls of scaffolding strategies**	303
12	**Professional development and scaffolding strategies**	320
	Index	331

ACKNOWLEDGEMENTS

There are many people we want to jointly thank for their contributions to this book.

Thank you to Brad, Edward and the team at Inner Drive for giving us this fantastic opportunity, for motivating us to finish when writers block and imposter syndrome hit, and for editing the tomes which needed taming.

Routledge, thank you for believing in this concept for a book and for giving us the space to share our thoughts on scaffolding.

So many experts have kindly shared their knowledge by providing a case study, and this book is all the richer for their insights. Thank you to Neil Almond, Sarah Bagshaw-McCormick, Elizabeth Brydon, Elliot Morgan, Ben Cooper, Eve Morton, Sarah Young, Jo Blackman, Elizabeth Johnston, Jovita Castelino, Fiona Leadbeater, Laura Solly, Emma Macaulay, Nikki Sullivan, Kieran Mackle, Sophie Morris, Steven Keary, Sarah Dennis, Paul Cline, David Preece, Ceri Boyle, Richard Wheadon and David Goodwin.

Finally, this book would not have made it to the publishers were it not for the support of our friends and family and the incredible people who have offered us advice throughout the process.

By Rachel: For Luke and Lois. Thank you for bearing with 'Mummy working again' and bringing joy and laughter to my life along the way.

Acknowledgements

For Lee. Thank you for always being at my side. For my family. Thank you for your support and love always. Dad, you are missed so much. For the Steplab Team. Thank you for making it possible for me to write a book at the same time as starting a new job and offering such amazing support and inspiration. I can't believe I get to work with you all every day.

By Alex: For Scott. Thank you for your constant support and love. You are my world. I promise one day that I will put the laptop down and switch off...

For my family, who champion all that I do. Mum, your memory is forever with me and is my inspiration. I love you, and I hope that I am continuing to make you proud.

Thank you to the phenomenal practitioners at Kings Priory School, who inspire and amaze me every day.

And finally, for Helen Snelson who I aspire to be more like with each day.

FOREWORD

The Scaffolding Effect

While we all want the best for the young people we teach, we also need support with clarifying how we can support them all to achieve, regardless of their starting points. There's long been a need for a book of this kind, and Alex Fairlamb and Rachel Ball have done the serious heavy lifting so that we can be both more efficient and more effective in helping pupils get the most from the curriculum we teach.

In *The Scaffolding Effect*, Alex and Rachel make it clear that the aim is not to make material easier, but rather to make it accessible. And they are also clear about the difference between scaffolding and differentiation.

Until relatively recently, there's been a ton of time wasted on differentiation. We need to keep under constant review the impact of the things we do. And the impact of differentiation is limited and often detrimental to learning. There are several reasons why differentiation doesn't usually work.

The first problem is that differentiation anticipates in advance what children are capable of – by giving them prepared worksheets according to their ability, we are limiting what they might be capable of because the work usually puts a cap on what they can do.

The next issue is that the materials prepared for differentiation are usually closed exercises. So all that pupils are required to do is complete these. Completion of a prepared material does not allow them to interrogate the material and make sense of it on their own terms. And they don't usually require them to think very much.

Since the materials have been prepared in advance for pupils to complete, they usually have less cognitive challenge in them. Cognitive challenge is at the heart of learning – if a pupil does not have the chance to struggle with demanding material, they are not really gaining new knowledge and developing skills.

The completion of the worksheet is often regarded as the work. Pupils finish something and are praised for it, without checking for sure that they have properly understood something. It is too easy to complete work which has been prepared in advance by guessing, prompting or copying from someone else. This places very little demand on them but has the superficial attraction of making them appear busy. Busy is not the point, learning is.

Finally, they create a lot of extra work for teachers. Extra work is fine if it results in better outcomes but is a waste of time when it doesn't.

What, then, is the difference between scaffolding and differentiation? Well, scaffolding consists of the live conversations and additional unpacking of the material, mostly live during the lesson. Differentiating materials in advance, on the other hand, predetermines what children can do.

The power of scaffolding is that we use solid strategies to help make the goal of true agency and inclusion a realistic prospect. Just as a physical scaffold allows builders to reach great heights while ensuring safety and stability, effective scaffolding allows learners to stretch beyond their current capabilities within a secure environment.

With scaffolding, the role of the teacher is to carefully determine the appropriate level of support necessary to elevate students' engagement and comprehension while gradually removing that support as their independence grows. What we need in order to open more intellectual doors for our young people is a proper guide to the range of scaffolds available to achieve this goal.

What is so helpful about Alex Fairlamb's and Rachel Ball's work is that they have dug deep into the research and have provided the rationale for the elements and strategies that underpin the principles of scaffolding: they have tracked down the hard evidence ranging from the testing effect to support for writing that gives us the confidence that scaffolding works and will make a difference to all learners.

However, it is one thing to know the 'why'; what we also need is the 'what' and the 'how'. And this is where *The Scaffolding Effect* supplies a magnificent boon to the profession. We've all sat in sessions where we've heard some powerful ideas, but have left frustrated, because we're left floundering in terms of how to use these ideas in practice. In this terrific book, we have two experienced, energetic and imaginative teachers and teacher-educators who have carefully identified how to bring scaffolding to life in our practice.

If you are looking for a synthesis of the theory, a decent road map to make it work in your practice and some examples of how teachers have incorporated scaffolding and its sensitive removal, then this book will fill your professional heart with joy!

Mary Myatt
Education writer and speaker
31 October 2024

SERIES EDITORS' FOREWORD

We have looked forward to writing this foreword for some time now. It is an incredible addition to the Teacher CPD Academy series. For us, this book signals a significant shift away from the dark days of differentiation gone wrong, towards a new era of optimism and belief that all of our students can thrive at the highest level.

For years, teachers have wrestled with one of the biggest challenges in education: how to support every student effectively while managing the realities of the classroom. The days of differentiation—once hailed as the answer—often left teachers drowning in unrealistic workload demands, creating multiple versions of resources and lesson plans for different students. And yet, despite the effort, the impact on student learning was questionable at best.

That's why *The Scaffolding Effect* is such an important and timely book. Rachel Ball and Alex Fairlamb have provided something that has long been missing from education—a deeply researched, highly practical, and genuinely sustainable approach to supporting all students.

There is a wealth of evidence in this book. Rachel and Alex have meticulously woven together decades of research from cognitive science, educational psychology, and classroom practice. They don't just scratch the surface; they go deep into what really works, offering clarity where confusion has long reigned. If you want to understand the 'why' behind effective scaffolding, this book has you covered.

But research alone isn't enough. What makes *The Scaffolding Effect* truly stand out is its practical application. This isn't just theory—it's an actionable guide that teachers can use immediately. From expertly designed strategies to real-world examples, the book ensures that scaffolding becomes a tool that enhances teaching rather than adding to workload.

More than anything, this book brings fresh hope. It offers a way forward that is both evidence-based and manageable. It acknowledges the realities of the classroom while equipping teachers with the tools to better support all students. In a profession where time is precious and impact is everything, *The Scaffolding Effect* is must-read. If you are looking for a book that will truly make a difference to your teaching and your students, you won't find a better one than this.

Bradley Busch and Edward Watson, Directors of InnerDrive

Introduction

Education can be frustrating. This is particularly the case when some pedagogical approaches, which are hailed to be panaceas, are adopted whole scale across a school, despite shaky evidence. Schools are often high accountability, high pressure environments, and so the temptation to try to resolve the monumental issue of how to support the broadening and often complex range of students we serve can result in us reaching for the wrong tools. We are both experienced teachers and leaders who have taught during the era of differentiation. Differentiation has become the hydra of the education world, the nine-headed beast who haunted Lyrna using its venom to do so. When the hydra had one of its heads cut off, in an attempt to slay it, two new heads grew in their place; it appeared as seemingly invincible to anyone who tried to rid Lyrna of this danger as it mutated and grew. How this has manifested with differentiation is a littered landscape of lethal mutations such as differentiated learning objectives, flight paths and separate curriculums for 'more' or 'less able' students. We felt frustration at the low expectation culture this created and the inordinate amount of teacher's time wasted through the creation of multiple levelled worksheets, for example.

Thankfully, much has changed in the education landscape over the past decade or so, and many more schools have a better understanding of cognitive science and the danger an approach like this can create. Differentiation in this form has therefore been phased out in many schools; the heads of the hydra being cauterised in some contexts. With its

DOI: 10.4324/9781003467069-1

continuing demise, many teachers have been left with questions about what comes next. If not differentiation, then what does support look like that ensures that all students can learn effectively? A clear part of this answer is adaptive teaching and scaffolding. However, in spite of the evidence which demonstrates the power of scaffolding, this is an area of a teacher's toolkit which is not only tricky to manage, but it is also an area where many misconceptions persist. These are misconceptions which we will explore and bust in the chapters of this book. Part of this limited knowledge and practice of scaffolding can be linked to it being an area of expertise often lacking in practical development for teachers as there is a 'lack of specific examples and tips in teacher's editions of textbooks' (Fisher & Frey, 2010).

This book is our attempt to define what scaffolding is, and what is not, and to give some accessible and practical strategies of what it looks like across the curriculum. We wanted to include a focus on scaffolding in practical subjects, such as DT (Design Technology) and PE, as much of the literature in this area is sparse. We also felt it was important to include examples of scaffolding approaches at KS1 and KS5 because scaffolding here *can* and *should* look different. We are therefore very grateful to all of the teachers who have contributed case studies to ensure the book caters for teachers in all backgrounds. Scaffolding continues to be an ongoing dialogue, and one that needs to be carefully considered in its implementation, taking into account the context of a school and the potential varying readiness of teachers to thread it effectively into lessons. To support this context-specific dialogue, at the end of every chapter there are reflection questions to enable teachers and leaders to reflect meaningfully about any gaps in current approaches to scaffolding and plan some concrete actions.

This book is not a 'pick up and go' guide to scaffolding. Our belief is that scaffolding is context and student specific. In addition, in a high accountability culture, it can be tempting to seek out a silver bullet and put strategies in place (with the best intent) without carefully considering their purpose and implementation. The shortcuts offered by snake oil salesmen can tempt us to swiftly adopt strategies and not consider the subject and phase specifics of our schools. Consequently, it is likely that lethal mutations in scaffolding will appear (explored further in Chapter 11). Be on guard against seductive and slick 'scaffolding strategies' that are rolled out without careful consideration and that are often scant in evidence. Evidence interpreted through the lens of your particular context will always be one of your best weapons against the Hydra.

Some other key principles to consider as you read the book and that are further explored through later chapters:

- The specific scaffolding strategy, or how much scaffolding is needed is best determined by the teacher in response to assessment of learning.

- Although scaffolding does involve planning for potential barriers students may have, a large chunk of a scaffolded approach means adapting in the moment during the lesson. It is not always something which can be planned or scripted in advance.

- If scaffolding requires live adaptations, you will make mistakes. Effective scaffolding means adding or withdrawing support at the right time, neither allowing students to become too reliant or not allowing them enough support to achieve. We won't always get this right, and it's important to make peace with the fact that misjudging the amount of support needed at a certain time is likely to happen. What is crucial is to continue reflecting and learning from such moments.

- Scaffolds are not intended to be permanent. If everyone has a scaffold all of the time, it's not a scaffold, it's just your lesson plan.

- Scaffolding should not be hugely labour intensive. Many of the scaffolding strategies we explore in this book involve pedagogy which does not require hours of planning! Verbal cues, live modelling or pre-teaching vocabulary for example are hugely important scaffolding approaches.

- Scaffolding can be a specific student, group or a whole class approach. At the beginning of a new unit with new exam questions for example, the whole class would need a scaffolded approach. However, as students become more confident and secure that scaffold can be removed whilst for others it may need to remain or even be increased.

Our hope for this book is that it allows you as the teacher to see how you can embed high expectations for all your students, whilst still ensuring those that need additional support receive it in the most helpful ways possible.

Reference

Fisher, D. & Frey, N. (2010) *Guided Instruction: How to Develop Confident and Successful Learners*. ASCD

1 Differentiation, adaptive teaching and scaffolding

> The most effective way to differentiate is through Dylan Wiliam's responsive teaching – preparing for the top and supporting students to get there, rather than deciding in advance which pupils will perform which tasks. We must resist the temptation to dumb down.
>
> *(Myatt, 2020)*

All: Describe what was agreed at the Treaty of Versailles
Most: Explain why it was so difficult to agree on the terms of the Treaty
Some: Evaluate who would have been happiest with the Treaty

What's wrong with differentiation?

I'm sure we would all agree now that the differentiated learning outcomes at the start of this chapter are pretty misguided. Several years ago, this approach was very commonly seen in schools as part of an umbrella of strategies called 'differentiation'. You may have come across 'chili challenges' with tasks identified by how 'hot' or challenging they were. Or perhaps your learning outcomes were identified as Must, Should, Could or even Bronze, Silver, Gold. An extreme example of this was a school that had six learning objectives: three objectives with a stretch objective each. Imagine starting your lesson by explaining outcomes like this to your class!

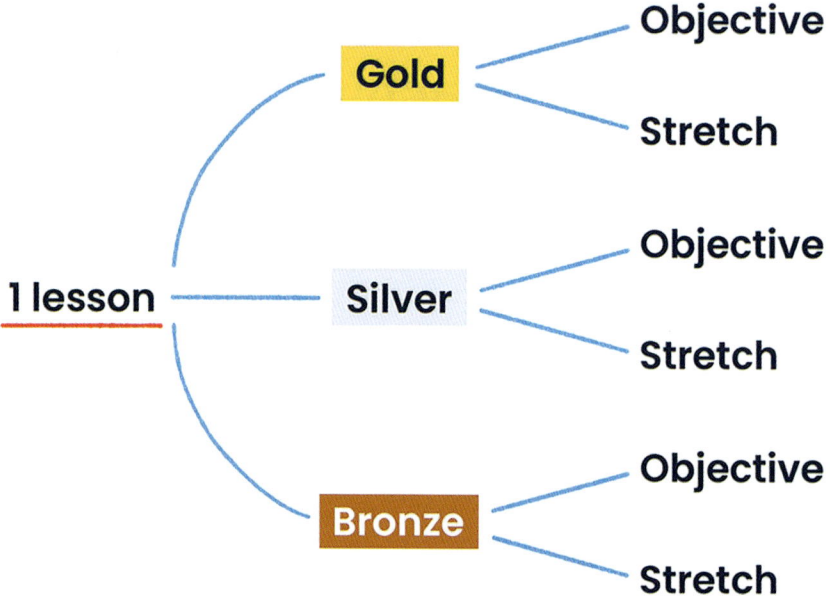

FIGURE 1.1 Differentiation

There may also have been three different worksheets designed and given out to students (perhaps distributed by identifying target grades in advance of the lesson), or you may have been asked to arrange students into three ability groups (one English department called their three Shelley, Orwell and Byron and an RE department called their three Jesus, Mary and Joseph!). Colour coding or adding symbols to these worksheets made it even more obvious to students what was really going on here. There may also have been different tasks set with students choosing which activity they completed based on their own confidence. School leaders would look for evidence of 'differentiation' in book looks, and perhaps you would even be graded on these books or what was seen in lessons.

Thankfully, this limiting approach to learning intentions and to differentiated work is far less popular than it was, although there are still some schools who still persist on holding onto this practice, with teachers caught in the hangover of a differentiation frenzy in the last decade or more. Most of us have come to realise the low expectations these strategies promote:

> When we use 'Gold-Silver-Bronze' or 'All-Most-Some' or 'Mild-Medium-Extra Hot' differentiated learning outcomes, we are saying that we expect much less from some students than others. We are advertising our low expectations to the class . . . The impact on motivation, effort levels and outcomes are catastrophic.
>
> (Roberts, 2022)

As discussed later in the chapter, we know there is a wealth of psychological research that makes the link between how able a teacher thinks a student is and what their outcomes are. Our expectations as teachers feed into a students' self-efficacy and beliefs about their own capabilities, and therefore can be extremely damaging.

Another method used by teachers across the country to differentiate involved adding extra challenge to lessons. You might add a 'challenge question' to your powerpoint slides or hand out extra worksheets to those 'able' students who finish before others. What we should focus on, is instead of adding this additional challenge on, why not embed the challenge for all from the very start of the lesson? 'Cognitive challenge is at the heart of learning – if a child does not have the chance to struggle with demanding material, they are not really gaining new knowledge and developing skills' (Myatt, 2020). Roberts (2022) goes on to explain the damage done through adding these 'extension' tasks. Although referring here to boys, many of these consequences apply to all students:

1. Extension tasks advertise a teacher's belief that some children deserve harder work in lessons than others.
2. Extension tasks provide boys with an opt-out.
3. Extension tasks discourage boys from following mastery goals.
4. Extension tasks can frustrate and confuse those that complete them.
5. Extension tasks deepen attainment gaps.

Differentiation, at its heart is no bad thing of course. It means thinking about the needs of your individual students and adapting your lesson so that it helps them learn most effectively; taking account of reading ages or lack of prior knowledge for example. However, during this recent period of education the, practice of differentiation has become lethally mutated and morphed into some kind of monster (remember the Hydra?), which not just put a ceiling on students' progress, but also created an unwieldy burden on staff workloads.

Teachers have spent many wasted hours on the practice of differentiation. Vicious, tick-box and time wasting accountability systems were all invented which aimed to prove differentiation was happening:

> Differentiation tends to focus on working with individuals or small groups of learners. While it can be a useful approach when understood and deployed well – for example in special schools – when used in mainstream it can lead to teachers juggling multiple 'microlessons' during a class or delegating teaching tasks to others.
> (Mulholland, 2022)

Little wonder then that differentiation has been referred to as 'one of the darkest arts in teaching' (Didau, 2015).

So if we're not supposed to differentiate in the way the term has become synonymous with, how do we ensure that all our students are challenged and supported? First, comes consideration of challenge, or the approach of 'Teach to the Top'.

'Teach to the top'

'Teach to the Top' is an expression which has become more commonly used in teaching over the last few years as an alternative way of thinking about the challenge and subsequent adaptation of lessons for learners. This approach to teaching is 'a mindset that should underpin the way we teach, an ideology that should shape the way we conceptualise education and a practical strategy for ensuring the richest, most productive educational experience for our students' (Mansworth, 2021).

'Teach to the Top' is about planning your lesson to push students just out of their comfort zones, being unapologetic about encouraging intellectual curiosity and having the highest expectations about what students can do. Instead of planning with students with lower prior attainment in mind and adding on additional challenges or extension tasks, 'Teach to the Top' means keeping your pitch high and supporting all students to reach the same highest learning intentions. It's about being ambitious with students; ensuring that learning is satisfyingly challenging.

> Teaching to the Top - when the top signifies the highest attaining students in the group - is at its core, simply logical. If teachers aren't teaching to the top, then some students are learning nothing at all; some of the class are inevitably held back and restricted from making progress.
>
> (Mansworth, 2021)

Indeed, all of our students need to feel challenge, to make mistakes, to be stretched beyond their comfort zone. Professor Robert Coe (2013) has explained that this kind of challenge is essential to learning.

> Learning happens when people have to think hard. Obviously this is over simplistic, vague and not original. But if it helps teachers to ask questions like, Where in this lesson will students have to think hard? it may be useful.

Importantly, this challenge must be accessible, not unpleasant, and come with support. We could phrase this as 'satisfyingly challenging'. But as teachers we do our students a disservice if we do not allow them to struggle. 'If your pupils aren't struggling and making mistakes, perhaps you're not doing your job. The only way to prevent struggle is to lower expectations. And as the clichÈ goes, nobody rises to low expectations' (Didau, 2015).

One example of the evidence base behind Teach to the Top is of course the work of Robert Bjork and the theory of Desirable Difficulties (Bjork, 1994). The concept describes the idea that for students to learn to their maximum capability, tasks should be designed to be challenging. Tasks are desirable because they lead to long-term learning and memory retention, but difficult because these are the very tasks as learners we don't find easy: 'Conditions of learning that make performance improve rapidly often fail to support long-term retention and transfer, whereas conditions that create challenges and slow the rate of apparent learning often optimise long-term retention and transfer' (Bjork & Bjork, 2011).

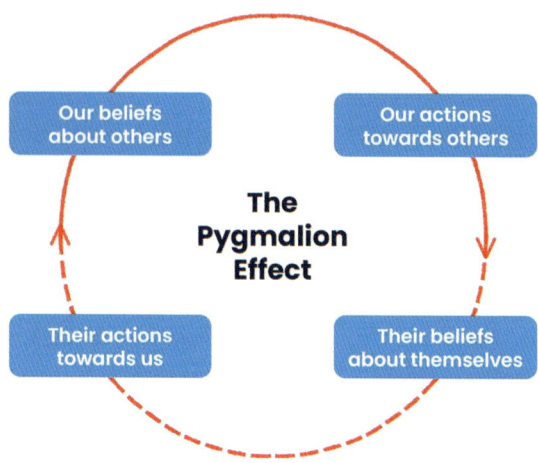

FIGURE 1.2 The Pygmalion effect

This 'Teach to the Top' mindset is important because we know there is a clear link between teacher expectations and student outcomes, especially when teachers are explicit about this with their classes (Peterson et al., 2016). Rosenthal's research, now referred to as the Pygmalion effect or Rosenthal effect, shows this clearly. Rosenthal and Jacobson (1968) researched the effect of teacher expectations on motivation and performance. Students at an elementary school were given an IQ test and their teachers were told that some students in their class were particular high achievers or 'Bloomers'. After eight months they returned and retested the students. The 'Bloomers' showed more increased IQ scores than the other students, despite the students actually being chosen randomly. The experiment showed that teacher expectations are crucial and become a self-fulfilling prophecy. High expectations lead to stronger performance, something many of us can echo in our own experience. As an 11 year old student being told I had no artistic skills at all has become ingrained in my memory to the point where I rarely help with my primary school age children's homework projects; 'Mummy's rubbish at Art'. Conversely, the history teacher who believed in me and told me I could pursue the subject at university instilled a huge amount of confidence and self-belief.

> When others believe in our potential, they give us a ladder. They elevate our aspirations and enable us to reach higher peaks. Dozens of experiments show that at work, when leaders hold high expectations, employees generally work harder, learn more, and perform better. In schools, when teachers set high expectations, students get smarter and earn higher grades – especially if they start out with disadvantages . . . low expectations tend to hold us back – it feels like our boots are made of lead. It's called the Golem effect: when others underestimate us, it limits our effort and growth.
>
> (Grant, 2023)

This low expectation culture has a limiting impact on all students, but perhaps most specifically on boys:

> Low expectations of boys is a destructive cycle. Saying boys can achieve is not enough. Believing boys can achieve is not enough. Actually doing it and showing it day-in day-out in every single lesson is what will make the difference.
>
> (Pinkett & Roberts, 2019)

So how can we practically focus on and show high expectations in schools? Here are some suggestions:

1. Carefully consider the use of language

As well as removing any lingering signs of differentiation such as deciding in advance which students will be capable of certain work or letting students choose the difficulty level of their work, schools can also review their use of language. Use of terms such as 'low ability' or 'less able' are not helpful and do not communicate high expectations. I would urge schools to think about what these terms mean and communicate to the students themselves. A student could be labelled 'less able' because of some disappointing SATs scores in Year 6. They could carry that term around with them throughout school, perhaps placed in lower sets or even put on a different curriculum path or barred from certain options choices. For the student, the daily cycle of feeling that your teacher/s have low expectations of you will not surprisingly press heavily upon the mindset, motivation and confidence of a child. For the teacher, who even may not use these terms aloud, the unconscious and conscious impact of having such terms in your head will naturally limit what you expect the child to do. It is this kind of language choice that leads to comments like 'They wouldn't be capable of this work' or 'She can't do that'. As we've seen already in the chapter, labelling a child from a snapshot of their education like this can be extremely damaging. A better replacement might be 'lower prior attainment'. A snapshot perhaps showed lower than expected attainment, but that does not preclude future high attainment. Great schools will pursue the highest expectations of all, no matter what a slip of paper shows their previous grades as.

2. Remove target grades and flight paths

Schools should also think carefully about their use of target grades on an individual level. For some, they can be aspirational, but for others they place limits on learning. Target grades are also problematic in their link to teacher expectations even in the post-differentiation landscape.

> Less is expected of a child who performs comparatively poorly in their KS2 tests, for whatever reason, than of one who performs well. They are generated a lower target grade, likely to be put in lower sets and almost certainly given easier work to do.
>
> (Newmark, 2017)

Ever wondered why KS3 assessment scores seem bang on target? Target grades also provide teachers with a short cut when marking work and submitting data unless strict blind marking and moderation takes place, often unlikely with workload demands. And then there is the association with flight paths, a practice still common in many schools where a student's suggested final grade is plotted and predicted based on prior attainment.

Ofsted's National Director for Education, Sean Harford has said, 'Flight paths in secondary are nonsense and demotivating for pupils.' When predictions are made about individual students' performance these predictions can become self-fulfilling. If students (or teachers) believe that they can't do better than a Grade 4, many will stop trying. Why would we ever want to convince anyone that children are less capable than they might be?

(Didau, 2019)

3. Focus on a challenging curriculum

It is our belief that schools should also ensure that the work on building and maintaining a challenging curriculum remains a high priority and concentrate on embedding this in classroom practice, using challenging questioning, developing teacher subject knowledge, having one challenging learning intention or goal and using challenging texts 'above their pay grade' (Myatt, 2021).

Adaptive teaching

So now we have established a culture of high expectations, how do we give support to those that need it without it drifting into unhelpful differentiation? The answer lies in the use of 'adaptive teaching' instead. The term adaptive teaching has been around as a concept since the 1980s (Hatano & Inagaki, 1986) but has now become more familiar, partly due to its use in the Early Career Framework (2024) for example. Adaptive Teaching as a term encapsulates the importance of responding to need, without deciding need in advance. Adaptive Teaching could look like this as a three-step process:

- Anticipate barriers
- Use assessment to elicit understanding
- Make in the moment adaptations (Eaton, 2022)

To help us understand more about what that looks like, let's consider the analogy of a home-cooked meal:

> Before I start cooking, I will think carefully about what ingredients I need, whether I need to preheat my oven and whether I have the right equipment available. I will use a recipe as my starting point, the building blocks of my meal that I know mean it's more likely to be palatable. My oven runs hot so I'll also consider how I need to adapt the timings slightly.
>
> During the making and cooking, I will regularly taste-test to check whether the cooking is beginning to form and taste as it should. I might add a little more salt or stir as needed. I'll check the oven to see if it's burning and might turn the food over at regular points.
>
> Once the meal has been made I will evaluate what worked and what I might do differently next time, using my understanding of how the meal has been received. I might realise the food needed longer in the oven, or that the vegetables should have been chopped up into smaller pieces. This will give me important guidance for when I make the meal again.

In other words, I prepared and pre-empted barriers. I made adjustments as I went along based on taste and appearance. Finally eating the meal allowed me to see what areas needed further adapting for next time. So how does this relate to the adaptation needed in teaching?

First, anticipate barriers, for example difficult or unfamiliar vocabulary or common misconceptions that students might encounter, and plan to address them.

Second, use assessment during the lesson to elicit understanding: cold calling, hinge questions and circulation are good ways to find out how much students know and understand.

Third, add in the moment adaptations. These could be stopping to show what a good example looks like, providing prompts or analogies or adjusting the level of challenge slightly. It is these adaptations which can be termed *scaffolds*.

Reading exercise books or looking at lesson footage after the lesson can then lead to further understanding of what students understand, leading to more adaptation or scaffolds as needed as you continue to teach the class.

Why is scaffolding important?

Over the last few years I have begun to strength-train regularly. Mastering some of the lifts and exercises set by my coach has been a real challenge at times! One of the most difficult moves for me to learn early on, with very little upper body strength, has been the progress to a full press up. I watched the video my coach shared of a perfect push up. I really wanted to do it, but needless to say I was pretty pathetic on my first attempt!

My coach then encouraged me to start with elevated push ups. Using a bar for this on a squat rack (or the back of a chair) and gradually lowering it as I became stronger massively scaffolded my progress, enabling me to eventually be able to do multiple push ups from the floor. My coach gave me a physical scaffold, in the form of the moveable bar, and she *scaffolded* my push up progression. I was never told I wouldn't be able to do a push up, or given lower expectations of a kneeling push up. Instead I was supported with the explanation that my progress to full push ups might take a little longer. In much the same way, scaffolding represents the temporary support that can be given to students to enable them to meet the high expectations we have addressed earlier in the chapter.

What is scaffolding?

The term 'scaffolding' was first used by Wood et al. (1976) as a way to describe the support or assistance that means a student is able to do a task which they would have struggled with on their own. The term is also linked closely to the work of Vygotsky (1984) who wrote about the zone of proximal development – the difference between what a student can master on their own, and what they can achieve with the support from an expert. This support, to help students gain more knowledge and skills and become more independent, was then described by Bruner as temporary scaffolds where as expertise grows, the expert can gradually challenge the student more; 'a process of "setting up" the situation to make the child's entry easy and successful and then gradually pulling back and handing the role to the child as he becomes skilled enough to manage it' (Bruner, 1983). In a classroom context therefore, a teacher can support a student to learn and understand a task by providing scaffolds such as models or questions. These supports are then removed as the student becomes more proficient.

The analogy of scaffolding in construction works well here: scaffolding supports the work and materials whilst a building undergoes repair. Similarly, the analogy of a child learning to ride a bike helps us understand the temporary role of scaffolding in teaching and learning.

> For example, in teaching a child to ride a bike, the training wheels serve as a scaffold. The adult running alongside the bike serves as another. In other words, the adult handles the harder parts temporarily, while allowing the child to try out the easier parts.
> (Fisher & Frey, 2010)

Stabilisers can also provide support to children learning to ride a bike; once balance and pedalling have been mastered, the stabilisers can be removed.

A 'Teach to the Top' approach will quickly flounder without the appropriate support for students to meet these highest expectations. Support and high expectations go hand in hand.

> A much better, wiser and more effective notion of differentiation is that it applies to the level of support and scaffolding learners need

to reach common, aspirational learning goals. We're all aiming for the top of the mountain – but some of us will need more help, more guidance, more time.

(Sherrington, 2019)

In the classroom, scaffolding requires the teacher to be responsive to the needs of students and understanding the barriers students may face to meet the challenge of the 'Teach to the Top' approach: 'Scaffolding is a metaphor for temporary support which is removed when no longer required. It may be visual, verbal or written' (EEF, 2020). Scaffolding is therefore a key part of adaptive teaching, of making the high challenge learning accessible to all; 'Scaffolding provides a gentler entry, but the destination remains the same. Lower-attainers may take longer and need more help, but the job of teachers is to "disrupt the bell curve", not just to preserve it' (Coe et al., 2020; William, 2018).

Although much of the early work on scaffolding was done with regard to individual students, research since then has developed into its use with groups of students. The research base on scaffolding shows that 'scaffolding is an effective teaching strategy' (Van der Stuyf, 2002). Murphy and Messer found that 'scaffolding was effective' based on a study involving over 100 children where scaffolding was provided in order to provide verbal explanations of balancing in terms of weight and distance. Children who received a scaffolded approach made significant improvements between the pre and post tests (Murphy & Messer, 2000). After observations of two classrooms another study noted: 'Scaffolding is an important instructional tool because it supports students' learning . . . Students whose learning is helped by scaffolding in socially constructed environments will have an advantage over students who do not' (Roehler & Cantlon, 1997). The authors observed that five main types of scaffolding were evident including offering explanations and modelling of desired behaviours.

In another study involving 13 teachers from KS2 classes it concluded that: 'Teachers need to believe that children can learn difficult and complex ideas; this is what school is about. But they must be content that often pupils can only do this one step or a few steps at a time' (Bliss et al., 1996). Another study concluded that in situations where independent work requirements were high, 'high contingent support was more effective than low contingent support in fostering students' achievement' (Van de Pol & Elbers, 2013). In other words, teacher adaptation and support by teachers was crucial to achievement; 'when teachers are taught how to scaffold, their degree of contingency increased but the independent working time for students increased as well'.

A common misconception here is that scaffolding is just adding a writing frame or a worksheet to a lesson, but the research shows this would be wrong; 'Scaffolding is more than just a worksheet' (Aubin, 2022). Instead, modelling, metacognitive thinking and specific vocabulary instruction are all shown to be effective scaffolding strategies. 'When introducing a new task or working format, it is indispensable that the learners be able to see or hear what a developing product looks like' (Walqui, 2008). The EEF (2020) explain this further in their report, suggesting that scaffolding could involve a glossary of key words, sentence starters, a modelled example, a class 'We write', a diagram on the board to prompt students' schema or even a conversation with a student using metacognitive talk; 'How did we approach this question last time we had a go?' 'How do you think we could start?' and so forth. Rosenshine confirms this, exploring scaffolding as one of his principles of instruction where he writes that teachers should 'provide scaffolds for difficult tasks' outlining suggestions such as guided practice, modelling, thinking aloud, pre-empting misconceptions and the use of checklists or success criteria (Rosenshine, 2012).

Why is adaptive teaching and implementing scaffolds so hard to get right?

The research on teacher wellbeing and workload tells us that adaptive teaching and consequently scaffolding is one of the hardest aspects of teaching to get right.

> Scaffolding is a highly complex process requiring a wide range of skills from the instructor or teacher. To properly scaffold, the teacher needs to possess and show a range of emotional skills such as empathy and patience. (S)he also needs to know when and how to provide close support and also when and how to take it away. Finally, they need to be able to hold two mental models at once; their own mental model of the overall problem to be solved and crucially, the child's mental model to be solved.
>
> (Kirschner & Hendrick, 2024)

The working lives of teachers and leaders report of April 2023 showed that of over 11,000 respondents, approximately 27% showed lack of confidence in adaptive teaching in comparison to aspects such as implementing behaviour rewards and sanctions or assessing student's progress (DfE, 2023). Understanding of scaffolding is a key aspect of teaching which separates 'novices' from 'expert' teachers:

> Novice teachers tended to think of scaffolding as a way in which teachers made work easier for students, whereas the expert teachers had the long-term goal of subject agency for their students, and so they understood the metaphor of scaffolding as the 'something' that they did in the process of teaching to move students towards independence.
>
> (Shires, 2020)

Therefore, scaffolding is an area of practice which must be prioritised by school leaders, mentors and subject leads for professional development, in order that students are adequately supported; 'what the research also finds is that getting adaptive teaching right is hard. It is a particularly complex approach that requires good professional development and support for the teacher, and also quite a bit of teaching experience and expertise' (Mujis, 2023).

It is important that an approach utilising scaffolding does not become a return to an approach of overly prescriptive differentiation as described above. The danger is that the swingometer swings too far, with an

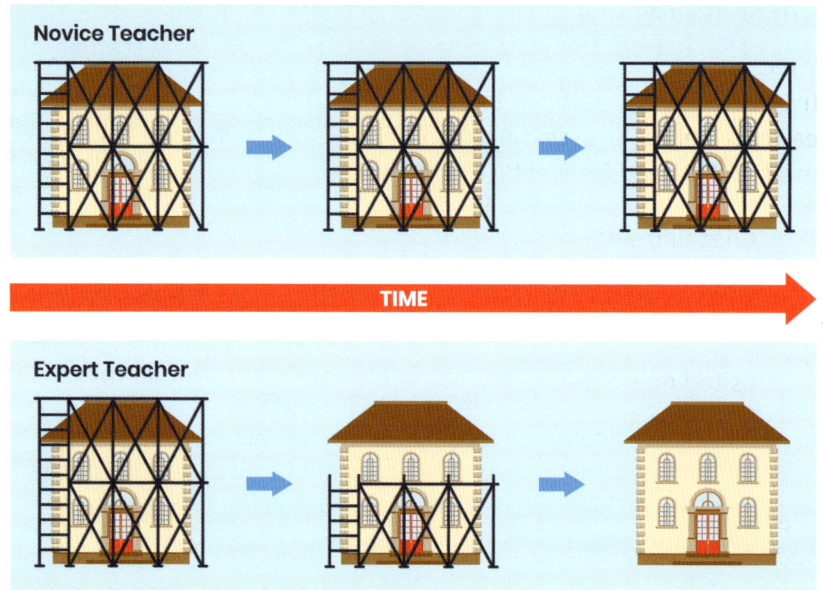

FIGURE 1.3 Novice vs expert teacher

unmanageable workload for staff and the limiting of challenge for students. So we need to think carefully about our scaffolding strategies themselves, who receives support, and fundamentally, we must have a clear plan for removal of this scaffolding. We should also be careful to ensure that the same dangerous practices associated with differentiation do not simply start with adaptive teaching. Tick boxes on lesson plans or leaders searching for adaptive teaching in exercise books will not help anyone; when we observe lessons we should be 'looking at, not looking for' (Didau, 2020).

Additionally, we must be on our guard about viewing scaffolding as a 'catch all'. It won't replace the need for comprehensive, targeted support for some students. 'Adaptive teaching is not a miracle cure. There will always be a very small minority of learners whose learning needs are very, very different and for whom all the scaffolding in the world won't be enough' (Sealy, 2024).

Checking for understanding comes first

What is important to note here, and is perhaps one of the reasons adaptive teaching is so difficult to get right, is that scaffolding is unlikely to be most helpful if assessment and checking for understanding is not used skilfully and frequently by the teacher.

> Checking For Understanding allows us to gauge the temperature in the room in terms of student learning. This, similarly to the second and fourth principles (small steps and providing models, respectively), helps us know what to do next. It allows us to know when to remove the stabilisers and encourage them to ride solo.
>
> (Inner Drive, 2022)

If as teachers we are not using techniques of formative assessment such as frequent questioning, how do we know how much or the exact nature of the scaffolds needed, or indeed which students require the support?

How then can we summarise the benefits of scaffolding for students?

- Scaffolding helps students to understand new knowledge and material
- Scaffolding increases student independence over time
- Scaffolding helps connect prior and new learning so that students can build their knowledge meaningfully to build schema
- Scaffolding allows just the right amount of struggle, meaning students feel less frustrated
- Scaffolding builds engagement through success which has a positive effect on motivation

Scaffolding is a crucial aspect which teachers must get right in order to best challenge and support students. The aim of this book is to go some way to providing examples of what scaffolding may therefore look like in practice.

Chapter 1 Self-Reflection Questions

Take a few minutes to reflect on the questions below and jot down your answers...

1. Do you possibly have any hangovers from "The dark art of differentiation?"

2. How confident are you at adapting your teaching using scaffolding where appropriate?

3. Are you rigorous in checking for understanding so that you know which students need scaffolding and how much?

References

Aubin, G. (2022) *EEF Blog: Scaffolding – More Than Just a Worksheet* (Online). Available at https://educationendowmentfoundation.org.uk/news/scaffolding-more-than-just-a-worksheet. Accessed 9th October 2023

Bjork, E. L. & Bjork, R. A. (2011) Making Things Hard on Yourself, but in a Good Way: Creating Desirable Difficulties to Enhance Learning. *Psychology and the Real World: Essays Illustrating Fundamental Contributions to Society*, 2, 59–68

Bjork, R. A. (1994) Memory and Metamemory Considerations in the Training of Human Beings. In J. Metcalfe & A. Shimamura (Eds.), *Metacognition: Knowing About Knowing*. MIT Press

Bliss, J., Askew, M. & Macrae, S. (1996) Effective Teaching and Learning: Scaffolding Revisited. *Oxford Review of Education*, 22(1), 37–61 (Online). Available at https://doi.org/10.1080/0305498960220103

Bruner, J. (1983) *Child's Talk*. New York: Norton

Coe, R. (2013) *Improving Education: A Triumph of Hope Over Experience*. Inaugural Lecture of Professor Robert Coe, Durham University, 18th June (Online). Available at http://eachandeverydog.net/wp-content/uploads/2015/05/ImprovingEducation2013.pdf. Accessed 28th March 2024

Coe, R., Rauch, C. J., Kime, S. & Singleton, D. (2020) *Great Teaching Toolkit Evidence Review* (Online). Available at https://assets.website-files.com/5ee2872 9f7b4a5fa99bef2b3/5ee9f507021911ae35ac6c4d_EBE_GTT_EVIDENCE%20 REVIEW_DIGITAL.pdf. Accessed 10th November 2023

DfE (2023) *Working Lives of Teachers and Leaders Wave 1* (Online). Available at https://assets.publishing.service.gov.uk/government/uploads/system/uploads/attachment_data/file/1148571/Working_lives_of_teachers_and_leaders_-_wave_1_-_core_report.pdf. Accessed 9th October 2023

Didau, D. (2015) *What if Everything You Knew About Education Was Wrong?* Crown House

Didau, D. (2019) *How Do We Know Pupils Are Making Progress? Part 1: The Madness of Flight Paths* (Online). Available at https://learningspy.co.uk/assessment/how-do-we-know-pupils-are-marking-progress-part-1-the-problem-with-flightpaths/#:~:text=Ofsted's%20National%20Director%20 for%20Education,prediction%20can%20become%20self%2Dfulfilling. Accessed 11th July 2024

Didau, D. (2020) *Intelligent Accountability: Creating the Conditions for Teachers to Thrive*. Woodbridge: John Catt Educational

Early Career Framework (2024) (Online). Available at https://www.gov.uk/government/publications/early-career-framework. Accessed 9th August 2024

Eaton, J. (2022) *EEF Blog: Moving from Differentiation to Adaptive Teaching* (Online). Available at https://educationendowmentfoundation.org.uk/news/moving-from-differentiation-to-adaptive-teaching. Accessed 3rd April 2024

EEF Report (2020) *Special Educational Needs in Mainstream Schools* (Online). Available at https://educationendowmentfoundation.org.uk/education-evidence/guidance-reports/send. Accessed 9th October 2023

Fisher, D. & Frey, N. (2010) *Guided Instruction; How to Develop Confident and Successful Learners*. ASCD

Grant, A. (2023) *Hidden Potential: The Science of Achieving Greater Things*. Penguin Random House

Hatano, G. & Inagaki, K. (1986) Two Courses of Expertise. In H. W. Stevenson, H. Azuma & K. Hakuta (Eds.), *Child Development and Education in Japan*. W. H. Freeman, Times Books, Henry Holt & Co

Inner Drive (2022) *What Is the Most Important of Rosenshine's Principles of Instruction?* (Online). Available at https://blog.innerdrive.co.uk/most-important-rosenshine-principle. Accessed 9th October 2023

Kirschner, P. A. & Hendrick, C. (2024) *How Learning Happens: Seminal Works in Educational Psychology and What They Mean in Practice* (Second edition). New York: Routledge

Mansworth, M. (2021) *Teach to the Top*. Woodbridge: John Catt Educational

Mujis, D. (2023) *Is It Time to Ditch Differentiation?* (Online). Available at https://www.tes.com/magazine/teaching-learning/general/adaptive-teaching-ditch-differentiation-teachers. Accessed 9th October 2023

Mulholland, M. (2022) Adaptive Teaching; Why It Matters. *TES Magazine* (Online). Available at https://www.tes.com/magazine/teaching-learning/specialist-sector/adaptive-teaching-why-it-matters-SEND-teachers-school. Accessed 19th July 2023

Murphy, N. & Messer, D. (2000) Differential Benefits from Scaffolding and Children Working Alone. *Educational Psychology*, 20(1), 17–31 (Online). Available at https://doi.org/10.1080/014434100110353

Myatt, M. (2020) *Death by Differentiation* (Online). Available at https://www.marymyatt.com/blog/death-by-differentiation. Accessed 10th November 2023

Myatt, M. (2021) *Above Their Pay Grade* (Online). Available at https://www.marymyatt.com/blog/above-their-pay-grade. Accessed 4th October 2023

Newmark, B. (2017) *Why Target Grades Miss Their Mark* (Online). Available at https://bennewmark.wordpress.com/2017/02/22/why-target-grades-miss-their-mark/#:~:text=I%20learned%20that%20Target%20Grades,a%20target%20for%20other%20subjects. Accessed 9th April 2024

Peterson, E. R., Rubie-Davies, C., Osborne, D. & Sibley, C. (2016) *Teachers' Explicit Expectations and Implicit Prejudiced Attitudes to Educational Achievement: Relations with Student Achievement and the Ethnic Achievement Gap* (Online). Available at https://www.cuesta.edu/about/documents/vpaa-docs/7_Teachers_Explicit_Expectations_and_Implicit_Prejudiced_Attit_2016_Learning.pdf

Pinkett, M. & Roberts, M. (2019) *Boys Don't Try*. Routledge

Roberts, M. (2022) *The Boy Question*. Routledge

Roehler, L. R. & Cantlon, D. J. (1997) Scaffolding: A Powerful Tool in Social Constructivist Classrooms. In K. Hogan & M. Pressley (Eds.), *Scaffolding Student Learning: Instructional Approaches and Issues*. Cambridge: Brookline Books

Rosenshine, B. (2012) Principles of Instruction: Research-Based Strategies That All Teachers Should Know. *American Educator*, 36(1)

Rosenthal, R. & Jacobson, L. (1968) *Pygmalion in the Classroom* (Online). Available at https://gwern.net/doc/statistics/bias/1968-rosenthal-pygmalionintheclassroom.pdf

Sealy, C. (2024) *Adaptive Teaching – The Four Verbs Approach* (Online). Available at https://primarytimery.com/2024/03/29/adaptive-teaching-the-four-verbs-approach/. Accessed 3rd April 2024

Sherrington, T. (2019) *Rescuing Differentiation from the Checklist of Bad Practice* (Online). Available at https://teacherhead.com/2019/01/24/rescuing-differentiation-from-the-checklist-of-bad-practice/. Accessed 19th July 2023

Shires, L. (2020) Scaffolding by Novice and Expert Teachers: The Difference. *Impact* (Online). Available at https://my.chartered.college/impact_article/scaffolding-by-novice-and-expert-teachers-the-difference/. Accessed 9th October 2023

Van de Pol, J. & Elbers, E. (2013) Scaffolding Student Learning: A Microanalysis of Teacher-Student Interaction. *Learning, Culture, and Social Interaction*, 2, 32–41 (Online). Available at https://doi.org/10.1016/j.lcsi.2012.12.001

Van Der Stuyf, R. R. (2002) Scaffolding as a Teaching Strategy. *Adolescent Learning and Development*, 52, Section 0500A

Vygotsky, L. S. (1984) Interaction Between Learning and Development. In *Mind in Society: The Development of Higher Psychological Processes*. Cambridge: Harvard University Press

William, D. (2018) *Creating the Schools Our Children Need*. Learning Sciences International

Wood, D., Bruner, J. & Ross, G. (1976) The Role of Tutoring in Problem Solving. *Journal of Child Psychology and Child Psychiatry*, 17, 89–100

2 Scaffolding of retrieval practice and verbal prompts

> It seems that in order for retrieval practice to work well with students of any age, we need to make sure that students are successful.
>
> *(Sumeracki, 2017)*

In recent years, cognitive science has been brought to the forefront of education, meaning that teaching has become more evidence-informed. Teachers now understand that in order to achieve the best outcomes for students, the wider use of reliable evidence is crucial to classroom practice. It is not uncommon now for Professional Development (PD) sessions to start with pre-reading or explanation of research such as Sweller's Cognitive Load Theory, Ebbinghaus' Forgetting Curve or Rosenshine's Principles of Instruction in order to make the 'why' clear when introducing strategies.

Therefore, when considering ways to scaffold in the classroom and beyond, it is important to consider some key principles about what we know about learning first. Without considering these principles, it is likely teachers will lack understanding of effective scaffolding approaches or use scaffolding in ways which don't best support students (the idea of lethal mutations around scaffolding is explored later in this book).

The 'Simple Model of the Mind' (Willingham, 2010) gives us a really practical and accessible model to help us understand how students learn and

DOI: 10.4324/9781003467069-3

therefore how we can best scaffold. This has been exemplified in the diagram shown in Figure 2.1 (Cavigioli, 2019).

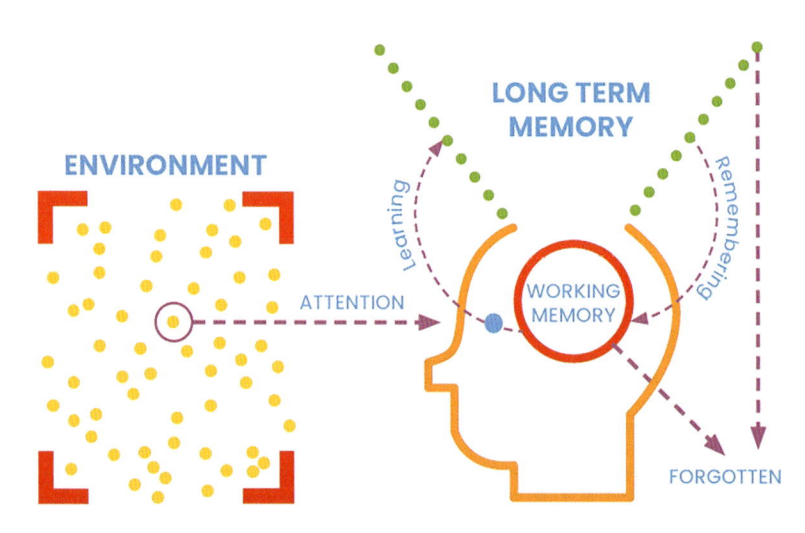

FIGURE 2.1 Memory model

Jamie Clark (2024) has then helpfully distilled this model into these key principles.

1. **Secure attention:** 'Students remember what they attend to' (McCrea, 2017). For learning to take place, students need to be paying attention to what is taught and thinking hard. We need to keep students focused on learning by reducing environmental distractions and embedding routines such as accountable questioning, that help students to focus on challenging cognitive work.

2. **Building memory:** Sweller's Cognitive Load Theory (1988) shows that 'our memory is divided into long-term and working memory, where 'learning requires a change in long-term memory' (Kirschner et al., 2006). Our working memory is only able to hold a small amount of information at any one time. If our working memory then becomes overloaded with too much information, learning is reduced. As teachers we therefore need to be deliberate about avoiding overloading

students in order to maximise learning. This could relate to the design of our tasks, or the way we present information.

3. **Building knowledge:** Constructing knowledge means developing schema; mental frameworks that help us organise and process information. We need to provide opportunities for students to make links with prior knowledge in order to build schema through our organisation of the curriculum and chunking of new learning.

4. **Cognitive Engagement:** 'Learning requires a change in long term memory' (Kirschner et al., 2006). To ensure learning happens therefore, we need to ensure students are 'cognitively active' as much of the time as possible. (Everett, 2020). Questioning and other formative assessment strategies will help us assess what this looks like.

5. **Generative Processes:** 'When we generate information, learned material is reactivated, thus enabling memory consolidation' (Shimamura, 2018). As teachers we should plan for generative activities and retrieval to help students to build schema.

Planning for cognitive load in particular can help us to scaffold more effectively. For example, in task design we might consider chunking explanations, giving student-friendly definitions and ensuring any slides are uncluttered. 'Scaffolding reduces the cognitive load on a learner because the elements that are initially out of the learner's capacity can be controlled by the scaffolder' (Trickey, 2020). An expert exemplification can be seen here: Instead of a teacher adapting a lesson on the Five Pillars of Islam by reducing the focus to two or three (as was apparently suggested to a teacher in their lesson observation feedback once to reduce cognitive demands), some concrete alternative scaffolding approaches which reduce memory demands are suggested:

- Having really clear, succinct explanations
- Chunking explanations so that the whole class learn about and then apply their learning one pillar at a time
- Ensuring learner understood terms like pillar both literally and metaphorically

- Using clear, legible, uncluttered visual information which adds to your spoken explanation without introducing extraneous visual noise
- Giving learners more permanent access to this information via written materials

(Sealy, 2024)

Our understanding of Cognitive Load and the other principles above are a solid foundation in helping us to scaffold more effectively. In the next part of the book, we will explore some of these discrete scaffolding approaches in more detail.

It is important to state that each of these elements could span a whole book in themselves, and that what this book contains is an overview of some selected scaffolding strategies rather than an exhaustive account.

Retrieval practice

Research shows that Retrieval Practice is one of the most effective learning strategies for students. 'Testing is a powerful means of improving learning, not just assessing it' (Roediger & Karpicke, 2006). We know that 'retrieving information from memory is one of the most powerful ways to enhance learning' (Carpenter, 2023). Low stakes testing in order to support the long-term retention of knowledge has therefore become a staple part of classroom practice, with many schools advocating that this is a mandatory part of each lesson. Whilst many different retrieval practice activities exist, it is important that for some students this is carefully scaffolded, and not so difficult that students become demotivated. We've all felt the dauntingness of a blank piece of paper, and therefore strategic scaffolding in Retrieval Practice can increase success where appropriate for all students. Rosenshine (2012) suggests around an 80% success rate is optimal to ensure students are effectively challenged, but also leads to increased confidence and therefore motivation – 'the sweet spot where students are challenged, but not so much that they cannot answer any of the questions' (Inner Drive, 2021). We also know that for certain students, such as younger groups or some students with SEND (Special Educational Needs and Disability) and/or EAL, additional adaptations or scaffolds may need to be provided to support them to feel this success. In the rest of this chapter we will explore what the evidence says and some potential ways teachers can do this.

The scaffolding of retrieval practice

1. Consider the order of the task

A recent study concluded that the ordering as well as the pitch of the retrieval questions was important. It seems that retrieval can be scaffolded to support students by ordering from easiest to hardest: 'In the field experiment, we find that ordering the questions from easiest to most difficult yields the lowest probability to abandon the test as well as the highest number of correct answers' (Anaya et al., 2021). Craig Barton (2023b) also advises scaffolding in the form of asking the easiest question first on a task, including retrieval. This meant more students completed the task, and interestingly students scored higher marks: 'Probably because an easy first question helps students overcome any initial reluctance to start, and then that initial taste of success generates the momentum needed to keep them putting in effort for longer.'

Example of retrieval questions which build in difficulty: (Norman England)

A. In what year did the Norman Conquest of England take place?

B. Name a contender to the throne who was not at the Battle of Hastings.

C. Describe why William wanted to create the Domesday Book.

D. Give one change William the Conqueror made to English castles and fortifications.

E. Describe one impact that the Norman conquest had on the lives of English peasants.

2. Use hints to scaffold, but only after an appropriate wait time

We've all been in the moment where we are struggling to remember something and someone gives us a nudge word or hint, and immediately

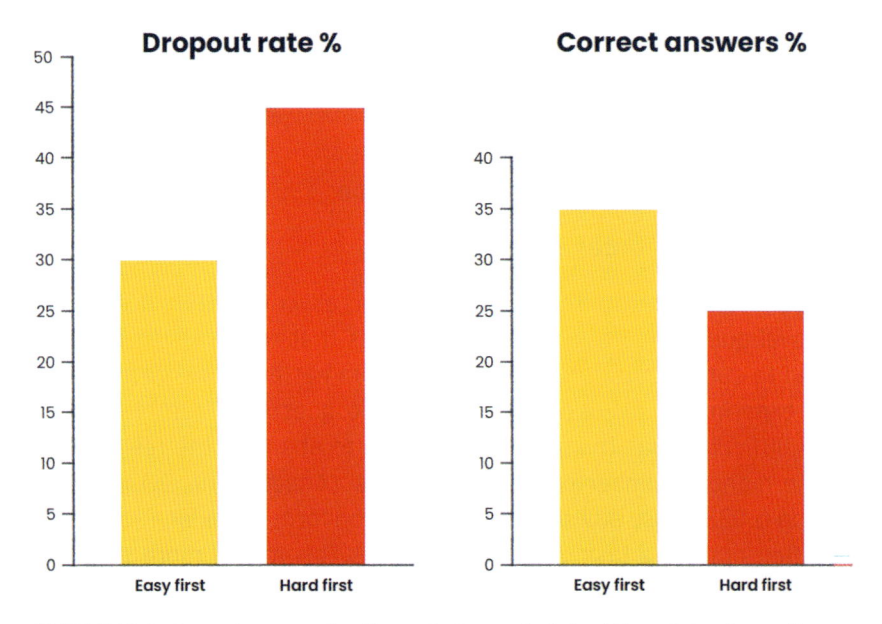

FIGURE 2.2 A graph comparing the ordering and pitch of the retrieval questions

we can then make the connection. Recent research on the use of hints in retrieval practice also suggests that weak hints may be an appropriate scaffold for some students (Vaughn et al., 2022). 'Hints are probably especially important when pupils would otherwise fail to answer most of the test questions without them' (Still, 2022). The study also showed that we need to be careful to ensure these are *weak* hints and that we don't go too far with our scaffolding 'participants who received weaker hints showed better performance on delayed post-tests . . . stronger hints led to better immediate recall due to the ease of retrieval, they did not support long term retention as effectively as weaker hints did' (Inner Drive, 2024).

Raichura (2018) advises that it is also important to take the time to think about meaningful cues and is why hints such as 'it rhymes with . . . ' or 'it begins with . . . ' are unhelpful if we want students to understand rather than just parrot back.

For example, students could be struggling to recall the term for the foreign policy used by the US during the Cold War to prevent the spread of communism (Containment). I could suggest that it begins with 'C' or make an action with my arms to show how I am encircling an object. However, it would be better to use examples of hints like this:

A. What is the term for the foreign policy used by the US during the Cold War to prevent the spread of Communism?
B. Hint: The Korean War was an example of where we see the US employ this strategy by sending soldiers as part of NATO.
C. Hint: It is associated with President Harry Truman and his 1947 Truman Doctrine.

> It is tempting, when you really want your pupils to give the correct answer, to keep adding in clues – but this must be done in a way which makes them think about the content itself rather than artificial clues. Otherwise they are retrieving without context and are performing, not demonstrating understanding; they are giving the illusion of understanding. It is preventing them from making valuable connections with various pieces of information.
> (Raichura, 2018)

The use of wait time when students are struggling to remember is a further scaffold of retrieval practice, remembering that Retrieval Practice is a 'desirable difficulty' (Bjork, 1994). 'Validate that retrieval is hard, remind them that taking a "mental moment" will boost their long-term learning... encourage students to sit with the struggle a little longer' (Agarwal, 2023). It is important that even when hints or cues may be needed, that teachers don't rush into this, allowing some struggle to take place. It can be tempting as teachers to fill this time of silence, but we help improve student independence if we push students out of their comfort zone a little. It's also true that not all students will need cues or hints and even those that do will not need them every time. Any form of scaffold such as this must be added in response to what your assessment in the lesson shows you, rather than predetermining who will need it in advance.

> The solution, I think, is to refrain from giving hints and cues so students can see what they can do without them, but have them available when students need them. So, in the Do Now example, the

hints could be on the back of the piece of paper, or only revealed on the board after 5 minutes. Or when setting students off to answer a question, we refrain from giving a verbal or written hint to the whole class, and instead save it for the specific students who we identify as needing it as we circulate the room.

(Barton, 2023a)

It is also important that over time any hints or cues are gradually reduced to fit with the principles of the scaffolding approach.

3. Model and guide where appropriate

Retrieval can be further scaffolded in the same way as any other task, which could be as simple as modelling through some pre-completed examples, or live modelling of one or two questions. In some cases, particularly with younger students, guided retrieval practice rather than free recall might be a more appropriate approach to promote success (Karpicke et al., 2014). For example, providing a partially completed knowledge organiser or concept map may be a useful scaffold for some students, seen in another experiment by Karpicke.

> To help guide the students to recall information, students were given partially completed concept maps – or diagrams that help to represent relationships among ideas about a given topic. . . . Students were first allowed to fill out the concept maps with the text in front of them then the researchers took away the texts, and had the students complete these partially completed concept maps by recalling the information from memory. Using this scaffolded retrieval activity, the 4th grade students were much more successful on a learning assessment later.
>
> (Sumeracki, 2017)

Figure 2.3 shows an example of a partially completed retrieval grid (Fairlamb, unpublished).

The area of Retrieval Practice and SEND students in particular is one in which there is still a gap in research (Jones, 2021), and obviously each

Chronology Connection

Put the dates and events in the correct chronological order.

Hint? Bank of Dates and Events

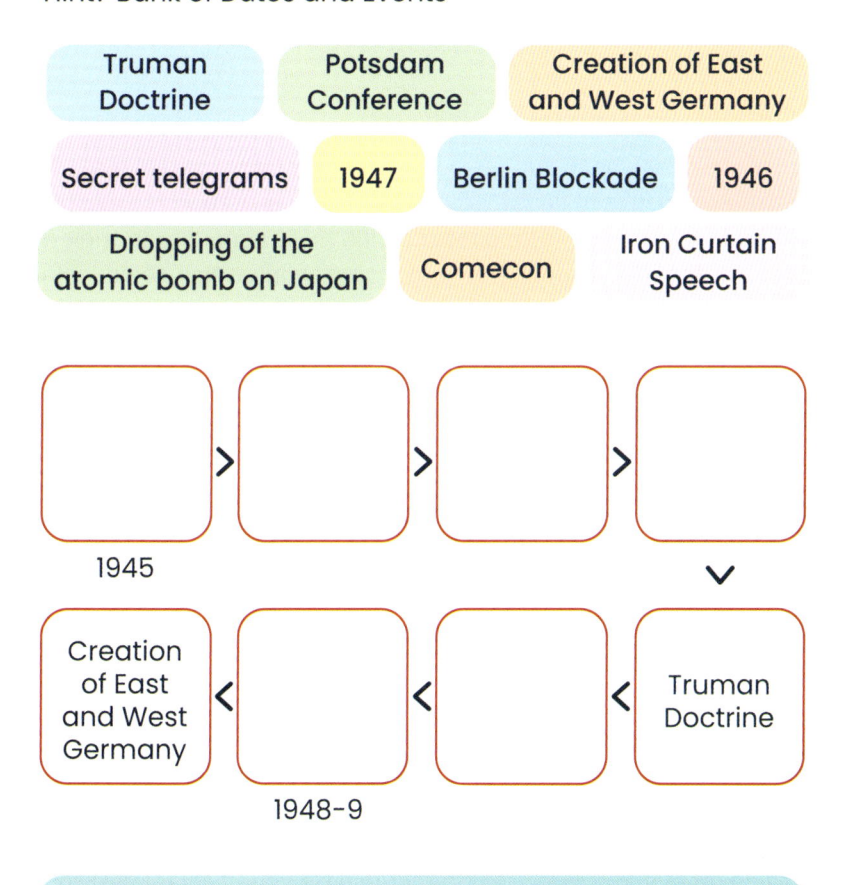

Truman Doctrine	Potsdam Conference	Creation of East and West Germany
Secret telegrams	1947	Berlin Blockade	1946
Dropping of the atomic bomb on Japan	Comecon	Iron Curtain Speech

[ ] > [ ] > [ ] > [ ]
1945

[Creation of East and West Germany] < [ ] < [ ] < [Truman Doctrine]
           1948–9

Misconception alert: Consider how we know which came first between the atomic bomb on Japan and the Potsdam Conference.

FIGURE 2.3 Chronology connection

individual's needs are different. It may be that further cues, or prompts, are needed, and we should definitely ensure that support staff working with students with additional needs are trained in retrieval practice in the same way as teachers are. However, recent research seems to provide evidence that retrieval is universally useful (Carpenter, 2023). 'The current research and evidence should give us the confidence to persevere with this strategy with all the learners in our classroom' (Jones, 2021).

Use of verbal prompts

Much of what has been suggested here as scaffolds for retrieval practice involves the use of verbal prompts or cues, an area worth exploring as an often overlooked form of scaffolding more generally. In their five a day tool, the EEF recommend verbal scaffolding which could include 'reteaching a tricky concept to a group of pupils or using questioning to identify and address any misconceptions' (EEF, 2022). However, a prompt may be much less formal than this. A student struggling to start a task may just need a verbal reminder such as 'How did we tackle this task last time?' or 'What is the first step in this experiment based on the model we just looked at together?' A useful definition of this kind of prompt is of 'statements made by the teacher to focus students on the cognitive and metacognitive processes needed to complete a learning task' (Fisher & Frey, 2010). This can be in the form of a question such as the above, or a declarative statement: 'Ensure you start the paragraph by declaring your argument just as we practised.'

Fisher and Frey continue by dividing prompts into those which deal with cognition (to trigger academic knowledge) and metacognition (to think about thinking). So for a student needing some scaffolding support in a DT lesson, 'What kind of tool would be best to cut this material?' would be a cognition prompt, whereas 'Don't forget to have your diagram next to you so you know which materials need joined together first' would be a metacognitive prompt. It may be that as teachers we jump too quickly by default to thinking written or visual scaffolds may be needed, but in fact a little verbal prompting may be all that a student needs to learn complex content.

Chapter 2 Self-Reflection Questions

Take a few minutes to reflect on the questions below and jot down your answers...

1 How much do you currently scaffold Retrieval Practice for students?

2 What are the pitfalls of providing too much support or scaffolding for students in Retrieval Practice?

3 Which one of these strategies might you try with an upcoming class? What would this look like? Script it out where appropriate.

References

Agarwal, P. (2023) *What Should You Do When Your Students Can't Retrieve Anything?* (Online). Available at https://www.retrievalpractice.org/strategies/scaffold-retrieval-practice. Accessed 27th October 2023

Anaya, L., Iriberri, N., Rey-Biel, P. & Zamarro, G. (2021) *Understanding Performance in Test-Taking: The Role of Question Difficulty Order* (Online). Available at https://www.edworkingpapers.com/sites/default/files/ai21-392.pdf. Accessed 13th December 2023

Barton, C. (2023a) *Don't Make Hints Unavoidable* (Online). Available at https://tipsforteachers.substack.com/p/40-dont-makes-hints-unavoidable. Accessed 25th June 2024

Barton, C. (2023b) *#43 Ask the Easiest Question First* (Online). Available at https://open.substack.com/pub/tipsforteachers/p/43-ask-the-easiest-question-first?r=cdzzi&utm_campaign=post&utm_medium=email. Accessed 27th November 2023

Bjork, R. A. (1994) Memory and Metamemory Considerations in the Training of Human Beings. In J. Metcalfe & A. P. Shimamura (Eds.), *Metacognition: Knowing About Knowing*. The MIT Press

Carpenter, S. K. (2023) Encouraging Students to Use Retrieval Practice: A Review of Emerging Research from Five Types of Interventions. *Educational Psychology Review*, 35, 96 (Online). Available at https://doi.org/10.1007/s10648-023-09811-8

Cavigioli, O. (2019) *Willingham's Simple Memory Model* (Online). Available at https://www.olicav.com/#/diagrams/. Accessed 26th June 2024

Clark, J. (2024) *Teaching One Pagers*. John Catt Educational

EEF (2022) *The 5 a Day Principle: Scaffolding Tool* (Online). Available at https://d2tic4wvo1iusb.cloudfront.net/eef-guidance-reports/send/5-a-Day_Reflection_Tool_2023.pdf. Accessed 27th June 2024

Everett, L. (2020) *Incremental Improvement so All Pupils Are Cognitively Active All of the Time* (Online). Available at https://justonethingafteranotherblog.wordpress.com/2020/12/21/incremental-improvement-so-all-pupils-are-cognitively-active-all-of-the-time/. Accessed 17th June 2024

Fairlamb, A. (unpublished) @alex.fairlamb@hotmail.com

Fisher, D. & Frey, N. (2010) *Guided Instruction: How to Develop Confident and Successful Learners*. ASCD

Inner Drive (2021) *Rosenshine's Seventh Principle of Instruction: Obtain a High Success Rate* (Online). Available at https://blog.innerdrive.co.uk/rosenshine-seventh-principle-of-instruction. Accessed 28th October 2023

Inner Drive (2024) *Effective Questioning for Retrieval Practice: What Does the Latest Research Say?* (Online). Available at https://www.innerdrive.co.uk/blog/effective-questioning-retrieval-practice/. Accessed 1st July 2024

Jones, K. (2021) *Retrieval Practice 2: Implementing, Embedding and Reflecting*. John Catt Educational

Karpicke, J., Blunt, J., Smith, M. & Karpicke, S. (2014) Retrieval-Based Learning: The Need for Guided Retrieval in Elementary School Children. *Journal of Applied Research in Memory and Cognition*, 3(3), 198–286

Kirschner, P., Sweller, J. & Clark, R. E. (2006) Why Minimal Guidance During Instruction Does Not Work: An Analysis of the Failure of Constructivist, Discovery, Problem-Based, Experiential, and Inquiry-Based Teaching. *Educational Psychologist*, 41(2), 75–86

McCrea, P. (2017) *Memorable Teaching: Leveraging Memory to Build Deep and Durable Learning in the Classroom*. CreateSpace Independent Publishing Platform

Raichura, P. (2018) *Retrieval Cues: Do Your Questions Help or Hinder* (Online). Available at https://bunsenblue.wordpress.com/2018/03/19/retrieval-cues-do-your-questions-help-or-hinder/. Accessed 25th June 2024

Roediger, H. L. & Karpicke, J. D. (2006) Test-Enhanced Learning: Taking Memory Tests Improves Long-Term Retention. *Psychological Science*, 17(3), 249–255 (Online). Available at https://doi.org/10.1111/j.1467-9280.2006.01693.x

Rosenshine, B. (2012) Principles of Instruction: Research-Based Strategies that all teachers should know. *American Educator*, 36(1)

Sealy, C. (2024) *Adaptive Teaching – The Four Verbs Approach* (Online). Available at https://primarytimery.com/2024/03/29/adaptive-teaching-the-four-verbs-approach/. Accessed 3rd April 2024

Shimamura, A. (2018) *MARGE: A Whole -Brain Learning Approach for Students and Teachers*. (Online). Available at https://shimamurapubs.wordpress.com/wp-content/uploads/2018/09/marge_shimamura.pdf. Accessed 17th June 2024

Still, K. (2022) *A Teacher's Guide to Retrieval Practice: Feedback and Elaboration* (Online). Available at https://www.sec-ed.co.uk/content/best-practice/a-teacher-s-guide-to-retrieval-practice-feedback-and-elaboration/. Accessed 25th June 2024

Sumeracki, M. (2017) *How to Create Retrieval Practice Activities for Elementary Students* (Online). Available at https://www.learningscientists.org/blog/2017/4/6-1. Accessed 26th June 2024

Sweller, J. (1988) Cognitive Load During Problem Solving: Effects on Learning. *Cognitive Science*, 12(2), 257–285

Trickey, S. (2020) *Scaffolding* (Online). Available at https://www.teachwithmrst.com/post/scaffolding. Accessed 20th June 2024

Vaughn, K., Fitzgerald, G., Hood, D., Migneault, K. & Krummen, K. (2022) The Effect of Hint Strength on the Benefits of Retrieval Practice. *Applied Cognitive Psychology*, 36(2) (Online). Available at https://onlinelibrary.wiley.com/doi/10.1002/acp.3929. Accessed 27th October 2022

Willingham, D. (2010) *Why Don't Students Like School?* Jossey-Bass

3 Scaffolding through modelling

> A central feature of an instructional teaching process is for a teacher to show their students how to do something so that they can do it themselves.
> *(Sherrington, 2022)*

A second scaffolding approach which has its roots in cognitive science is modelling, defined as 'a demonstration of a skill or problem-solving strategy by an expert' (Fisher et al., 2009), and 'Modelling describes the process of learning or acquiring new information, skills, or behaviour through observation, rather than through direct experience or trial-and-error efforts' (Eggen & Kauchak, 2001). Modelling is equally as beneficial in practical subjects such as PE and Drama, as it is in written subjects such as English and History because

Models can be;

- Physical representations of completed tasks – exemplars that can be used as scaffolds, such as a model paragraph for opening a history essay
- Conceptual models – such as the one we need to form to understand the behaviour of particles in solids, liquids and gases
- Explicit narration of our thought processes when thinking through how to solve problems or undertake a creative activity.

(Sherrington, 2019)

DOI: 10.4324/9781003467069-4

Modelling can be used where teachers show students 'what a good one looks like' or can be a joint construction with students such as a paragraph written jointly with the teacher and students together: 'When introducing a new task or working format, it is indispensable that the learners be able to see or hear what a developing product looks like' (Syarifah & Gunawan, 2016). Bandura (1977) outlines modelling as playing a key part in how and why people learn. 'Fortunately, most human behaviour is learned observationally through modelling: from observing others one forms an idea of how new behaviours are performed, and on later occasions, this coded information serves as a guide for action.'

In his fourth principle of Instruction, Rosenshine writes that teachers should 'provide models: providing students with models and worked examples can help them learn to solve problems faster' (Rosenshine, 2012).

In his eighth principle, Rosenshine expands further, noting modelling as an effective form of scaffolding: 'Scaffolds include modelling the steps by the teacher, or thinking aloud by the teacher as he or she solves the problem.' It seems entirely reasonable and logical that providing good examples, or letting students see us complete a process step by step would benefit students in mastering a skill independently.

> From writing a poem to factoring an equation, from passing a rugby ball to designing a website, students in school are constantly in the process of in the process of creating products and performances. However, these do not reach a high standard by magic. They are always the result of combinations of procedures, some relatively simple, others extremely complex. As teachers, it is our responsibility to show students how to use and manipulate their knowledge to form these end products, and just as importantly to ensure they are of as high a standard as possible.
>
> (Allison & Tharby, 2015)

It is important to emphasise here that models must be chosen carefully. There is a risk that students can become demotivated if they feel such a model is beyond their capability, and therefore breaking down the process through metacognitive talk and joint construction of a task alongside thoughtful selection is crucial. In fact, merely watching a model in itself will not lead to learning.

> In the absence of the expert pointing out what to notice, it is likely that the student will notice the wrong things, or even come away from the demonstration with a misconception of what took place . . . students need to witness the teacher's thinking firsthand and see the interaction of both the cognitive and metacognitive aspects required to successfully apply the skill or action.
> (Fisher & Frey, 2010)

Visualisers

Visualisers have become a popular feature in the classroom, used as an effective way to support modelling. Many visualisers have the technology to support photos and videos of models, which is a useful way to support absent students as well. The idea of a 'visualiser book' has become more common, and many teachers are now seeing the benefits of this as an effective scaffold:

1) It sets the standard for presentation/organisation
2) I put notes in it about where we are up to/what next
3) It helps me model text annotation or exam questions.
4) It helps absent students catch up.
(McGee, 2023)

Visualisers help students to see a process from start to finish and to gain concrete knowledge of expectations and is therefore not surprising that many schools now have a visualiser in each classroom.

So how can we put modelling into practice in the classroom, whether through a visualiser or other method?

1. Worked examples

One key way teachers can model for students is the provision of worked examples, a learning effect predicted by cognitive load theory (Sweller, 1988). A worked example is a pre-solved problem or completed task: 'this means giving a step by step demonstration of how to complete a task or solve a problem, with each stage thoroughly explained' (Inner Drive, 2021).

Worked examples act as an effective scaffold for students, especially novices (Clark et al., 2012) because they free up working memory to think about the steps involved in solving a problem, rather than on working out the answer. Consequently, 'students learn to recognise which moves are required for particular problems, which is the basis for developing knowledge and skill as a problem solver.'

We can all perhaps identify with this if we think about following a recipe step-by-step when making a dish for the first time. Not only does this mean the 'how' of the task is carefully scaffolded, it takes account of cognitive load theory.

'The *worked example effect* occurs when learning is enhanced by studying worked examples to problems rather than by trying to solve the original problems' (Ayres, 2012). The EEF review in cognitive science (2021) showed 22 studies which showed the positive impact of worked examples on learning outcomes, although these were particularly focused on secondary students and students in subjects such as science and maths.

One useful way to use worked examples is the FAME approach, as explained by Bob Pritchard writing for the EEF:

- F – **Fading:** Fading away steps in a process after full worked examples, to increase complexity
- A - **Alternating**: Alternating worked examples with opportunities for students to try a similar independent example

M – **Mistakes:** Include mistakes in worked examples so that students develop deeper understanding

E – **Explanation**: Teachers can use a think-aloud process to help students make sense of the model

(Pritchard, 2022)

Worked examples might include therefore a number of maths or science problems with the solutions and working out provided. Students can then interrogate the example and be questioned about their understanding – 'Why is X my first step?' 'Why would it be a mistake to do x' or 'Would I have got the same result if I'd done y?'.

In English or Psychology for example, a modelled paragraph might be shown to students, who then deconstruct what makes it successful, perhaps alongside success criteria. This can be really successfully done in conjunction with the teacher by using the visualiser to underline, highlight or annotate key parts of the answer.

In Maths this might be the presentation of several worked examples of a mathematical process, with the teacher deconstructing each step in a formula using metacognitive oracy, for example the steps in working out the answer to a complicated equation (with misconceptions and potential error points highlighted and discussed).

In Art or Design Technology, creating a model in advance, for example a pottery piece or birdhouse, allows students to see what an excellent example looks like, and teachers can then question students about the techniques which have been applied to create it (exemplified in the case study in Chapter 8).

The other benefit to creating a pre-prepared model example is that 'you are compelled to see the task through the eyes of your students before the lesson. This means you can nip in the bud any potential misconceptions and pre-empt any potential icebergs that students can run aground on' (Allison & Tharby, 2015). I recently visited an Art lesson for example, where the teacher had recorded a video of himself modelling a particular shading technique. After watching and discussing as a class, the teacher was able to leave the video playing on silent to give students an extra scaffold to refer to, should they need it.

Another way that modelling can scaffold learning for students is through **'backwards fading',** steadily removing some of the modelled work so that students can start to independently solve the problem. We can see the concept of backwards fading illustrated in this diagram (Clark et al., 2006).

One way to do this is to use completion tasks. A worked example is provided but with some elements missing, for example a maths problem with a couple of steps missed out. 'These are a great way to advance the knowledge of students who are nearly experts in a particular topic, but still need a little bit of help and guidance' (Inner Drive, 2021). In addition,

Transitioning from worked examples to problem assigments

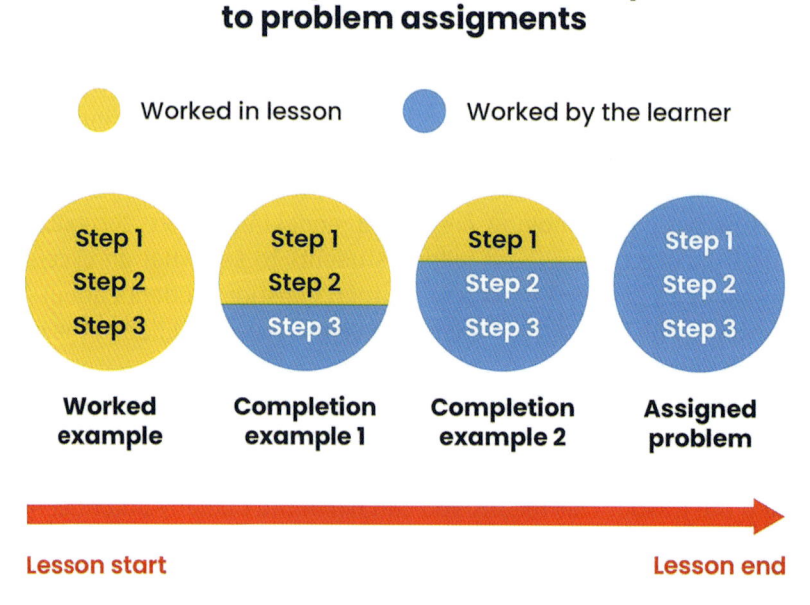

- Worked in lesson
- Worked by the learner

Worked example	Completion example 1	Completion example 2	Assigned problem
Step 1 / Step 2 / Step 3	Step 1 / Step 2 / Step 3	Step 1 / Step 2 / Step 3	Step 1 / Step 2 / Step 3

Lesson start → Lesson end

FIGURE 3.1 A diagram demonstrating backwards fading

Effective teachers will tend to provide students with many worked examples so that the general patterns are clear, providing a strong basis from which to learn. The trick is then to gradually reduce the level of completion, leaving students to finish problems off and ultimately do them by themselves.

(Sherrington, 2019)

Comparative modelling can also be a useful way of scaffolding using worked examples. In this strategy, a couple of examples are shared with students. Students could then identify which one is better, and this is best done alongside really clear success criteria which has already been shared with students. This is an opportunity for teachers to highlight common misconceptions or easy mistakes to make which affect the quality of their answers.

In History this might mean putting two paragraphs alongside each other and comparing to see which one contains the key vocabulary, which presents the better argument which evidence provided, or which one uses the greater depth of knowledge (as seen in the example below). In Maths it might be comparing two equations with the working out shown to see which one has reached the correct answer. In DT it might be comparing photographs of two finished products, or in PE you could use two video clips of a particular skill being demonstrated. Rather than simply pointing students to the answer about which one is better, it's useful to let students do this independently first to ensure students start to build their mental models of what excellence looks like.

2. Live modelling

Of course having pre-prepared modelled examples is great, but another way to scaffold for students through modelling is through live modelling. Live modelling is about taking what we do as teachers often automatically, choosing vocabulary, deciding upon a structure, planning and editing, and making these explicit to students. At first, you may want to do this on your own, taking each part of the problem, or each sentence

The Scaffolding Effect

Comparative Modelling

**Q1. Describe two features of the Babington Plot 1586
[4 marks]**

Success criteria:
- Point – stated, accurate feature
- Evidence – 2–3
- Evidence – SPET

Answer A:

One key feature of the Babington plot was that its aim was to remove Elizabeth I as Queen.

For example, the plan involved the the Duke of Guise invading with 60,000 men, then assassinating Elizabeth I and replacing he with Mary Queen of Scots.

A further key feature of the plot was that Mary Queen of Scots was implicated in the plot.

For example, Walsingham and his spies were watching Mary and intercepted her letters and read them, and they were then used to prove her guilt resulting in her execution in 1587.

Answer B:

One key feature of the Babington plot was that its aim was to remove Elizabeth I as Queen.

For example, the plan was to remove Elizabeth and replace her.

A further key feature of the plot was that MQS was implicated in the plot.

For example, letters were found in Throckmorton's house and this proved she was guilty and 11,000 others too.

SPaG
- Debt – not dept
- Catholic – capital C
- Elizabeth/Mary – capitals
- Legitimate – no 'e' before the 'm'

Common wrong phrasing
- Everyone in England / the public thought she was illegitimate
- She was unpopular with everyone
- All Catholics were involved in the plots

FIGURE 3.2 A diagram showcasing comparative modelling

and explaining aloud what you are doing and why. A visualiser is a really useful tool to use here so that students can see your writing process for example, at the same time as you explain aloud what you are writing and why.

We know that students find hearing teachers think aloud their processes and understanding is something which students find helpful (Block & Israel, 2004). Fisher and Frey determine three methods teachers could use when live modelling:

- The teacher alerts students to the methods used to form their initial understanding of the problem or task
- The teacher articulates how they know whether a decision is correct or not
- The teacher demonstrates how to use a particular process or procedure to complete a task

'Regardless of the discipline, the purpose of a think-aloud during guided instruction is to provide a well-timed scaffold to move the student to the next step or stage' (Fisher & Frey, 2010).

This is a bit of a daunting prospect for any teacher, particularly if you don't have a great deal of experience or are new to a particular topic. One good way to combat this is to either practise an example beforehand, script your explanations, or even to pre-prepare an example and have this next to you as a prompt during the live modelling process. You may not need it, but it acts as a comfort blanket in case you do.

As you become more confident with live modelling and as students begin to understand the process, the modelling can become more collaborative, and this also keeps students focused. The teacher can ask questions such as, 'What key piece of vocabulary is needed here?' 'What might my next sentence look like?' or simply 'What should I do next?' The live modelling process can also help build a supportive culture where, by adopting the role of the students facing a particular question, you can help them see that their emotions when faced with a similar task are natural.

Over time with repeated scaffolding like this, students' confidence should increase, and they should gain knowledge in how to approach tricky tasks; 'Live modelling shows that success isn't something that comes as the result of a click on a Powerpoint slide. Success is a process of thinking, editing and reflecting again. Importantly what it also shows is that mistakes are okay' (Roberts, 2022). Allison and Tharby (2015) suggest language such as 'I must say when I first looked at this problem I didn't know where to start. And then it hit me that I should.' 'It's ok to feel frustrated at this point, I often do. Now the best way to solve this is to . . .' 'I used to struggle with . . . but when I started to use this strategy I found it much easier.'

Live modelling can be particularly useful in highlighting misconceptions that students may hold about the subject. For example,

> In maths and science there are numerous well-known common misconceptions and errors; in writing, there are many common spelling and grammatical errors. A form of scaffolding is to tackle these things head-on, highlighting potential pitfalls and supporting students in checking their own work so that, ultimately, students have a sound knowledge of the pitfalls and are able to self-check and self-correct.
>
> (Sherrington, 2019)

Live modelling does not come without its pitfalls though. If we're not careful, students may end up simply copying out what teachers produce with no better understanding of what made it good in the first place or instead just passively listening (Atherton, 2024). Atherton goes on to share a clever strategy to prevent this, with students using an active margin to record interesting or important aspects of the model while it is being shared. The students are less passive, actively seeking out useful vocabulary or devices for example: 'In jotting down features of your own response, they have effectively created a marginal scaffold strip in their exercise book to help them write their own essay.'

3. Student models

An alternative to using teacher models, either live or pre-prepared is to use examples from the students themselves. This can be really motivating for students because it helps them feel that preparing such an answer is achievable by them all. One way to do this is to make sure your circulation of the classroom is purposeful and you are looking for brilliant examples of a problem solved, choice of vocabulary, succinct answer or whatever the key success criteria is. You can then use these under the visualiser to show the rest of the class what meeting that success criteria looks like. In a further step linked to feedback, students can then use this information to improve their own work. Students can also identify why the work is successful and perhaps add points for development. Managed well, this kind of activity can be immensely motivating as well as providing a scaffold for students.

'Even more interestingly, we can ask the individual themselves to talk to the class about the process of completing the work, refining exactly how they arrived at the successful end point. It all helps in assisting students' metacognitive capacity' (Thom, 2018).

If using student work there and then seems a little daunting or the relationship with the class is not yet built up, you can also do this anonymously. When reading the books or looking at work ready for feedback, you can easily photograph a couple ready to show the class in the next lesson. This is ideally part of a wider whole class feedback, where students then have time to implement improvements to their work or attempt a similar problem in order to put the feedback into action.

4. I, We, You

A final approach to modelling is a combination of several of the previous methods; the I, We, You approach. In the 'I' phase the teacher provides a pre-prepared model example, which as explained above is interrogated and annotated by students against success criteria. In this phase, although the teacher has done the heavy lifting, it's important to include checks for understanding along the way. In addition, the teacher may narrate their choices and processes at this stage. This rich discussion is followed by a 'We' joint construction of a second problem, a similar problem or a further paragraph in an extended answer. In this phase, responsibility begins to pass to students, working side by side with the teacher. Finally, students complete a similar problem independently. By this stage, students should be familiar with the material and able to complete problems with a fair amount of ease. This gradual release approach to modelling can be very effective as a scaffold as problems are broken down into chunks, and continual checks for understanding ensure that by the 'You' part of the model that students have the confidence and motivation to have a go at a problem independently.

I do	We do	You do
Fully demonstrate, explicitly break down the material, one step at a time.	Give partial examples, present material in larger chunks, introduce variation.	Give opportunities for independent problem solving of whole tasks.

Novice ←——————————————————→ Expert

FIGURE 3.3 Novice vs Expert

This process is modelled in the History example shown in Figure 3.4, where student practice is carefully scaffolded as they are novices to a particular style of exam question (Thornton, 2019). We can see a section for annotation of a completed model, a section for co-creating an answer together as a class and then a section of independent practice.

In practice, when teachers use this kind of 'gradual fading' (van de Pol et al., 2018), they may repeat several phases after checking for understanding reveals students need more modelling – perhaps I, we, I, we you or I, I, we, you may be more realistic:

> The trouble is that you can't know – and a student can't know themselves – if they are ready to be successful on their own until they give it a go. However, unlike a baton race, where you only get one chance

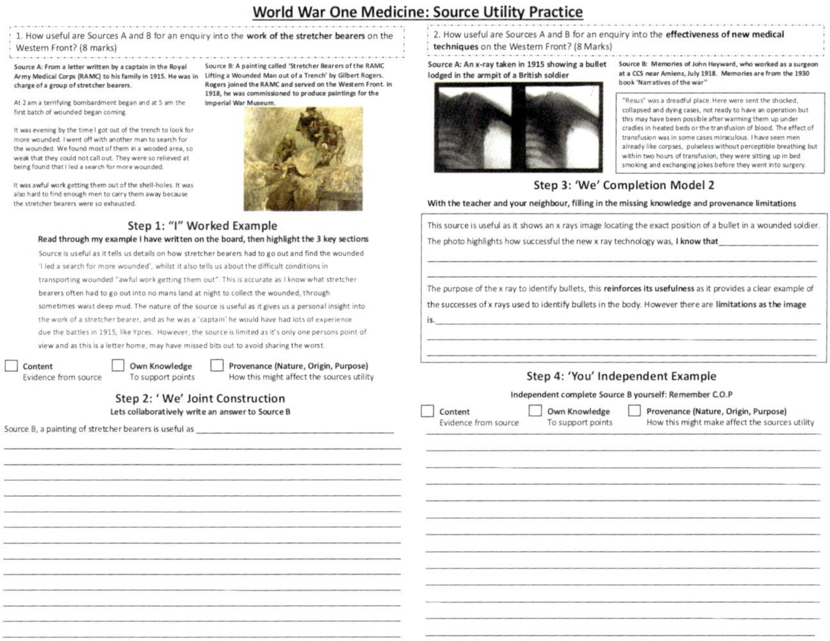

FIGURE 3.4 Example of I, We, You approach (Thornton, 2019)

FIGURE 3.5 The I, We, You approach

to get it right, in a modelling sequence in a lesson, you can try many times, making attempts at success an explicit part of the process.

(Sherrington, 2022)

A common mistake with this approach therefore can be that the teacher is too slow to move to the 'You do' stage and to over scaffold this, or equally to make the 'I do' so complicated that students struggle when moving to the independent stage. Moreover, it can be the case that 'I, we, you' becomes a static process which teachers take students through robotically, worried that going backwards from a 'we' or 'I' stage is not possible. Modelling can involve going backwards and forwards between the 'I, we, you' process as part of adaptive teaching and so it might be better to see modelling as Quigley (2022) has phrased it, as a 'continuum... whereby pupils may subtly slide along the continuum' with our checks for understanding helping us to determine where on the continuum they are currently residing.

> How long students spend on each stage of the continuum is an empirical question and will largely be determined by the quality of examples (and non-examples) and completion problems that you use as well as the proficiency and prior knowledge of the students. Feedback to the teacher is key here: if students are performing successfully on a stage, then you can make the transition to a lower level of support, increasing the number of steps that a student is expected to complete.
>
> (Needham, 2018)

Modelling does not come without its pitfalls though, and there are some to be aware of here:

- Be careful not to over-model and ensure that students do ultimately get to independent practice. It may be that you need to move back to more structured modelling and try again, but ultimately as with any scaffolding it must be removed.

- Be careful not to make assumptions about what students know and understand. When live modelling for example, be really explicit with students about what you are doing and why. It can be easy to assume students understand why you have selected particular vocabulary or structured your work in a certain way, but they may not.

- Be careful not to set students up simply to copy your model. Make sure the independent practice is of a different problem or a similar question.

- Don't 'dumb down' your model. Make sure you maintain your high expectations and ensure even students with high prior attainment are pushed.

- Ensure I, We, You does not become overly prescriptive. It is not a lesson structure, nor should it be used every lesson, but instead as appropriately determined by the teacher.

Chapter 3 Self-Reflection Questions

Take a few minutes to reflect on the questions below and jot down your answers...

1 What models of excellence do you use in your classroom?

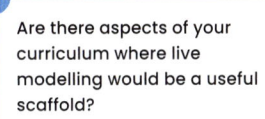

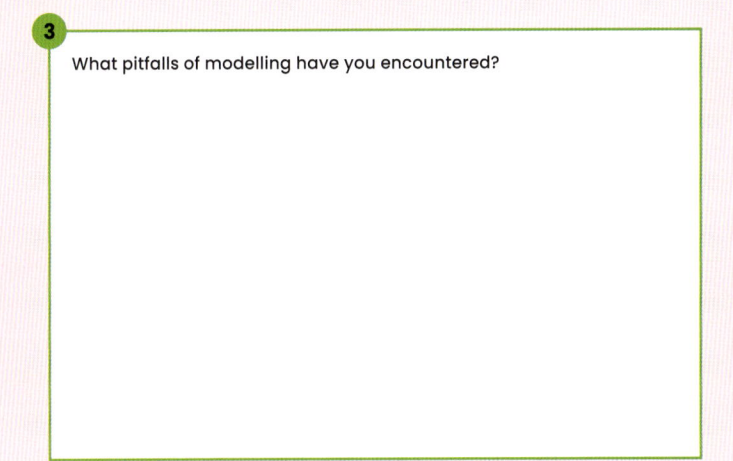

2 Are there aspects of your curriculum where live modelling would be a useful scaffold?

3 What pitfalls of modelling have you encountered?

References

Allison, S. & Tharby, A. (2015) *Making Every Lesson Count*. CrownHouse

Atherton, A. (2024) *Live Modelling, Maximising Student Thinking* (Online). Available at https://codexterous.home.blog/2022/05/29/live-modelling-maximising-student-thinking/. Accessed 9th January 2024

Ayres, P. (2012) Worked Example Effect. In N. M. Seel (Ed.), *Encyclopedia of the Sciences of Learning*. Boston, MA: Springer (Online). Available at https://doi.org/10.1007/978-1-4419-1428-6_20

Bandura, A. (1977) *Social Learning Theory*. Englewood Cliffs: Prentice-Hall

Block, C. C. & Israel, S. E. (2004) The ABCs of Performing Highly Effective Think Alouds. *The Reading Teacher*, 58(2), 154–167.

Clark, R., Kirschner, P. & Sweller, J. (2012) Putting Students on the Path to Learning: The Case for Fully Guided Instruction (Online). *American Educator*, 36(1), 6–11

Clark, R., Nguyen, F. & Sweller, F. (2006) *Efficiency in Learning: Evidence-Based Guidelines to Manage Cognitive Load*. John Wiley and Sons

EEF (2021) *Cognitive Science Approaches in the Classroom* (Online). Available at https://educationendowmentfoundation.org.uk/education-evidence/evidence-reviews/cognitive-science-approaches-in-the-classroom. Accessed 2nd August 2024

Eggen, P. D. & Kauchak, D. P. (2001) *Educational Psychology: Classroom Connections* (Fifth edition). New York: Macmillan

Fisher, D. & Frey, N. (2010) *Guided Instruction: How to Develop Confident and Successful Learners*. ASCD

Fisher, D., Frey, N. & Lapp, D. (2009) *In a Reading State of Mind; Brain Research, Teacher Modeling and Comprehension Instruction*. Newark: International Reading Association

Inner Drive (2021) Rosenshine's Seventh Principle of Instruction: Obtain a High Success Rate (Online) Found at https://blog.innerdrive.co.uk/rosenshine-seventh-principle-of-instruction Accessed 28th October 2023

McGee, N. (2023) *Twitter Post* (Online). Available at https://twitter.com/RE_McGEE/status/1722326296217141691

Needham, T. (2018) *Applying Cognitive Load Theory to English Part 4: Combining the Alternation Strategy and the Problem-Completion Effect – Examples from Teaching Writing* (Online). Available at https://tomneedhamteach.wordpress.com/2018/11/05/applying-cognitive-load-theory-to-english-part-4-combining-the-alternation-strategy-and-the-problem-completion-effect-examples-from-teaching-writing/. Accessed 2nd August 2024

Pritchard, B. (2022) *EEF Blog: Working with Worked Examples – Simple Techniques to Enhance their Effectiveness* (Online). Available at https://educationendowmentfoundation.org.uk/news/eef-blog-working-with-worked-examples-simple-techniques-to-enhance-their-effectiveness#:~:text=The%20EEF's%20Bob%20Pritchard%20introduces,of%20worked%20examples%20in%20teaching.&text=Worked%20Examples%20can%20help%20pupils,1%20in%20the%20science%20classroom. Accessed 21st January 2025

Quigley, A. (2022) *Closing the Writing Gap*. Routledge

Roberts, M. (2022) *The Boy Question*. Routledge

Rosenshine, B. (2012). Principles of instruction: Research-based strategies that all teachers should know. *American Educator*, 36(1),

Sherrington, T. (2019) *Rosenshine's Principles in Action*. John Catt Educational

Sherrington, T. (2022) *Five Ways to Secure Progress Through Modelling* (Online). Available at https://teacherhead.com/2022/06/15/five-ways-to-secure-progress-through-modelling/. Accessed 30th October 2023

Sweller, J. (1988) Cognitive Load During Problem Solving: Effects on Learning. *Cognitive Science*, 12(2), 257–285

Syarifah, E. & Gunawan, W. (2016) Scaffolding in the Teaching of Writing Discussion Texts Based on SFL Genre-Based Approach. *English Review: Journal of English Education*, 4, 39

Thom, J. (2018) *Slow Teaching*. John Catt

Thornton, G. (2019) *I, We, You* (Online). Available at https://mrthorntonteach.com/2019/10/05/i-we-you/. Accessed 27th November 2023

van de Pol, J., Mercer, N. & Volman, M. (2018) Scaffolding Student Understanding in Small-Group Work: Students' Uptake of Teacher Support in Subsequent Small-Group Interaction. *Journal of the Learning Sciences*, 28(2), 206–239 (Online). Available at https://doi.org/10.1080/10508406.2018.1522258

4 Scaffolding of explanations

> A good explanation is the beating heart of an effective learning sequence.
>
> (Boxer, 2021)

We present new knowledge and explain to students all the time. However, in order to make sure all students can access this information, it is important to make sure our explanations are also given in an effective way; when explaining new knowledge to students, it can be easy for them to become overwhelmed.

With our understanding of cognitive load, we need to make sure that our explanations are given in such a way that students can understand it more easily and that working memories do not become overloaded.

> If students are overwhelmed with too many new elements at once, it logically follows that intrinsic cognitive load can be reduced by breaking up the task into bite-sized chunks. Within the Cognitive Load Theory literature, this is referred to as the *isolated elements effect*.
>
> (Lovell, 2020)

1. Chunking

If I asked you to tell me your mobile phone number right now, you'd probably recount the numbers in groups or chunks, perhaps like this:

07777-777-777. You do this because grouping the numbers into sections like this makes it easier to remember. 'Chunking' makes information more easily digestible and memorable and is therefore an effective way to scaffold. Essentially this means as part of your explanation you group different bits of knowledge together and share them in stages in more meaningful or manageable sections or chunks.

> The more effective teachers do not overwhelm their students by presenting too much new material at once. Rather, these teachers only present small amounts of new material at any one time, and then assist the students as they practise this material. Only after the students have mastered the first step do teachers proceed to the next step.
>
> (Rosenshine, 2012)

This ensures that the working memory is not put under too much strain and allows for greater learning efficiency.

It is because of this that careful time investment is needed in breaking the curriculum down into manageable chunks, and spending time thinking about sequencing how this new material will be introduced to students. This can be aided with examples, particularly when they 'hook onto the previous knowledge of our students' (Quigley, 2016). Therefore teachers need to think carefully about not overloading students with information, whilst equally providing enough examples in our explanations so that students can make connections with prior knowledge.

This also applies to any other information we present to students. A video for example, should be presented in chunks, alongside questions to focus students and provide ways to check for understanding. Reading a text should also be chunked, with opportunities for check for understanding questions or for students to generate their own summary after each new section. It is better to break up a lesson into chunks of an explanation with time for modelling and independent practice after each new section of knowledge, such as the example shown in Figure 4.1,

60 The Scaffolding Effect

where the steps of a science practical are chunked, rather than to share huge amounts of knowledge in one go and leave the practice for the last part of the lesson.

Chunked Explanations

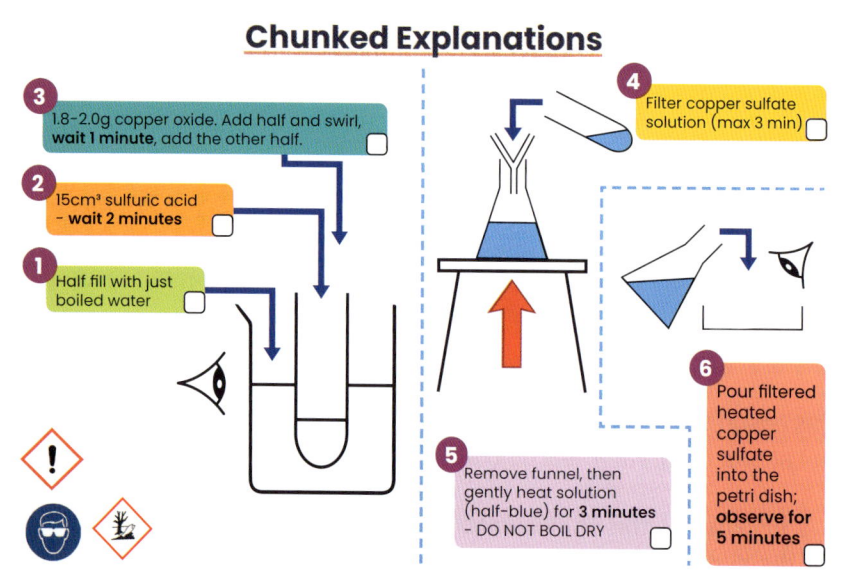

3 1.8-2.0g copper oxide. Add half and swirl, **wait 1 minute**, add the other half.

2 15cm³ sulfuric acid - **wait 2 minutes**

1 Half fill with just boiled water

4 Filter copper sulfate solution (max 3 min)

5 Remove funnel, then gently heat solution (half-blue) for **3 minutes** - DO NOT BOIL DRY

6 Pour filtered heated copper sulfate into the petri dish; **observe for 5 minutes**

FIGURE 4.1 Chunked explanation of a science practical (Paterson, 2019); integrated instructions – thoughts on chemistry and education (www.dave2004b.wordpress.com/integrated-instructions/)

2. Analogies

I recently lost my passport. I opened the cupboard of doom to start looking and quickly realised it was like finding a needle in a haystack. Analogies like this aid understanding. It didn't take you long for you to realise that my cupboard was a mess, that I didn't know where to start looking for my passport and finding it would not be easy. Therefore, a second way of scaffolding explanations is to ensure we use effective analogies. Analogies help us make a connection between an abstract concept and information they are already familiar with to help unlock understanding. Although there are pitfalls (choosing too unfamiliar an abstract which needs lots of explanation or allowing an analogy to

Scaffolding of explanations 61

embed a misconception for example), analogies can really help students to make sense of their learning.

Describing the journey through a student's GCSE (General Certificate of Secondary Education) being akin to a marathon rather than a sprint for instance, helps students see the value in revision that is chunked throughout the year. Showing how an electron orbits a nucleus in the same way that the earth orbits the sun helps students make sense of atomic structure.

Adam Boxer (2021) offers four helpful criteria for effective analogies. ('The source is the idea that is supposed to be more familiar to the student . . . and the target is the unfamiliar idea.')

a) Knowledge of the source: 'Analogies only work if the source is known to the students.' Comparing Winston Churchill in World War Two to being like a broken record because of his constant messaging about resilience and determination would not therefore be helpful as many students would not have knowledge of what a record is or why it would be broken. Indeed, many may think of a record as a time achieved in the 100m sprint instead of a vinyl record.

b) The analogy's limit: 'Sources and targets by definition will not map exactly onto each other – there will always be a point at which the analogy stops working . . . at some point the source and target become so dissimilar that the analogy becomes worthless.'

c) Do no harm: 'Some analogies can be actively harmful.' We must be careful to ensure our analogies do not promote misconceptions, or are so distracting that students spend more time thinking about the analogy than they do the content.

What's the challenge here? Analogies shouldn't 'trick you into ignoring the real difficulties in communicating the concepts' (Boxer, 2021). It's important to spend time thinking about what makes this concept so challenging and therefore what our analogy effectively needs to communicate.

3. Pre-teaching of vocabulary

In Chapter 5-7, we will discuss further the importance of scaffolds for Literacy. However, it is important to note here the value of pre-teaching vocabulary when explaining new concepts. An understanding of key vocabulary and this being explicitly taught will help to scaffold these new ideas for students. We know that the demands of disciplinary vocabulary are significant with students coming across multiple new examples of Tier 2 and 3 words each day, and therefore they will need support in unlocking those keywords in order to access the curriculum content.

In 'Closing the Vocabulary Gap' Alex Quigley explains a formula for how to do this well. The SEEC models suggests:

- **'Select** - Preview the reading material for the lesson or the topic or the scheme of learning at hand.' Teachers should think about the difficulty of the reading material and the vocabulary which might need to be taught explicitly.

- **'Explain** - Once you have selected the words to teach . . . we move onto explaining the word successfully' through a combination of writing the word and definition, saying it out loud and discussing examples.

- **'Explore**' - This could be done through a discussion about the etymology or morphology of the word for example.

- **'Consolidate** - We know that to deeply understand a word we need to be repeatedly exposed to that word.' Making sure the vocabulary is part of retrieval practice is essential.

(Quigley, 2018)

Another way to ensure vocabulary is explicitly taught is to use a Frayer model. These graphic organisers can be used across subjects to explicitly focus on keywords. These will be discussed further in the oracy chapter.

5. Visual scaffolds

Providing visual scaffolds can also be a really effective way to support students as they grasp new material. Vision is 'probably the best single tool we have for learning anything' (Medina, 2008). Visual scaffolds can be diagrams, pictures or illustrations which help students make sense of explanations and new knowledge. This is often referred to as dual coding theory:

> According to dual coding theory, if the same information is properly offered to you in two different ways; it enables you to access more working memory capacity. This means that you can benefit from access to both visual and verbal memory capacity.
> (Kirschner, 2019)

Using visuals can particularly support students in trying to understand a process or cycle, a diagram with arrows and pictures to consolidate an explanation of the life cycle of a butterfly for example.

Another example of a visual scaffold is a graphic organiser. As a history teacher helping students to understand the causes and effects of a particular event for example, I will regularly use a graphic organiser to support students' understanding. A science teacher may use a tree diagram to support students to see classification differences between different plants or animals. Graphic organisers such as the one shown in Figure 4.2 are really useful ways to help students organise their information and in turn supports understanding; 'graphic organisers present information in concise ways to show key parts of the whole concept, theme or topic and are highly effective for all students' (Fisher & Frey, 2010).

Examples of graphic organisers include flow diagrams, concept maps or tree diagrams and can be co-constructed with the teacher as part of live modelling or 'We do' activity. They can also be used to feed into retrieval approaches, such as asking students to finish a partially completed organiser (such as the Cold War example in Chapter 2).

Visual Scaffold

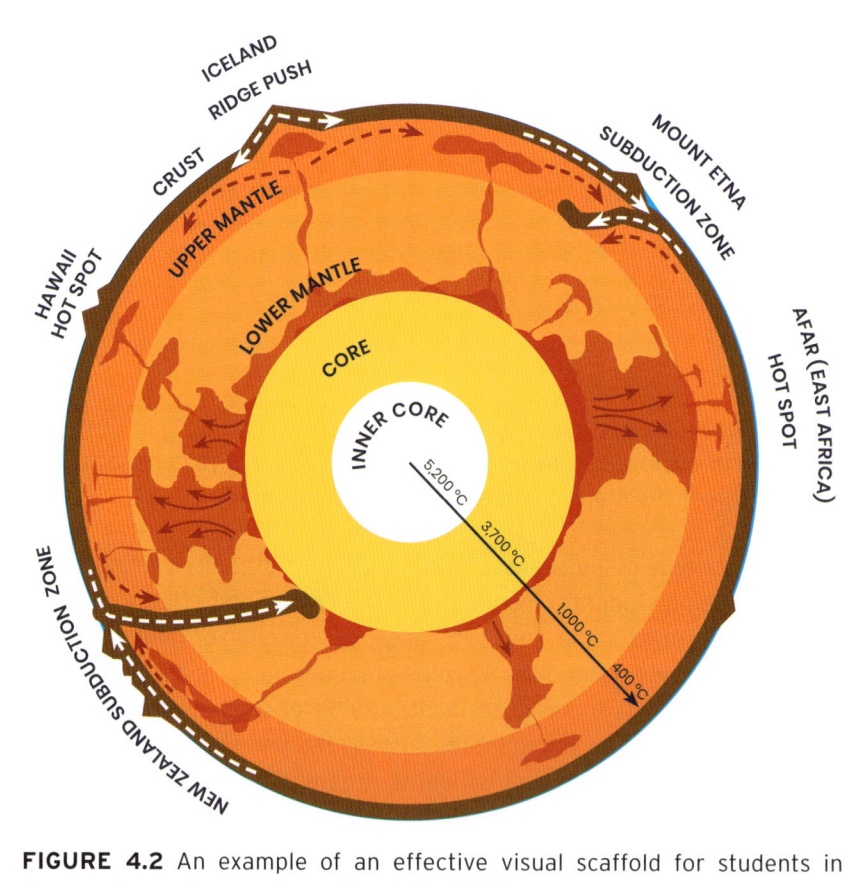

FIGURE 4.2 An example of an effective visual scaffold for students in Geography can be seen here (Goodwin, 2021)

Scaffolding of explanations 65

Why were there religious divisions in England?

Factor	Evidence	Explanation	Judge & Link
English reformation	· The Reformation was when Protestants challenged the Catholic Church across Europe. · Protestants believed that the Bible should be translated from Latin into English, that each Church should be simply decorated and that vestments should not be worn. · Henry VIII created a new Protestant Church in England in 1532 – the Church of England. · The Catholic Church felt threatened by this and so focused on strengthening their faith. Across Europe in Catholic countries, non-believers were put in prison or executed		

Mary I's reign	· Mary I changed England from Protestant (Church of England) back to Catholic.
	· Protestants were persecuted:
	  – 300 Protestants burned at the stake
	  – Many fleed to other countries to be safe (e.g Holland)
	· When Elizabeth I came to power in 1558, most of England's bishops were Catholic. To change the religion of the country she would need an **Act of Parliament** – the House of Lords was filled with many Catholic bishops <u>who would not</u> pass it.
	· Some priests changed their religion to Protestant but others continued to be devoted Catholics and refused to work in a Protestant Church.		

Geographical divisions	– Parts of England were more Catholic than others, meaning they were less likely to accept Protestantism. – The further from London an area was, the more likely it was to be a Catholic area e.g. Durham. – The closer an area was to London, the more likely it was to be Protestant.		

Puritans
(Radical Protestants)
	– When Elizabeth became queen, many Protestants in exile decided it was safe to return to England.
	– Puritans – they came back more **radical** and were known as **Puritans** because they wanted to '*purify*' the Christian religion.
	– They wanted to:
	  – Get rid of anything not written in the Bible.
	  – Churches to be simple and priests not to wear special clothes (vestments).
	– A lot of the other Protestants said that these Puritan ideas were too much.		

FIGURE 4.3 Graphic organiser example (Fairlamb, 2019) unpublished

Why did the Elizabethans want to explore the world more?

- Explain the six different reasons why Elizabethans wanted to explore the world more.
- Judge the different reasons (gr 6–7).
- Link the reasons (gr 8–9).

The Age of Exploration: Why did Elizabethans want to explore the world more?

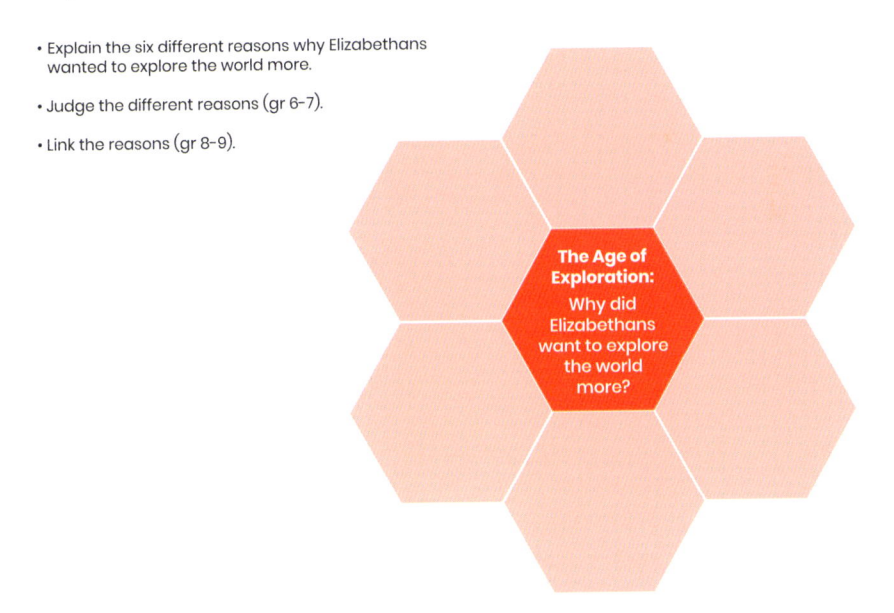

FIGURE 4.4 Graphic organiser (Fairlamb, 2019) unpublished

CASE STUDY: DAVID GOODWIN, TEACHING AND LEARNING TRUST LEAD @MRGOODWIN23

Scaffolding through Graphic Organisers

Writing can be difficult for students due to the limitations of working memory. When writing, students must hold and manipulate various pieces of information in their minds simultaneously – such as the content they are writing about, sentence structure, and spelling – while physically writing or typing. At a young age, students are still learning to master language rules, so constructing coherent and grammatically correct sentences adds extra cognitive load. The coordination between thinking of ideas, organising them logically, and then expressing them clearly in written form requires significant mental bandwidth.

Students need tools to help offload their thinking, providing a temporary cognitive boost. Graphic organisers, such as mind maps, concept maps, and flow diagrams, can help students generate sentences and narratives containing more complex structures of syntax and discourse. Think of these tools as an external workspace where students can select, organise, and integrate their ideas. When students offload their thoughts, they increase their chances of engaging in an iterative cognitive loop, where captured thoughts are reprocessed, refined, and expanded upon, fostering a deeper understanding and innovation.

When students organise and externalise their ideas, they reduce the cognitive load on their working memory. By putting their thoughts into an external space, students free up mental capacity, enabling them to focus on the writing process itself, rather than simultaneously managing the content and structure of their work.

Using graphic organisers to scaffold writing can be time-consuming, as students must learn to select and organise their ideas using a graphic organiser. You can mitigate this by providing templates and partially completed organisers. It is also worth considering using this technique towards the end of a learning sequence, when students have grasped the knowledge and you want to show them how to apply it in challenging ways, such as composing an essay or writing persuasively.

Another novel way of using this technique is to have students create their organiser incrementally as they progress through a topic. Students can add to their organiser every 1–3 lessons; this can save time, support students in consolidating their learning and help them explore the connections between the concepts they are learning.

Students are more likely to thrive when using and creating an organiser if they understand its value. Explain to your students why they are constructing the organiser and how it will support their writing. Also, mine the process for all it is worth – have students explain their organiser to a partner, and use cold-calling and checking for understanding techniques to assess students' evolving understanding. The key is to view the organiser as a servant of the learning process; it is not the intended outcome, but rather a technique to support students in complex thinking.

The following steps outline an example of how you might sequence the use of a graphic organiser to support writing.

Select an organiser that will best represent the information students are organising. In Organise Ideas, Caviglioli and Goodwin (2021) outline four types of diagrams, categorised by the language they represent.

- Mind maps and concept maps best represent the big picture. They reveal hierarchies and help classify ideas.
- Venn diagrams and the crossed-continua organiser are best used when comparing and contrasting ideas.
- Flow charts and cycle diagrams best represent sequences and temporal relations.
- Fishbone and relation diagrams depict causal relations.

Teach students to select their ideas. Using sticky notes can help students manipulate and organise their ideas more freely. You might also consider using retrieval practice to identify the most appropriate ideas for the question or problem students will complete.

Show students how to complete the first steps of their organiser using the ideas they have selected. Consider using templates and live-modelling the process under a visualiser. When ready, give students sufficient time to complete their organiser and circulate the room to get a visual check for understanding.

It is worth having students explain their organiser to a peer. Doing so will strengthen their understanding of the material as they begin to evaluate the accuracy of their organised ideas.

Model how to transform a completed diagram into a coherently structured piece of writing by revealing how each cluster can represent an individual paragraph. Do this under a visualiser and narrate your thinking. Check that students now know how to use their organiser, and when confident they will be successful, let them work independently.

Here is an extract from an example of how a Year 6 student used her mind map to write an introduction to her South America project. Notice how each branch is transformed into a paragraph.

Visuals such as pictures or diagrams should however, be used in a timely way, and we should also carefully consider the split attention effect. 'Information that must be combined should be placed together in space and time' (Lovell, 2020). One way to do this is to verbally explain an image or diagram rather than giving accompanying text. Lovell gives several examples of this such as. The same goes for learning from a map. Rather than reducing split attention by writing the names of the different landmarks *on* the actual picture, the teacher could eliminate split attention by *pointing* (visual) and *saying* (auditory), 'This is Mt Stellar' and 'This is Joan's cliff'. Any labels could then be added afterwards to check understanding.

Although visual scaffolds can be immensely helpful to scaffold explanations, we must also be careful not to make this part of education's 'lethal mutation'

Scaffolding of explanations 69

Here is an extract from an example of how a Year 6 student used her mind map to write an introduction to her South America project. Notice how each branch is transformed into a paragraph.

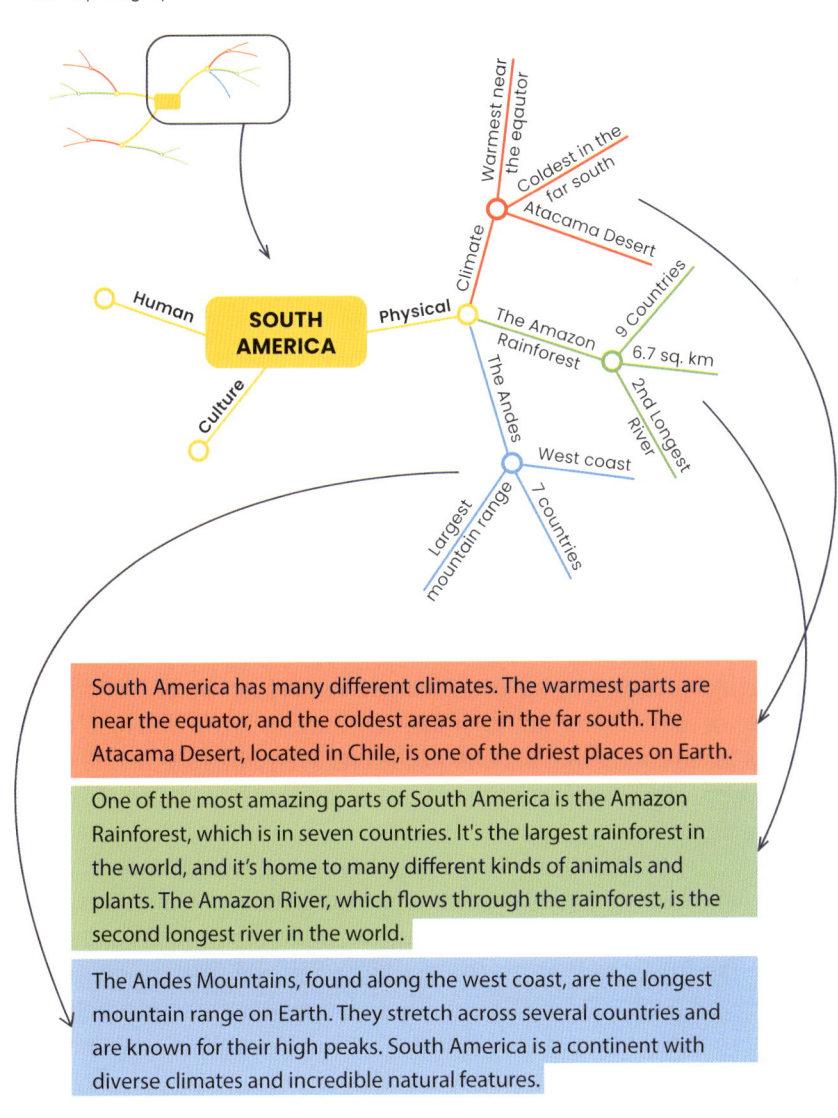

SOUTH AMERICA
- Human
- Physical
  - Climate
    - Warmest near the equator
    - Coldest in the far south
    - Atacama Desert
  - The Amazon Rainforest
    - 9 Countries
    - 6.7 sq. km
    - 2nd Longest River
  - The Andes
    - West coast
    - Largest mountain range
    - 7 countries
- Culture

South America has many different climates. The warmest parts are near the equator, and the coldest areas are in the far south. The Atacama Desert, located in Chile, is one of the driest places on Earth.

One of the most amazing parts of South America is the Amazon Rainforest, which is in seven countries. It's the largest rainforest in the world, and it's home to many different kinds of animals and plants. The Amazon River, which flows through the rainforest, is the second longest river in the world.

The Andes Mountains, found along the west coast, are the longest mountain range on Earth. They stretch across several countries and are known for their high peaks. South America is a continent with diverse climates and incredible natural features.

FIGURE 4.5 Example of a Year 6 student's mind map

culture, a term used by Ed Haertel (Brown & Campione, 1996) to describe the occurrence of teachers misunderstanding research and/or misapplying it in the classroom. This is something with dual coding is particularly susceptible to. For example, a teacher may apply lots of pretty icons to slides because they have heard about dual coding when in fact this is not helpful and in some cases may in fact *increase* cognitive load. 'Some approaches – like combining verbal explanations with graphical representations, also known as dual coding – are possible to implement poorly' (EEF, 2021).

6. Storytelling

In the collection of Middle Eastern folktales *One Thousand and One Nights* we read of the story of Scheherazade, a young woman who volunteers to marry King Shahyrar despite knowing he has been marrying a new bride each day and executing her the following morning. Scheherazade has a plan to avoid the same fate, a plan to captivate him with her powerful storytelling abilities. The story goes that that night Scheherazade tells her first story and stops before the ending of the story, leaving it on a cliff-hanger and totally captivating the king, who is desperate to know how the story ends. Her life is spared until the following day so that she can continue the story, and the pattern continues for 1001 nights, the king eagerly anticipating the conclusion of the previous night's story. The stories have a powerful effect on the king who changes his perspective on women and seems to become a reformed character. By the end of the 1001 nights, the king has fallen in love with Scheherazade and even when she tells him she has no more stories left, her life is spared permanently and she is made his queen. Stories are powerful.

Storytelling therefore can be an excellent scaffold of explanations. 'The human mind seems exquisitely tuned to understand and remember stories – so much so that psychologists sometimes refer to stories as "psychologically privileged" meaning that they are treated differently in memory than other types of material' (Willingham, 2009). Willingham goes on to explain why stories are beneficial:

- 'Stories are easy to comprehend because the audience knows the structure which helps to interpret the action'

- 'Stories are interesting'
- 'Stories are easy to remember'

Therefore using story as part of your explanation can ensure that students more easily understand the curriculum content. Research has shown that stories are 'sticky' (Quigley, 2023).

'Another research trial, based on the teaching of evolution in primary schools, showed that pupils learned more when they engaged with stories read by the teacher, rather than through doing tasks to demonstrate the same concept.'

There are a number of ways in which this can be implemented, suiting some subjects more easily than others. Mary Myatt (2023) offers some practical suggestions for embedding storytelling into our curriculums. For example,

> When we are developing a new unit, whether in primary or secondary, we might think about how a story (and this includes fiction and non-fiction) can be the starting point, or used for reading at home. To take an example in maths in primary, when we are teaching the Fibonacci sequence, we could tell the story of Fibonacci's three wishes. In secondary science, some schools are extending their reading through using extracts from Yuval Harari's Sapiens: A Brief History of Humankind.

Some key principles for the use of stories in the curriculum could be:

- Identify central characters for a given topic
- Measure your selections against Wilingham's 4 Cs – causality, conflict, complications and character
- Return to a central story throughout a topic
- Don't overload a topic with too many stories (Quigley, 2023)

The example below shows how storytelling can be used in KS1 History to teach students about local Black Victorians.

The Exciting Story of Ellen Craft, KS1 Local Black Victorians (Fairlamb, 2024) unpublished

> **Task 2: The Exciting Story of Ellen Craft (Teacher to Read Aloud)**
>
> Ellen Craft was a brave and clever woman. She was born in 1826 in Georgia, in southern USA, during a time when many people were not treated equally because of the colour of their skin. This is called racism.
>
> Ellen was born into enslavement, but didn't let that stop her from dreaming of freedom. She married another enslaved person named William Craft, and together, they came up with a daring plan to escape their owner and life elsewhere in freedom.
>
> Ellen and William knew that if they tried to escape together, it would be challenging because they might be recognised. So they came up with a very clever idea. Ellen, who had very light brown skin, but sometimes people thought that because her skin was light, that she was a white person.
>
> Using this to their advantage, Ellen disguised herself as a white gentleman, and William pretended to be her 'slave'. Ellen cut her hair short and wore men's clothing. They started their escape by saying at the train ticket office that Ellen needed to travel to Philadelphia (in northern USA) for medical treatment. Travelling by train and boat, facing many challenges and close calls along the way.

We must be careful, of course, to ensure that the curriculum is the driver of the story, particularly in subjects such as History and Religious Studies, so that students do not fall into the trap of forming snap judgements. We need to ensure that students still receive a variety of perspectives and maintain the rigour of the curriculum, not just listen to an exciting story! We should ensure content is paramount, and 'recognise narratives as curricular objects, not pedagogic tools' (Vallance, 2024).

Chapter 4 Self-Reflection Questions

Take a few minutes to reflect on the questions below and jot down your answers...

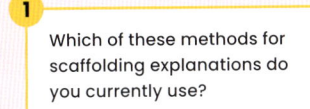

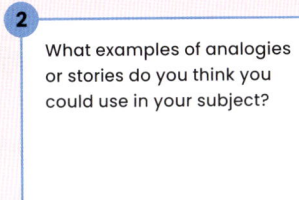

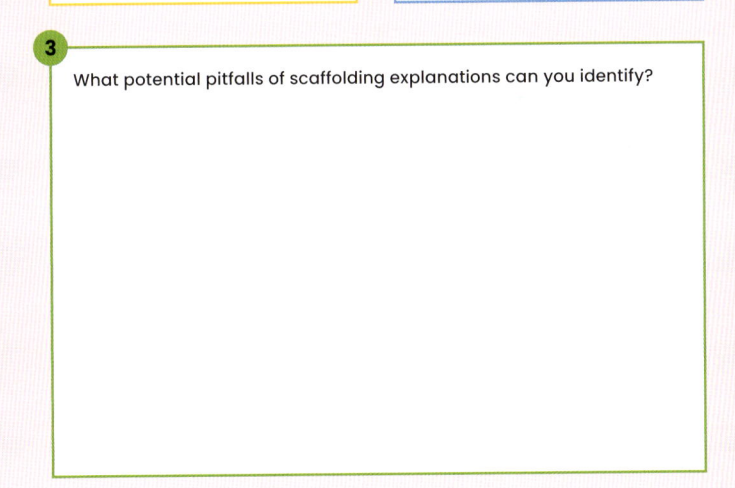

1. Which of these methods for scaffolding explanations do you currently use?

2. What examples of analogies or stories do you think you could use in your subject?

3. What potential pitfalls of scaffolding explanations can you identify?

References

Boxer, A. (2021) *Teaching Secondary Science: A Complete Guide*. John Catt Educational

Brown, A. L. & Campione, J. C. (1996) Psychological Theory and the Design of Innovative Learning Environments: On Procedures, Principles, and Systems. In L. Schauble & R. Glaser (Eds.), *Innovations in Learning: New Environments for Education*. Hillsdale, NJ: Lawrence Erlbaum Associates

Caviglioli, O. & Goodwin, D. (2021) *Organise Ideas: Thinking by Hand, Extending the Mind*. John Catt Education

EEF (2021) *Cognitive Science Approaches in the Classroom* (Online). Available at https://educationendowmentfoundation.org.uk/education-evidence/evidence-reviews/cognitive-science-approaches-in-the-classroom. Accessed 15th July 2024

Fairlamb (2019) unpublished. @alex.fairlamb@hotmail.com

Goodwin, D. (2021) *Diagram of the Earth, David Goodwin on X: "@geotayler @lcgeography @ThatBenRanson. An Updated Version Based on Your Feedback, Luke. Thank You* (Online). Available at https://t.co/xQvKJcGcEg"/ X. Accessed 15th August 2024

Kirschner, P. A. (2019) Dual Coding: Double-Barrelled Learning. In O. Caviglioli (Ed.), *Dual Coding with Teachers*. John Catt Educational

Lovell, O. (2020) *Sweller's Cognitive Load Theory in Action*. John Catt Educational

Medina, J. (2008) *Brain Rules: 12 Principles for Surviving and Thriving at Work, Home and School*. Seattle: Pear Press

Myatt, M. (2023) *Using Stories in the Curriculum* (Online). Available at https://www.marymyatt.com/blog/using-stories-in-the-curriculum. Accessed 10th November 2023

Paterson, D. (2019) Integrated Instruction. *Thoughts on Chemistry and Education* (Online). Available at https://dave2004b.wordpress.com/integrated-instructions/. Accessed 9th August 2024

Quigley, A. (2016) *The Confident Teacher*. Routledge

Quigley, A. (2018) *Closing the Vocabulary Gap*. Routledge

Quigley, A. (2023) How Sticky Stories Can Help Your Pupils to Learn. *TES Magazine* (Online). Available at https://www.tes.com/magazine/teaching-learning/general/how-sticky-stories-help-pupils-learn. Accessed 15th November 2023

Rosenshine, B. (2012) *Principles of Instruction: Research-Based Strategies That all Teachers Should Know* (Online). Available at https://www.aft.org/sites/default/files/Rosenshine.pdf. Accessed 21st January 2025

Vallance, J. (2024) *Storytelling: Pitfalls, Problems and Perspective*. Ark Soane History Conference Workshop

Willingham, D. (2009) *Why Don't Students Like School?* Jossey-Bass

5 Scaffolding and reading

> The reading rich get richer, the reading poor get poorer ... It is vital that at each step teachers recognise the fundamental causes of reading barriers faced by pupils, while helping our pupils negotiate the increasing trajectory of challenge in the texts they read, in school and beyond.
>
> *(Quigley, 2020)*

Introduction: literacy

We are **ALL** teachers of literacy. Let's make this a clear ethos from the start. Irrespective of phase, career stage, experience or subject, we are **ALL** teachers of literacy. And just like with our high expectations of our pupils in terms of developing their subject knowledge and skills, we must also have high expectations of the reading, writing and speaking that **ALL** of our students do throughout the entirety of their school career. Alex Quigley emphasises how important having literacy at the heart of a curriculum is, arguing that 'for our children to be able to access the curriculum that they are immersed in, and for them to become successful lifelong learners and future employable citizens, literacy is a passport which every child has a fundamental entitlement to' (Quigley, 2020).

Given that Key Stage 2 data from 2023 highlights that 'in reading, 73% of pupils met the expected standard, down from 75% in 2022' (DfE, 2023) and that amount of children (8–18 years old) who read for pleasure in their free time has dropped to 'just over 2 in 5... the lowest level of reading enjoyment we have recorded since we began asking this question in 2005' (National Literacy Trust, 2023), literacy leaders and classroom teachers face an increasing challenge of how to develop literacy and oracy skills both as a reading culture across a whole school and as part of disciplinary literacy. Resultantly, greater focus and effort has been placed on selecting and implementing high-impact, evidence informed literacy and oracy scaffolding strategies that can be deployed to help close the reading gap and support children to write effectively.

Secondary teachers and crossing the bridge . . . know-*what* to know-*how*

At secondary school level, explicitly teaching literacy can prove more daunting than for primary practitioners, given the difference in weighting afforded to literacy within the training programmes that practitioners undertook. In primary schools, the importance of literacy has always been a fundamental pillar of their curriculum – given their role in the delivery of phonics programmes and linked interventions, which ensure that children have the building blocks with which to develop their reading and writing through their continuing school career. Fidelity to a chosen phonics programme is an intrinsic part of the primary curriculum, and primary colleagues are trained to be proficient in identifying which children have not yet grasped the building blocks of reading.

For those secondary teachers who trained prior to the roll out of the new Early Career Framework (2024), when we began training, we were often told that we were training to be subject experts who must focus on continuing to develop our subject-pedagogical understanding. This meant that the vast majority of our focus was centred on ensuring that we had the requisite domain knowledge with which to plan, deliver and reflect upon the lessons that we taught. As part of this, our development plans were anchored on addressing knowledge gaps that we may have when teaching certain content or skills. With regards to the domain of literacy and disciplinary literacy, this was less so the case. This is not a criticism of training programmes prior to the ECF; evidence has moved on, and there has been a greater focus on ensuring literacy is the bedrock of secondary curriculums. We now have a greater appreciation and understanding of the integral part that literacy plays in our secondary curriculums.

When we trained, we became a 'science teacher' or a 'DT teacher'; we did not *explicitly* become a 'teacher of literacy' – someone whose role it is to be as responsible for the development of the reading, writing and speaking skills as we were for the knowledge and skills of our subjects. As a result, our knowledge of how to scaffold reading, writing and oracy remained limited, compounded by the previous era of limited professional development (PD) dedicated to it once within a school setting. Whilst our training and PD highlighted the need to develop the literacy of our pupils (and indeed, numeracy), it was often a tick box item that was an implicit part of a lesson; 'well, they're reading a textbook in a lesson which is reading, so that means I've taught literacy.' Sitting within this, there was a long-held general assumption for many that pupils arrive at the classroom door having learnt how to read and write in primary school, and that the role of the secondary English department and SEND team was to ensure that these skills progress to age-appropriate levels.

As a subject teacher, this meant that we were more focused on the knowledge and skill development, laying down textbooks plump with content from which we expect our pupils to extract the correct meaning and knowledge from the prose in front of them. Anecdotal information suggests that literacy training as an ITT and then PD training in school was shallow with stand-alone sessions focusing on generic approaches to developing literacy, such as providing students with key word banks or sentence starters.

As a result, strategies such as word banks tagged onto powerpoints and worksheets became a commonly perceived and used panacea for students to suddenly know how to understand and meaningfully use the new disciplinary tier 2-3 words placed in front of them. In short, we had the what, but not the why and how: why we need strategies such as word banks and how to use them with students in powerful ways. We knew that we should provide a bank and so we did, but we were not trained in explaining their purpose or how to scaffold students in accessing these word banks (including pronouncing them, due to assuming phonetic proficiency).

Gudmundsdatter Magnusson et al. (2023) outline this stating that:

> Research has shown that teachers can strengthen and develop literacy skills for adolescents through scaffolding practices (Fidalgo et al., 2015; Graham & Perin, 2007) However, research also show that scaffolding literacy is particularly challenging for teachers to integrate in daily teaching situations (Duffy & Roehler, 1987; Pearson & Cervetti, 2017; Pressley et al., 1989), and that teachers engage to a small degree in scaffolding practices in classrooms (e.g., Anmarkrud, 2009; Dignath & Veenman, 2020; Magnusson et al., 2019; Ness, 2011; Tengberg et al., 2022). Despite the fact that scaffolding literacy can be of great importance in classroom teaching, there are few studies on literacy professional development (PD) interventions targeting teachers' use of scaffolding. Moreover, we still know little about how PD efforts can be implemented in a way that effectively develops teachers' literacy practices and meet the individual needs of teachers.

In more worrying examples within school settings, the push for the evidencing of literacy taking place has often taken precedence over any form of formal literacy PD. I've experienced situations where practitioners were given time to simply identify on their schemes of learning where they already 'taught literacy' in the curriculum to prove that that the school was 'doing literacy' ('reading from a powerpoint – LITERACY' akin to 'using a graph on weapons in Year 7 History – NUMERACY').

Thankfully, this type of thinking is changing rapidly with training providers and in many schools, due in part to worrying findings regarding literacy levels. Research concludes that 'nationally 25% of 15-year-olds have a reading age of 12 or below, 20% a reading age of 11 and below and 10% a reading age of 9 and below' (Fernandes & Gallacher, 2020). Such data, alongside reading tests often conducted internally in Year 7, have drawn attention to the number of weaker readers within cohorts and helped to change the narrative as to who is responsible for developing the literacy levels of our pupils. Current providers of ITE and ECF have worked to ensure that the importance of literacy is a core part of the training programme that new teachers engage in. As part of their fidelity to the ITT Core Content Framework (2019), those who are new to the profession are focusing more closely on the theory of reading, writing and oracy.

Likewise, some schools have prioritised reading in their school development plans and have threaded whole-school reading strategies into PD sessions. The intent is clearly now there. But the devil is in the detail, and in the implementation. To what extent is this training focused on how to scaffold whole school literacy strategies and how to scaffold disciplinary literacy? When given the reading ages of pupils, how much time has been given to sequential PD aimed at training teachers and LSAs to confidently know and expertly use evidence-led literacy scaffolding strategies to support the weaker readers? And how much deliberate practice have they taken part in in order to avoid what McCrea (2023) has identified as a 'knowing-doing gap':

> The knowing-doing gap can emerge for a number of reasons. Sometimes it's because teachers are exposed to an idea but aren't helped to understand exactly *what to do* about it – how to put it into action. Sometimes it's because teachers know what to do, but haven't 'rehearsed' enough *outside* the classroom for it to manifest *inside* the busy context of a lesson.

As a result, those newly qualified or those who have engaged in whole-school literacy PD are often versed in the theory of reading (know-**what** literacy is and its importance), but left uncertain of the practicalities and know-**how** of how to be leaders of literacy within their *own subject domain*. In a nutshell, taking History as example, we want pupils to read, write and speak like a historian; we want them to use tier 2-3 terms in accurate, powerful and malleable ways in order to construct arguments; we want them to unlock inferences within complex sources, and be able to debate knowledgeably the varying interpretations of our past. For this to happen, teacher and TA PD must include greater opportunities for practitioners to become well-versed in disciplinary literacy and how to scaffold this, as well as have frequent opportunities to translate this knowledge into practice, within their own school context.

Consequently, when schools look to implement whole school literacy strategies (such as form time reading, DEAR) or task teachers with developing resources which promote literacy within their subject, there can be a disconnect between the intent and the implementation including how to scaffold literacy. This is why the literacy PD of practitioners must focus on empowering Heads of Department (HoDs) to lead their teams in driving disciplinary literacy with a key focus on rich texts and also the scaffolding of literacy so that ALL students can become stronger readers, writers and speakers.

Literacy as the bedrock of the curriculum

The next three chapters will explore scaffolding strategies around reading, explicit vocabulary instruction, writing and oracy within both primary and secondary contexts. At times in these chapters, there will be cross-over between strategies suggested for scaffolding reading, vocabulary, writing and oracy (including listening), as they are all symbiotic and tightly interwoven, like a rich tapestry of threads which form one beautiful, composite whole. Central to these approaches is the role of metacognitive oracy during the implementation of the literacy and oracy scaffolding strategies that we will explore, reinforced by the work of Sherrington (Rosenshine's Principles in Action, 2019) and Lemov (Teach Like a Champion 2.0, 2015) who have helped to improve practitioner understanding of the importance of modelling and questioning to support adaptive teaching.

For children to become strategic readers, writers and speakers, we need to explicitly model what this looks like including sharing the why we are doing it and the how, not just the what. We cannot act as magicians on a stage pulling a rabbit from the hat awaiting gasps of awe and wonderment. We must clearly, consistently and explicitly share how and why developing reading, writing and speaking skills is so important. This is important as sharing the why and illuminating the steps as to how will help to drive the motivation of pupils. Peps McCrae (2020) outlines this by saying that

> our motivation is heavily influenced by our anticipation of future success: the likelihood that we will reap the benefits . . . Securing success is not about making things easier for pupils. It is about helping them to do something they couldn't before.

Quigley (2020) too argues that motivation is central to successful reading, stating that 'reading habitually and seeing reading as a pleasurable, fulfilling and motivating activity matters'. Therefore, we need to ensure that we effectively scaffold literacy so that students experience success and a clear, known toolkit for accessing challenging texts and written responses, driving their motivation to want to grapple with texts more readily and heartily.

A final thing to outline before we explore the scaffolding strategies is that:

- Literacy is itself a scaffold for the curriculum – it is a way with which children can access the curriculum and successfully negotiate their way through subject progression models. Myatt (2022) outlines the importance of stories and rich texts as part of building up knowledge and skills through the reading of rich nonfiction and fiction texts to make learning more memorable.
- Literacy scaffolds act as a part of teaching and learning. Not only can literacy scaffolds develop literacy domain knowledge and skills (how to write for a particular purpose and audience, how to write

fiction) and subject domain knowledge and skills, but they also help students to interpret feedback, explain their thinking and how to ask and answer questions.

- The teaching of literacy skills needs to be scaffolded; for us to teach reading, writing and speaking skills, we need to ensure that we are providing children with the appropriate, targeted support that is needed for them to meet literacy milestones and develop competence and confidence over time.

Getting ready for reading

Broadly speaking, reading can be broken down into:

- Phonics
- Enjoyment/love of reading
- Disciplinary literacy
- Interventions

This chapter will focus on the enjoyment of reading and disciplinary literacy and will not focus on phonics (as fidelity is required for this) and interventions (which are bespoke to the school and cohort).

There are many different approaches to reading with children. In previous years, strategies have included 'popcorn'/'round robin' reading and 'DEAR' (Drop Everything and Read). In theory, these strategies have sound reasoning behind their use. With data from the National Literacy Trust (2023) report highlighting that just three in ten children read daily, the rationale was that the greater exposure that that child has to opportunities to read independently and to read aloud, then their ability to read and their confidence should improve. In primary schools, this has usually meant threading in independent reading as part of a diet of whole class reading and teacher-led modelled reading, with independent texts usually informed by UK Reading Levels (either levels or bands). In secondary schools, this has sometimes meant designating time in a school timetable for children to read independently or students taking turns to read aloud during form class or lessons.

However, this approach has limitations, particularly in secondary, if form time reading is stuffed into an already busy 15-minute registration period in a morning. In both of the below scenarios, imagine a child in Year 7 who has the reading age of a 7-year-old:

- **Scenario A. DEAR in form time.** Year 7 students can pick their own text and read in silence for 15 minutes a day during form time.
- **Scenario B. Popcorn reading.** Year 7 students all read the same text in a Religious Education lesson where they are learning about Judaism, and the teacher picks pupils who then take turns to read aloud. The student who has just finished reading then selects the next student to read aloud and so on.

What do you consider the likelihood that a child with the reading age of 7 years old is going to access and read the text successfully?

In scenario A, how do you know that they are successfully: decoding the words, have the required language comprehension, are drawing accurate meaning from the text (comprehension), and that they are reading with fluency? With 30 children all reading silently, how would we know who to support and how to support beyond any initial reading data that we had? Especially when a busy form tutor is unable to monitor the reading and provide scaffolding, due to contending with various administration and pastoral jobs to complete within such a narrow window of time. How could we instead approach form time reading, with scaffolds which unlock the words and meaning of the text?

In scenario B, asking a weaker reader to engage in popcorn reading can be incredibly daunting and demotivating. For them to read aloud a text that they have not encountered before, in front of 30 peers, when they are struggling to decode or read with fluency, could in fact have the opposite effect of building reading confidence. Added into that is a broad range of new vocabulary and concepts related to Judaism; how will the pupil know how to say Jewish words aloud? Whilst a teacher may in that moment be responsive and provide scaffolding to support the pupil in reading aloud, their difficulties with reading have become public. And with this being their singular lesson of the week in that subject, that is their lived experience until the next lesson. How could we instead approach disciplinary reading, with scaffolds which unlock the words and meaning of the text?

With this in mind, research has indicated that there are alternative approaches to reading as well as reading scaffolds which are more beneficial, including for weaker readers, which support a more strategic approach to teaching pupils how to read.

Detailed data

Before exploring these strategies, the role of reading data is an important aspect of scaffolding reading. Having data about the reading ages of pupils is a key part of knowing which pupils will require additional support in lessons when it comes to reading. However, a common error that is made is that generic reading tests such as the New Group Reading Test which produce a Standardised Age Score are used as the sole information used. Whilst these tests can act as a benchmark and help to determine which students are struggling most with reading, they do not diagnose the reason why the student is struggling to read.

If schools opt to use this information in isolation (shared with staff generically or used to create intervention groups), the issue is that the scaffolds put into place for the pupil may not be appropriate as they are not addressing the reading barrier of the child. Carrying out further diagnostic tests on weaker readers means that the reading barrier that a child faces can be determined, whether that be phonetical proficiency, comprehension and or fluency. Examples of such tests include FFT's Reading Assessment Programme at Primary and York Assessment of Reading Comprehension at Primary and Secondary. It is only by determining these individual barriers, and then sharing those barriers with teachers, that reading scaffolds can be used most powerfully as they help the practitioner to adapt the curriculum and their teaching and learning delivery to help address the barrier that the child experiences. This is furthered by the EEF who state that 'effective diagnosis of reading difficulties is important in identifying possible solutions, particularly for older struggling readers. Pupils can struggle with decoding words, understanding the structure of the language used, or understanding particular vocabulary, which may be subject specific'. The key, therefore, to scaffolding literacy, is to know the barriers and to whom those barriers apply.

Teacher-led modelled reading

One approach to scaffolding reading is through teacher-led modelled reading (or 'directed reading'). This is when the subject teacher (or in form class reading scenarios, the form tutor) reads aloud the determined passage or chapter to their pupils. This can involve pupils having a copy of the text in front of them, or having it displayed on the board using tools such as a visualiser.

As the teacher reads aloud, the pupils follow the text, and they may also annotate the text as the teacher does this. We can see within this approach the importance of metacognitive oracy as the

> development of reading comprehension then encompasses broader experiences of talk and listening. We should therefore tend to oral language development in our classrooms. Each interaction between teacher and pupil can lift the print from the page and make it better understood. This is why reading, and talking about reading, needs to play a fundamental role in *every* school day.... For most children, explicit structured and sustained reading instruction – early and for an extended period that spans primary *and* secondary schools – is essential for success.
>
> (Quigley, 2020)

The purpose of this is that teachers can:

- Model the enjoyment of reading
- Model expert reading
- Model fluency
- Model prosody – the intonation, stress, expression

- Model the purposeful annotation of the text (which parts, why)
- Model the use of keyword lists/banks or glossaries to unlock language comprehension

And as part of this, pupils can:

- Listen to the passage being read aloud and track the reader
- Enjoy the process of being read aloud to
- See new vocabulary and hear new vocabulary being read aloud (which they can then also say aloud), as well have the word explained, within the context of a passage

What would this look like?

Teacher-led modelled reading can support scaffolding in powerful ways:

Step 1: Prior to reading the lesson, the teacher uses their knowledge of their students to determine what template might be beneficial for the reading and breaking down of the next. Within that template, the teacher can pre-populate the template with questions, prompts (including bullet points) and/or dual coding. This takes into account that with scaffolding that 'some supports are planned prior to lessons and some are provided responsively during instruction' (McLeskey et al., 2017). I would advise that each pupil has a copy of the text/text in this template so that they can track the reader and annotate the text as they go.

Step 2: The teacher indicates to the pupil what the purpose of their reading is. The signposting of this means that we are supporting the students in knowing how to adapt their approach to reading a text in varying contexts and conditions, such as with unseen texts in examinations. Over time, we can reduce this scaffolding of signposting of the purpose as pupils become more confident and independent. This is why metacognitive oracy is central to teaching reading, where teachers model the process of reading the 'why we' as well as the 'how to'.

Step 3: As the teacher reads aloud, the teacher demonstrates how to chunk the text, breaking down a wall of words into digestible paragraphs, as part of 'granular chunking' (McCrae, 2020). These paragraphs can then be given a subtitle or summarised one by one in the margins.

The extent of modelling provided as part of this is based upon the knowledge of the students and checks for understanding as part of adaptive teaching, moving from heavy scaffolding of leading the subtitle and summary activities to lighter scaffolding where students determine their own subtitles and produce their own summaries.

Step 4: Moving through the texts, the teacher pauses at determined points and can use strategies such as reciprocal reading to unlock the meaning of the text and check for understanding. Teachers can 'plan concisely to explain vocabulary, ask questions or offer clarifications' (Quigley, 2020) including predetermining which pupils to call upon. Teachers can pause to highlight new vocabulary and explain what the word means, as well as pupils to chant the word aloud so that they verbalise it and develop confidence in using it during questioning.

Step 5: With the teacher directing the reading and pausing to check for understanding, opportunities for further scaffolding can be identified through inclusive questioning. This informs and empowers the teacher to adapt their reading delivery live in the moment, either at whole class or individual level.

Step 6: At the end of the reading, it is advisable to then summarise the text as a whole, using the mini margin summaries to inform this. By doing so we are ensuring 'granular chunking. Breaking ideas and processes so they can be learned in small parts before being built back up' (McCrae, 2020).

Step 7: Moreover, the teacher may also model the annotation of the text as they read, using metacognitive oracy to explain what they are annotating or summarising and why.

A common question I get from teachers and from pupils is that, if they are fluent readers, why do they need to take part in teacher-led modelled reading; 'Why can't I just read it on my own?' For me the answer is that they may be more fluent readers than the other students in the class, but that does not necessarily mean that they are *strategic* readers. By this it means that they cannot often read for purpose, annotate, summarise or ask the right questions of the text.

Therefore, through directed reading, a teacher will provide heavier scaffolding for students with lower reading ages/may struggle more through

Scaffolding and reading 89

Directed Reading

Subtitle and dual code	Reasons she was a threat	Summarise each reason into 3 bullet points
	• Mary, Queen of Scots, was a Catholic with a strong claim to the English throne. She was Henry VII's great granddaughter, Elizabeth I's second cousin. There were no issues about her legitimacy.	
	• She became Queen of Scotland at six days old after her father, King James V, died. Her mother, Mary of Guise, was from a very powerful Catholic, French, noble family. She married King Francis II of France. This was a Catholic country who Elizabeth had previously had problems with as she had agreed to support the French Protestants in 1562. With French help, Mary could take Elizabeth's throne.	
	• In 1560, Elizabeth helped Scotland's Protestant Lords defeat Mary of Guise (ruling Scotland for her daughter). The rebellion ended with the Treaty of Edinburgh in 1560 – it said that Mary, Queen of Scots, would give up her claim to the English throne. Mary did not agree with the treaty. Dec 1560, King Francis II died so Mary returned from France to Scotland. Although she was queen, the Protestant lords controlled the Scottish government. Mary had never approved the Treaty of Edinburgh 1560, so she continued to claim she still had a right to the English throne. She wanted to be named as Elizabeth's heir.	
	• Elizabeth did not want to name an heir. She was becoming more worried about the threat from foreign Catholic powers (France, Spain) and Catholics in England. If she made her Catholic cousin Mary her heir, it would make religious divisions in England worse OR it might encourage Catholics to try to make Mary the queen of England instead. She could not risk this.	
	• Mary married her second husband, Lord Darnley. She gave birth to a son, James. In 1567, Darnley was murdered. Mary was suspected of being involved. The scandal led to the Protestant Scottish Lords rebelling again. They forced Mary to abdicate* in favour of her baby son, James. She was imprisoned but escaped in 1568 and raised an army in an attempt to win back her throne. Mary's forces were defeated and she fled to England, seeking Elizabeth I's help against the rebels.	
	• When Mary fled and arrived in England in 1568, she was a problem for Elizabeth. Elizabeth did not think it was right for anyone to overthrow their monarch BUT she also knew Mary was a threat and had a claim to her throne. She kept Mary under guard until a court was held to hear evidence about the murder of Darnley. Mary disagreed with her being put on trial as she was a monarch. She said she would not offer a plea unless Elizabeth guaranteed that Mary's verdict would be 'innocent'. Elizabeth refused to do this. Elizabeth still had a problem though – she did not want to support the overturning of a monarch but she also did not want to set Mary free as she would then be free to raise an army and threaten Elizabeth's claim to the throne. She stayed a prisoner of Elizabeth's.	
	• In 1569 a plot was hatched against Elizabeth I. The plot was to marry Mary to the Duke of Norfolk (England's most senior noble) who was also a Protestant. This would mean any children they had would be Protestant and they would have a claim to the throne (and it would help solve the problem that Protestants would challenge her being a queen as she was Catholic). However, Elizabeth heard of this plan and it proved how dangerous Mary was – even when she was a prisoner. She was moved to another prison.	

39

FIGURE 5.1 Guided reading of Mary Queen of Scots with examples of a lower attaining student with significant literacy barriers and a higher attaining student, (Fairlamb, 2023) unpublished

90 *The Scaffolding Effect*

Subtitle and dual code	Directed Reading Reasons she was a threat	Summarise each reason into 3 bullet points
Claim throne ♛	Mary, Queen of Scots, was a Catholic with a strong claim to the English throne. She was Henry VII's great granddaughter, Elizabeth I's second cousin. There were no issues about her legitimacy.	– Catholic – no legitimate claims
Became Queen	She became Queen of Scotland at six days old after her father, King James V, died. Her mother, Mary of Guise, was from a very powerful Catholic, French, noble family. She married King Francis II of France. This was a Catholic country who Elizabeth had previously had problems with as she had agreed to support the French Protestants in 1562. With French help, Mary could take Elizabeth's throne.	– Queen 6 days old. – powerfull mother – french would help mary
King † died	In 1560, Elizabeth helped Scotland's Protestant Lords defeat Mary of Guise (ruling Scotland for her daughter). The rebellion ended with the Treaty of Edinburgh in 1560 – it said that Mary, Queen of Scots, would give up her claim to the English throne. Mary did not agree with the treaty. Dec 1560, King Francis II died so Mary returned from France to Scotland. Although she was queen, the Protestant lords controlled the Scottish government. Mary had never approved the Treaty of Edinburgh 1560, so she continued to claim she still had a right to the English throne. She wanted to be named as Elizabeth's heir	– mary did not agree. – king francis died – never aproved the Treaty of england
religious devision	Elizabeth did not want to name an heir. She was becoming more worried about the threat from foreign Catholic powers (France, Spain) and Catholics in England. If she made her Catholic cousin Mary her heir, it would make religious divisions in England worse OR it might encourage Catholics to try to make Mary the queen of England instead. She could not risk this.	– didnt want her name in heir – religious devision
Imprisond	Mary married her second husband, Lord Darnley. She gave birth to a son, James. In 1567, Darnley was murdered. Mary was suspected of being involved. The scandal led to the Protestant Scottish Lords rebelling again. They forced Mary to abdicate* in favour of her baby son, James. She was imprisoned but escaped in 1568 and raised an army in an attempt to win back her throne. Mary's forces were defeated and she fled to England, seeking Elizabeth I's help against the rebels.	– She gave birth – husband death – Imprisond
No Trile Still Prisoned	When Mary fled and arrived in England in 1568, she was a problem for Elizabeth. Elizabeth did not think it was right for anyone to overthrow their monarch BUT she also knew Mary was a threat and had a claim to her throne. She kept Mary under guard until a court was held to hear evidence about the murder of Darnley. Mary disagreed with her being put on trial as she was a monarch. She said she would not offer a plea unless Elizabeth guaranteed that Mary's verdict would be 'innocent'. Elizabeth refused to do this. Elizabeth still had a problem though – she did not want to support the overturning of a monarch but she also did not want to set Mary free as she would then be free to raise an army and threaten Elizabeth's claim to the throne. She stayed a prisoner of Elizabeth's.	– mary fled – not right to overthrow – refused to trile – not setting mary free
Plot ♛♛♛ ✗✗✗	In 1569 a plot was hatched against Elizabeth I. The plot was to marry Mary to the Duke of Norfolk (England's most senior noble) who was also a Protestant. This would mean any children they had would be Protestant and they would have a claim to the throne (and it would help solve the problem that Protestants would challenge her being a queen as she was Catholic). However, Elizabeth heard of this plan and it proved how dangerous Mary was – even when she was a prisoner. She was moved to another prison.	– Plot faild – proved how dangerous mary was

39

FIGURE 5.2 Guided reading of Mary Queen of Scots with examples of a lower attaining student with significant literacy barriers and a higher attaining student, (Fairlamb, 2023) unpublished

a greater level of clarification of the text or modelling in greater depth how to summarise a paragraph, but use lighter scaffolding for more fluent readers whereby they will be prompted to do these things. Scaffolding is a means by which we can teach to the top, and even the most fluent of readers can and need to be pushed to continue to improve with guided instruction from teachers.

Research also suggests that if we are using videos or recordings in lessons, that turning on the subtitles on the board can help to scaffold reading. Goldenberg (2024) has summarised the potential positive impact of using subtitles by stating that

> a longitudinal study of continuous use of subtitles at home, showed that children who watched television with subtitles scored significantly higher on word identification and comprehension tests than children who did not use subtitles.
>
> (Koskinen et al., 1997)

Reciprocal reading

Reciprocal reading is an approach that involves metacognitive oracy and the modelling of reading using determined strategies with pupils so that they read more strategically. The process of reciprocal reading is a scaffold for reading, but it is also something to be scaffolded; children cannot be expected to suddenly know how to use reciprocal reading strategies via osmosis, and need supporting in developing these skills. Using six key strategies, the teacher is able to model to pupils how they engage with a text, helping to create structured opportunities for 'purposeful speaking and listening activities support which pupils' language development' (EEF, 2021). The EEF report (2021) and Lemov et al. (2016) recommend the below approach:

- Predict what may happen
- Apply prior knowledge to the text to draw out meaning and build understanding

- Identify new vocabulary and see vocabulary in context
- Clarify the meaning of the text
- Summarise the salient points of the text
- Ask questions about the text (pre-planned and responsive). Carefully crafted pre-planned questions are central to this, as 'text-dependent questions are specific and can be answered only when students have carefully read and understood the author's specific arguments. They do not preclude other worthy questions; in fact they often precede them' (Lemov et al., 2016)

The EEF recommendations (2018) highlight how reciprocal reading can develop literacy in both primary and secondary schools

> To comprehend complex texts, students need to actively engage with what they are reading and use their existing subject knowledge. Reading strategies, such as activating prior knowledge, prediction and questioning, can improve students' comprehension.

This aligns with Lemov et al.'s (2016) argument of the importance of frequent close reading opportunities across the curriculum, arguing that:

> Breaking down . . . If you work with engines, you must be able to take one apart to understand fuel enters the cylinder, expands, drives the piston and moves the crankshaft. Close reading involves taking apart a complex passage . . . [it] is a set of tools for unlocking complex texts.

For me, reciprocal reading is that toolkit for pupils to practically break down texts through close reading in accessible steps. It provides various scaffolds for teachers to empower students to be able to do this, using metacognition and a success criteria to be able to chunk and make meaning of a text. The EEF (2021) has produced an effective overview of questions and prompts for Reciprocal Reading which are also useful as scaffolding, with the teacher reducing the prompts used over time.

Scaffolding and reading 93

Teacher prompts (Questions)
- Keep a note of the questions you have as we are reading. I'm recording mine on the whiteboard.
- Where is the story set? What do I know about that country/time?
- Why did the author choose that word? What does this word tell me about the character?
- I wonder if...

Teacher prompts (Predict)
- What do the title and front cover tell me about the book and what to expect?
- Is the author leaving me hints about what might happen next?
- Can I find and use the hints and clues to make my predictions?
- On no, I didn't expect that to happen... Can I 'squeeze' more evidence from what I've read to make new predictions?

Teacher prompts (Activate Prior Knowledge)
- What do you know about the setting of this story?
- What have we learnt about this in our science/topic lesson?
- Can you make a link to other texts we've read?
- That's right, you learnt about this in Year 3. Before we reading what do you remember?

Reading Comprehension Strategies: QUESTIONS, ACTIVATE PRIOR KNOWLEDGE, SUMMARISE, CLARITY, PREDICT

Teacher prompts (Clarity)
- Keep a careful eye on what's happening if you get lost, look for the words or phrases you're unsure of.
- It helps to go back and re-read if we're not quite sure what happened or why.
- Let's annotate any words of phrases we're unsure of.

Teacher prompts (Summarise)
- To really enjoy this text it's important to take a summary away after each chapter.
- Your summary could be five key words.
- A summary could be a quick picture with some annotations.
- A post-it note summary can help you take our story home so you can share it with a grown-up in your house.

Explicitly teaching children these strategies supports them to become strategic readers. What does a strategic reader do before, during, and after reading?

Before reading...	During reading...	After reading...
• Asks questions about the text. • Activates prior knowledge. • Makes predictions.	• Monitors understanding. • Makes connections within and beyond the text. • Makes mental models of the text. • Updates and makes new predictions.	• Clarifies understanding of the text. • Revisits and revises predictions. • Asks further questions. • Reflects on their own reading. • Summarises key points from the text.

FIGURE 5.3 Reciprocal comprehension strategies with prompts to support practice, Education Endowment Fund (2021)

Shanahan (2017a) outlines the approach that should also be taken when reducing scaffolding with reciprocal reading, whereby once the strategies have been secured by the students the scaffolds should decrease so that the students are applying them with greater autonomy and independence:

> Teachers tend to over-support kids' reading. We teacher educators tend to provide a lot of guidance and support for scaffolding – but we are less explicit about withdrawing this support. But, withdrawing support and just going cold turkey may not be the best bet. Reciprocal teaching is a good model of withdrawal of scaffolding, so I wouldn't hesitate to use that. Initially, the teacher guides the reading process . . . The teacher not only does everything but explains why she is doing it and how it is supposed to help . . . Then, the teacher starts to shift the responsibilities to the children, and to withdraw support.

Heavy, Medium, Light Scaffolding (Fairlamb, 2023) unpublished, based on the template and concept by Ball (2022)

Strategy	Heavy	Medium	Light
Predictions	Bank of predictions to select from Prediction sentence starters or prediction cues Greater depth of questioning by the teacher around the elaboration of predictions made and why	An example of a prediction Prompts/cues of prediction sentence starters	Create own predictions
Knowledge	In-depth recaps of prior knowledge supported with cues and prompts	Recaps of prior knowledge supported with some cues and prompts	Recaps of prior knowledge

(Continued)

(Continued)

Strategy	Heavy	Medium	Light
	Graphic organisers with key knowledge to support recapping prior knowledge and processing new information. Gaps are left to support recall and for new information to be added to from the reading Character and/or plot summaries	Prompts of the character's names and/or plot summaries	Blank graphic organisers which students build up using recall and add to during their reading
Vocabulary	A list of key words with definitions and/or dual coding (per page/or chapter): Tier 2 and 3 vocabulary Heavier use of knowledge organisers with key words and definitions and/or dual coding (directed more so by teacher) Frequent, repeated choral repetition of key words (said 3 or more times) Greater elaboration of the word being used in differing, accessible contexts (real world or prior knowledge) Teacher modelled underlining of new vocabulary and annotation of this	A shorter list of key words with definitions and/or dual coding: more focused on Tier 3 vocabulary Medium use knowledge organisers with key words and definitions and/or dual coding Frequent choral repetition of key words Explicit teacher-led links made between the word and prior knowledge	Sharing of key words for the lesson: more focused on Tier 3 vocabulary. Definitions for some Low scaffold knowledge organisers with key words and definitions (student more independent in accessing these and understanding them more successfully) Choral repetition of key words

(Continued)

(*Continued*)

Strategy	Heavy	Medium	Light
		Reduction of teacher modelling of underlining and annotation and greater independence in accessing tools to find out the definition	Students link the word with prior knowledge and/or other relevant links to other examples Independent in identifying new vocabulary and accessing tools to find out the definition
Summarise	Short reading loops - determined boxes of summary areas after chunks of information. This can involve cues and prompts added, including things such as bullet points Shared success criteria (see image: Tom's example) Teacher modelling of the summaries including prompts and cues	Short reading loops - determined areas where chunks of information are to be summarised Shared shortened success criteria/ working as a class to create a shared success criteria Teacher modelling of the summaries	Students able to self-chunk texts and identify where to summarise Students suggest own success criteria

(*Continued*)

(*Continued*)

Strategy	Heavy	Medium	Light
Clarify	Higher level of use of metaphors and analogies to explain words/text Repeated teacher-led reading of determined areas or repeated reading by the student A title for each paragraph is given or co-constructed Targeted written questions Signposting pupils to discourse markers (Quigley, 2020) Signposting helpful text features (Quigley, 2020) such as the glossary Heavier use of dual coding and/or visuals	Use of metaphors and analogies to explain words/text Use of repeated reading Reminding pupils of discourse markers (Quigley, 2020) Reminding of helpful text features such as the glossary	Students can suggest own metaphors and analogies Students independently approach discourse markers Students independently use text features
Questioning	Bank of question stems and example questions Teacher led recording of questions Examples from the teacher of questions to prompt further questions	Bank of question stems	

Whole class 'round-robin'/popcorn

As discussed earlier, whole class 'Round-Robin' or 'popcorn' reading can have its pitfalls. This approach usually involves a teacher selecting pupils to read aspects of a text or in the 'popcorn' sense it is the students who select the next person to read. Given the range of reading ages and barriers, this can be a very daunting experience for weaker readers, particularly if there is tricky and/or new vocabulary or new concepts within the reading.

Moreover, there is little opportunity to provide meaningful feedback to the student about their reading. Resultantly, round robin/popcorn reading has proven to be quite divisive in education as it has been commonly used in many schools, with some arguing that it supports oral reading and therefore oral fluency.

When asked about round robin reading and whether it could support oral fluency, Shanahan (2017b) argues that it should not be used as 'It is terribly inefficient. The person who is learning during the round robin is the reader – which means 25 other kids are sitting there waiting for their turn.' He furthers this by arguing that in subjects such as social studies that this method of reading would have little impact given

> let's face it, in a 30-minute social sciences lesson, each kid would typically get to read a minute or less. This means that social studies would add fewer than three hours of reading time per year – not enough to help the kids.
>
> (2019)

Shanahan (2019) suggests that a better approach, which would support oral fluency and provide greater opportunities for scaffolding and reciprocal reading strategies, would be to instead have

> the kids read sections of the text aloud to each other (partner reading) and then discuss and answer your questions. You should circulate among the partners making sure that they are reading

well and when they are not, they need to reread; such repeated reading is effective in promoting fluency.

Repeated reading

Repeated reading involves a student rereading a selected piece of text. The purpose of this is to build confidence and fluency so that we can provide structured practice opportunities for 'building up pupils' reading stamina, while offering repeated practice where they can focus on each aspect of fluency reading. 'The teacher role in providing scaffolding for this practice is key' (Quigley, 2020).

The process of repeated reading means that students can break down the words and develop their range of vocabulary, using existing or growing schema to help them to make sense of the words in front of them and to attach greater meaning to them. By then rereading the information with this heightened level of knowledge of the words and having removed the decoding barrier, a student can then read the information more fluently and aim to break down the information into chunks by which they can draw meaning and comprehension. This approach aligns with Afflerbach et al. (2017) research that 'deliberate, goal-directed attempts to control and modify the reader's efforts to decode text, understand words, and construct meanings of text support students in developing their reading comprehension and fluency skills'.

The EEF (2021) echo this by stating in their Improving Literacy in KS2 guidance report, stating that the recommendation that there should be 'guided oral reading instruction – teachers model fluent reading, then pupils read the same text aloud with appropriate feedback'.

How then can we scaffold repeated reading?

Scaffold 1: Teacher-led modelled reading. Frequent teacher modelling of repeated reading and reinforcing the purpose of why this reading strategy is being used; for some students this might require heavier scaffolding or repetition of the modelling to a greater level.

The impact of explaining and exposing to them opportunities of breaking down challenging texts through repeated reading means that we can cultivate greater resilience with reading and motivation amongst our students. This can be harnessed in examinations/tests where unseen texts are used.

Scaffold 2: Echo reading. With the initial reading of the text, the teacher reads it aloud. The students then repeat the same passage. This gives the students the opportunity to hear unfamiliar words read aloud and also have the prosody, pace and intonation modelled to them. Teachers can further scaffold this through: size of the chunk of text before the echo, depth of annotation of the text during the process, which reciprocal reading strategies deployed and their depth, use of linked tools such as word banks, glossaries and knowledge organisers.

Scaffold 3: Layered reading. 'Layered readings . . . Students need to read a challenging text more than once. Ideally, each reading would be different, with the changes in approach modelling the kind of problem solving implicit in deciding how to reread a passage when it proves difficult' (Lemov et al., 2016).

Scaffold 4: Use of reciprocal reading strategies with short reading loops. Students are directed to annotate a chunk of text on the first read (such as new vocabulary) then create summaries of the chunk after the second read. This can be repeated for determined chunks, with varying levels of direction and support from the teacher depending on the need of the student.

Scaffold 5: Dual coding. Use of pre-given symbols/images next to the text to help during the first read, or asking pupils to add dual coding during the first or repeated read, in order to develop comprehension. Asking pupils to transform the text into images/symbols enables a teacher to determine whether the reader really understands the crux of the chunk they have just read.

Scaffold 6: PEER. Using the EEF's PEER framework (EEF, 2021) when adults read to students so that they can 'prompt the child to say something about the book. Evaluate their response. Expand their responses by rephrasing. Repeat the prompt to help them learn from the expansion'.

Scaffold 7: Reader's Theatre. Using the EEF's 'Reader's Theatre' (EEF, 2021). This is a step-by-step approach which takes students through the process of reading moving from adult reading to text allocation, practice and culminating with reflection.

Something to note when using strategies such as teacher-led modelled reading, reciprocal reading and repeated reading is that the explicit instruction that teachers are providing means that more challenging texts can be read as a class. Myatt (2022) argues that all curriculums should be rooted in rich, challenging texts, and teacher-led modelled reading means that we can 'introduce new, challenging vocabulary and language, while modelling the strategies a more reader undertakes with seeming effortlessness'.

Paired reading

Schools can approach paired reading in differing ways. Paired reading within a classroom setting whereby peers of the same age group are paired; paired reading where peers from older year groups can be invited into classrooms to form the reading pair; or with an adult (teacher, TA, tutor etc.) being the paired reader. This particular section will focus on peer paired reading.

Paired peer reading is an approach where students read aloud to one another in pairs. In a form of coaching partnership, each will take turns reading whilst the other listens and provides support and/or feedback to their peer. The purpose of this is to create low-stakes reading opportunities for students whereby they can develop their fluency and also create a reading environment where each pupil is required to 'think hard' as one must read and the other must actively listen. Quigley (2020) highlights that this approach can be powerful in both the primary and secondary classroom, but also reminds us that the purpose of selecting paired reading and when to use it must be given ample consideration:

> For example, a Year 4 teacher seeking to introduce a challenging informational text for the new topic of climate change, with

challenging vocabulary and lengthy sentence structures, may likely deem 'teacher-led whole class reading' necessary in order to ensure the focus is on comprehension. After reading multiple texts on the same topic, the teacher then may seek to deploy paired reading, to shift the emphasis on to reading practice and developing reading. 'Paired reading' here can allow for multiple texts to be read at once. The teacher can circulate and monitor for both fluency and comprehension.

Moreover, Shanahan (2017) advocates using this approach in place of traditionally used strategies such as popcorn reading, stating that we should promote 'paired reading or reading while listening. Have kids do this with texts at their frustration level, practising repeatedly two or three times. The idea is to start with text that you struggle a bit with, but practising to the point of being able to read the text well. That oral reading improvement will transfer to silent reading'.

Paired reading within a year group requires careful pre-work in terms of ensuring that there is appropriate scaffolding in place. In one sense, paired reading is the scaffold as weaker readers can be paired with stronger readers, and so the stronger reader is able to model the fluency, prosody and expression to the other. However, we cannot rely on the stronger reader to be the 'expert' and so we must create an environment whereby we scaffold this reading strategy.

Scaffolding can take the form of:

Scaffold 1: Pre-teaching key vocabulary and concepts. Taking note of Quigley's caution about when to use paired reading and what level of challenge the text is – has sufficient groundwork been carried out so that the foundations of the knowledge required to access the paired reading text are secured. Does each student have the readiness to carry out paired reading on this topic, and what adaptations will be put in place to ensure that they are ready?

Scaffold 2: Pairing choices. Deciding if pairs will read simultaneously at first, then moving to them taking a turn at a time to read.

Scaffold 3: Text length. Deciding the length of chunks that are to be read aloud before they swap over. For example, a paragraph, page or chapter.

Scaffold 4: Text allocation. Deciding if the stronger reader will reduce their amount of reading aloud in the pair over time so that the weaker reader is given greater practice time.

Scaffold 5: Changing pairs. Changing the pairs to provide varied feedback; Shanahan (2009) says, 'A second rule is not to pair up the same kids all the time; they differ in their ability to give feedback, so share the wealth.'

Scaffold 6: Reciprocal reading. Using Reciprocal Reading strategies as part of this paired reading (ensuring scaffolding is in place for both of the pairs to carry this out effectively and successfully).

Scaffold 7: Teacher circulation, questioning and support. Where the teacher may sit with the pair and either model the paired reading† strategy itself (including feedback) or support the weaker reader† in breaking down the text. The teacher asks questions to check for comprehension in order to determine if text needs to be reread.

Scaffold 7: Repeated reading. Determine if repeated reading needs to take place; Shanahan (2014) says, 'I'd follow the research: we'd engage in paired reading and echo reading with repetition and feedback. Our purpose would be to practice the reading of demanding texts (texts which the students can't already read well) until we could read them at high levels of proficiency.'

Independent silent reading

Independent silent reading is an integral part of learning to read, and students should be exposed to increasingly challenging texts which they can draw meaning from for themselves. How to approach independent reading and how much should be carried out in school and beyond school has again created discussion in the education community. The DfE Reading Framework (2023) states that at KS3 students should 'develop an appreciation and love of reading, and read increasingly challenging material independently through . . . choosing and reading books independently for challenge, interest and enjoyment'.

Some schools have chosen to adopt whole-school strategies such as DEAR (Drop Everything and Read) in order to provide time within the curriculum for silent reading practice. Some argue against this (see our earlier discussion of the pitfalls and the scenario of DEAR time), such as Shanahan (2016) who states that

> DEAR, SSR, SQUIRT or any of the other 'independent reading time' schemes are tiny when it comes to reading achievement. Many of those studies have not been particularly well done, but even when they have been, the learning payoffs have been tiny.

In secondary school contexts, this has included concerns about ensuring if the student has an appropriate text (not too easy, not too difficult they can't access it) given that most will be asked to select their own book.

In addition, if silent reading is taking place without teachers circulating and checking for understanding of the text, students could be passively looking like they are reading when in reality they have mentally checked out. This can prove difficult if the independent silent reading is taking place during a form period (15 minutes, for example) or short period of time as the teacher cannot circulate sufficiently. Therefore, the difficulty can be, how can we hit the sweet spot with ensuring successful independent silent reading and effective scaffolding of this to ensure high expectations?

Shanahan (2019) argues that we should

> Talk to your kids about the importance of silent reading, tell them why you want to get some practice in doing it. . . . Initially, keep the segments brief – maybe a paragraph each, just as you

were doing with your round robin reading. This will allow you to question the kids about the content and you'll be able to tell them how they are doing. When they have trouble with it, have them read it again. Once the kids start having some success, move the goal. If they can read single sentences with comprehension, then have them try paragraphs.

Such (2021) furthers this by arguing that

> there is insufficient evidence to suggest that silent reading supports the development of initial reading fluency . . . such opportunities are only of benefit to those who have developed a level of reading fluency that allows for them to enjoy independent reading; those who will not will simply embed their disfluency or . . . will present to read during this part of the school day and begin to associate reading with a sense of shame;

suggesting that once students are more fluent in reading and are equipped with strategies to read more challenging texts, then the level of independent reading can be increased with reduced teacher modelling, as outlined in the EEF (2021) diagram demonstrating 'a process from transferring responsibility from an adult to a child'.

How can we scaffold independent silent reading?

Scaffold 1: Adopting Shanahan's (2019) approaches of the below, and using knowledge of reading progress from reading aloud opportunities which are built into the repertoire of reading strategies:

i) chunking lengths of text to be read independently, building it up incrementally

ii) pre-teaching of reciprocal reading strategies so that students can deploy these methods to break down the meaning of the text and support comprehension. Teacher circulation and questioning is used to determine if additional scaffolds need putting into place and if support is required with implementing reciprocal reading strategies

iii) repeated reading after teacher questioning

iv) use the above to help determine the progress a student is making and increase the challenge of texts when appropriate to do so.

Scaffold 2: Supporting the students to select texts with purpose with an appropriate level of complexity. Using Library sessions to scaffold student understanding of how to find a text and ones which are appropriately pitched. This could be carried out in pairs to drive motivation and promote discussion, as well as create opportunities for targeted levels of heavy, medium or light scaffolding to small groups or students who are picking out a text. This builds on arguments that we need to pitch independent reading accurately as more challenging texts require greater instruction and support.

Scaffold 3: As students become more fluent then increase the amount of independent reading time that they engage in (whilst those not yet fluent continue with strategies to build fluency, such as paired or repeated reading). To assess fluency, assessment using Zutell and Rasinski (1991) 'fluency rubric' can be useful.

Scaffold 4: Parent/carer workshops or support materials. Independent reading needs to take place at home and so we should consider how we can empower parents/carers to create the conditions for this. We need to ensure that we are equipping parents with the knowledge of how to set up an effective independent reading environment at home and support their children to carve out time to read daily. This could include providing training to parents/carers (such as Shanahan's approach above) on how to work with their children to chunk their silent reading and have check-in questioning carried out by the parent.

Exam questions

When in a state of heightened anxiety during timed examination/test conditions, students can find that they stumble over the questions set. They will either completely misread them, misread a concept/date/

event, or misread or confuse a command word (confusing it perhaps with other subjects). To support students in avoiding this pitfall, a helpful strategy can be to get them to RUSS the question:

- Read the question. Then re-read it.
- Underline the key aspects of the question: command word, concept, date, event, diagrams it refers to using, marks etc.
- Summarise. What is it that the question is therefore demanding. Translate it into a sentence of your own and then map out your plan for that question.
- Solve it. Using the plan created above, move onto solving the question.

This technique requires a lot of scaffolding and modelling at the start, with the teacher breaking it down for students before coaching them towards greater autonomy in timed conditions.

However, it can be a useful strategy for carrying out practice questions in lessons too, using mini whiteboards as a way for students to show if they understand what the question is asking for before they attempt to answer it, as part of metacognition. By doing this, teachers can also work out in advance to the pupils starting the question, if it is a case that it is the inability of the student to understand the question that is the barrier to success in their answer, or if it is the skill or content that is the barrier.

As part of adaptive teaching, teachers can then provide additional support and scaffolding to the pupils based on which one/or combination of factors caused the student to not address the question accurately. This strategy can be particularly useful for long prose mathematics questions as they have to simultaneously grapple with a situation where they have to 'decipher word problems, translate the words into operations and more' (Quigley, 2020).

108   The Scaffolding Effect

Planning my response

> 'The role of local communities was the most important factor affecting law enforcement during the Middle Ages.'

How far do you agree? Explain your answer.

You may use the following:
- Tithings
- Trial by Ordeal

You **must** also use information of your own. [16 marks + 4 SPaG]

RUSS the question:
Read, Underline, Summarise, Solve

What period of years is the Middle Ages?

Define 'law enforcement':

Define 'tithings':
Support or challenge statement.

Define 'trial by ordeal':
Support or challenge statement.

FIGURE 5.4 RUSS the question (Fairlamb, 2022), unpublished

PRIMARY CASE STUDY: READING IN PRIMARY
NEIL ALMOND (DEPUTY HEAD TEACHER)
@MR_ALMONDED

Learning to read requires understanding two main areas: language comprehension and word recognition, illustrated by Hollis Scarborough's 'The Reading Rope' (Scarborough, 2001).

Mastering word recognition involves:

1. **Phonological awareness**: Recognising sounds in words (e.g. syllables, phonemes).
2. **Decoding**: Converting spellings into sounds.
3. **Sight recognition**: Reading words without decoding each sound.

Language comprehension includes:

1. **Background knowledge**: Facts and concepts.
2. **Vocabulary**: Number of words known and depth of understanding.
3. **Language structures**: Semantics, clauses, sentence structures.
4. **Verbal reasoning**: Understanding metaphors.
5. **Literacy knowledge**: Concepts of print, genre, text structures.

The difficulty with language comprehension when compared to word recognition is that the ability for pupils to utilise their language comprehension can often be dependent on the texts that they are being applied to. Pupils may have enough knowledge to understand book A but not book B. This has ramifications on how teachers can scaffold reading. Teachers need to consider if the required scaffolding is tied to a particular text (for example, looking at the requisite background knowledge to understand a certain text) and/or if they require more general scaffolding to help them break down sentence structures of a particular text. However, the latter could, inadvertently, support pupils in understanding other texts too (for example, by breaking down multi-clause sentences).

Pupils' reading mileage will vary throughout their time in school so their experience of decoding and coming across words that pupils know how to pronounce will differ between pupils. Therefore, when pupils are reading, it is important to consider in advance which words may prove tricky for pupils to read (though it is impossible to know every word that pupils will struggle to read). The number of syllables, rarity of the word and the rarity of a particular sound-spelling correspondence is a useful heuristic to help decide on choosing these words.

Consider the sentence below:

> 'The flowers bloomed beautifully in the garden, and their vibrant colours made the whole place feel magical.'

Using the heuristic above, 'beautifully' could be a word that pupils could struggle to read as it contains four syllables and a rare sound-spelling correspondence where <eau> spells /ue/. So how can we scaffold student errors in pronunciation? There are four steps that can be used.

i. Isolate the sound-spelling correspondence.
ii. Build the word up from its component parts accumulatively.
iii. Re-read the clause and/or phrase with the word.
iv. Re-read the whole sentence with the target word

Let's look at each step in turn.

English orthography is tricky as the same spelling can represent multiple sounds or some sound-spelling correspondences are not used regularly. Isolating the pronunciation error that a pupil has made is a key first step when scaffolding their decoding. It is better to tell the pupils what the sound-spelling correspondence is, rather than getting the pupil(s)s to continue guessing. Tell the pupil(s) that this is e-a-u spelling of /ue/ and get them to repeat it.

Step two allows the pupil(s) to have plenty of practice of pronouncing the target sound while building up the word through its syllables. An important aspect of this step is that the word needs to be built up cumulatively and the pupil looks at the word. Get the pupils to repeat each syllable after you have pronounced it. For example, the teacher says 'beau', and then the pupil repeats it. The teacher says 'beau-ti', and then the pupil repeats. This continues until the whole word has been built. Corrective feedback must be provided when needed.

It is important to note that in step two, a pupil is likely not reading the word, but merely repeating what is said. This means that the orographic processing that needs to happen may not be taking place. By ensuring the pupil looks at the word, we are encouraging them to link the sound-spelling correspondence, but there is no guarantee that this is happening. To counter this, step three allows the pupil(s) to read the clause or phrase (this may need to be pointed out). This provides an opportunity to see if the pupil(s) can read the word within context without having to navigate multiple clauses and provides some time to pass since they said the word. This is important as the word may have dropped from working memory and so pupil(s) will hopefully be reading the word. Again, the teacher may need to scaffold even further by modelling the reading of the phrase/clause.

Finally, at step four, pupils need to read the whole sentence again so that they can build up their understanding of what they have read and read that word in the context that it has been written. The whole interaction may go something like this:

Teacher: This is a rare spelling. It is the e-a-u spelling of ue. What is it?
Pupil: The e-a-u spelling of ue.
Teacher: Excellent. Let's build the word up from its syllables. Beau (point to pupil).
Pupil: Beau.
Teacher: Beau-ti (point to pupil).
Pupil: Beau-ti
Teacher: Beau-ti-full (point to pupil).
Pupil: Beau-ti-full

Teacher: Beau-ti-full-y (point to pupil).
Pupil: Beau-ti-full-y
Teacher: Good. Now read from that word to 'garden'. Go.
Pupil: Beautifully in the garden
Teacher: Good. Now read from 'the' to 'garden'. Go.
Pupil: The flowers bloomed beautifully in the garden.
Teacher: Now the whole sentence.
Pupil: The flowers bloomed beautifully in the garden, and their vibrant colours made the whole place feel magical.

Unlike some scaffolding that may be provided in the mathematics classroom – such as times table grids – that should be faded out, errors in mispronunciation will inevitably happen, no matter the expertise of the reader. However, you know that scaffolding is successful if pupils are mispronouncing fewer words that were tripping them up, or that pupils are beginning to internalise the process above, where they may try to break the word into syllables independently.

Taking all that we have discussed in this chapter, it is clear to see that there is much food for thought when it comes to the different types of reading strategies and how we can scaffold each of those. At the centre of this is the need for the recognition that reading requires scaffolding, both in primary and secondary contexts. Ample time must be given to practitioners to understand the progression model of reading, the barriers that children can face and which scaffolds can help to overcome those barriers. PD time should be dedicated to KS2 learning about the EYFS and KS1 reading journey, as should secondary learn from primary, beyond just one-off phonics sessions. This in turn will help to minimise the risk of transition points (between year groups, between educational institutions) exacerbating the gap between the stronger and weaker readers. For our students to read right, they need practitioners who are secure on their reading scaffolding strategies.

Chapter 5 Self-Reflection Questions

Take a few minutes to reflect on the questions below and jot down your answers...

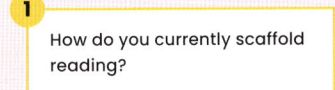

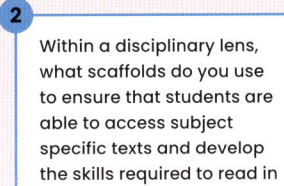

1. How do you currently scaffold reading?

2. Within a disciplinary lens, what scaffolds do you use to ensure that students are able to access subject specific texts and develop the skills required to read in your subject?

3. Which one of these strategies might you try with an upcoming class? What would this look like? Script it out where appropriate.

References

Afflerbach, P., Pearson, P. D. & Paris, P. (2017) Skills and Strategies: Their Differences, Their Relationships, and Why They Matter. In K. Mokhtari (Ed.), *Improving Reading Comprehension Through Meta-Cognitive Reading Strategies Instruction*. Rowman and Littlefield

Ball, R (2022) Scaffolding; How to use it well, TES Online (Online) https://www.tes.com/magazine/teaching-learning/secondary/curriculum-feedback-planning-scaffolding-how-use-it-well

Department for Education (2019) *ITT Core Content Framework* (Online). Available at https://assets.publishing.service.gov.uk/media/6061eb9cd3bf7f5cde260984/ITT_core_content_framework_.pdf. Accessed 12th March 2024

Department for Education (2019) *ITT Core Content Framework* (Online). Available at https://assets.publishing.service.gov.uk/media/6061eb9cd3bf7f5cde260984/ITT_core_content_framework_.pdf. Accessed 12th March 2024

Department for Education (2023) *Key Stage 2 Attainment* (Online). Available at https://explore-education-statistics.service.gov.uk/find-statistics/key-stage-2-attainment. Accessed 12th March 2024

Early Career Framework (2024) (Online). Available at https://www.gov.uk/government/publications/early-career-framework. Accessed 9th August 2024

Education Endowment Foundation (EEF) (2018) *Improving Literacy in Secondary Schools* (Online). Available at https://educationendowmentfoundation.org.uk/education-evidence/guidance-reports/literacy-ks3-ks4. Accessed 16th April 2024

Education Endowment Foundation (EEF) (2019) *Reciprocal Reading* (Online). Available at https://educationendowmentfoundation.org.uk/projects-and-evaluation/projects/reciprocal-reading. Accessed 16th April 2024

Fairlamb, A. (2022) *RUSS the Question*, unpublished

Fairlamb, A. (2023) *Guided Reading of Mary Queen of Scots*, unpublished

Fairlamb, A. (2023) *Heavy, Medium and Light Scaffolding* - Reading, adapted from Ball, R. (2022) Scaffolding and how to use it well, TES Online. Available online at: https://www.tes.com/magazine/teaching-learning/secondary/curriculum-feedback-planning-scaffolding-how-use-it-well. Accessed on 21st July 2024

Fernandes, C. & Gallacher, T. (2020) *Why Reading Is Key to GCSE Success, GL Assessment* (Online). Available at https://reports.gl-assessment.co.uk/whyreading/. Accessed 14th March 2024

Goldenberg, G. (2024) *Can Turning on the Subtitles Really Improve the Literacy Levels of Millions of Children?* Chartered College of Teachers (Online). Available at https://my.chartered.college/research-hub/can-turning-on-the-subtitles-really-improve-the-literacy-levels-of-millions-of-children/#:~:text=Therefore%2C%20the%20data%20suggests%20that,done%20for%20the%20weakest%20readers. Accessed 9th April 2024

Gudmundsdatter Magnusson, C., Luoto, J. & Blikstad-Balas, M. (2023) Developing Teachers' Literacy Scaffolding Practices – Successes and Challenges in a Video-Based Longitudinal Professional Development Intervention. *Teaching and Teacher Education*, 133, 104274, October (Online). Available at https://www.researchgate.net/publication/374356540_Developing_teachers'_literacy_scaffolding_practices-successes_and_challenges_in_a_video-based_longitudinal_professional_development_intervention. Accessed 9th April 2024

Higgins, S., Martell, T., Waugh, D., Henderson, P. & Sharples, J. (2021) *Improving Literacy in KS2 Guidance Report*. Education Endowment Fund (Online). Available at https://educationendowmentfoundation.org.uk/education-evidence/guidance-reports/literacy-ks2. Accessed 18th April 2024

Koskinen, P. S., Bowen, C. T., Gambrell, L. B., Jensema, C. J. & Kane, K. W. (1997) *Captioned Television and Literacy Development: Effects of Home Viewing on Learning Disabled Students*. Paper presented at the Meeting of the American Educational Research Association, Chicago, IL

Lemov, D. (2015) *Teach Like a Champion 2.0. 62 Techniques That Put Students on the Path to College*. San Francisco: Jossey-Bass

Lemov, D., Driggs, C. & Woolway, E. (2016) *Reading Reconsidered: A Practical Guide to Rigorous Literacy*. San Francisco: Jossey-Bass

McCrae, P. (2020) *Motivated Teaching. Harnessing the Science of Motivation to Boost Attention and Effort in the Classroom*. CreateSpace Independent Publishing Platform

McCrea, P. (2023) *The Knowing-Doing Gap: A Barrier to Teacher Improvement* (Online). Available at https://snacks.pepsmccrea.com/p/the-knowing-doing-gap. Accessed 1st November 2023

McLeskey, J. & Brownell, M. T. (2017) *Fig 67 High-Leverage Practice 15 SEN in Mainstream Schools Evidence Review*. EEF, 2020 (Online). Available at https://eef.li/D4821h

Myatt, M. (2022) *Using Stories in the Curriculum* (Online). Available at www.marymyatt.com/blog/using-stories-in-the-curriculum. Accessed 12th March 2024

National Literacy Trust (2023) *Children and Young People's Reading in 2023* (Online). Available at https://literacytrust.org.uk/research-services/research-reports/children-and-young-peoples-reading-in-2023/. Accessed 1st November 2023

Quigley, A. (2020) *Closing the Reading Gap*. Abingdon, Oxon: Routledge

Scarborough, H. S. (2001) Connecting Early Language and Literacy to Later Reading (Dis)abilities: Evidence, Theory, and Practice. In S. Neuman & D. Dickinson (Eds.), *Handbook for Research in Early Literacy*. New York: Guilford Press

Shanahan, T. (2009) *FAQ on Oral Reading Fluency*. Shanahan on Literacy (Online). Available at https://www.shanahanonliteracy.com/blog/faq-on-oral-reading-fluency-instruction. Accessed 16th April 2024

Shanahan, T. (2014) *Do You Want Your Husband to Remember Your Birthday or Anniversary?* Shanahan on Literacy (Online). Available at https://www.shanahanonliteracy.com/blog/do-you-want-your-husband-to-remember-your-birthday-or-anniversary. Accessed 16th April 2024

Shanahan, T. (2016) *Does Independent Reading Time During the School Day Create Lifelong Readers*. Shanahan on Literacy (Online). Available at https://www.readingrockets.org/blogs/shanahan-on-literacy/does-independent-reading-time-during-school-day-create-lifelong-readers. Accessed 17th April 2024

Shanahan, T. (2017) *I Get What You Want Us Not To Do, But What Should We Do? Getting Higher Test Scores*. Reading Rockets (Online). Available at https://www.readingrockets.org/blogs/shanahan-on-literacy/i-get-what-you-want-us-not-do-what-should-we-do-getting-higher-test. Accessed 1st July 2024

Shanahan, T. (2019) *Is Round Robin Reading Really That Bad? Reading Rockets*. Launching Young Readers (Online). Available at https://www.boredteachers.com/post/round-robin-reading-is-harmful-what-you-can-do-instead. Accessed 16th April 2024

Sherrington, T. (2019) *Rosenshine's Principles in Action*. Woodbridge: John Catt Educational

Such, C. (2021) *The Art and Science of Teaching Primary Reading*. London: Sage

Zutell, J. & Rasinski, T. V. (1991) Training Teachers to Attend to Their Students' Oral Reading Fluency. *Theory into Practice*, 30, 211-217 in Higgins, S., Martell, T., Waugh, D., Henderson, P. & Sharples, J. (2021) *Improving Literacy in KS2 Guidance Report*. Education Endowment Fund (Online). Available at https://educationendowmentfoundation.org.uk/education-evidence/guidance-reports/literacy-ks2. Accessed 18th April 2024

6a Scaffolding and writing

> You can shrink the amorphous challenge of poor literacy into manageable and meaningful goals and practical solutions. You can make a start on narrowing the gap for those pupils who will rely on the skill of writing to succeed in school. Every pupil leaving school as a confident, skilled writer should prove a priority that is within our gift to address.
>
> *(Quigley, 2021)*

The barriers that writing presents

Let's be honest, writing is TOUGH. Even the most expert of writers with a wealth of writing experience can experience barriers which hamper the writing process. As someone who has written essays at university and continued to write for educational audiences, this chapter has still taken a lot of time, cognitive effort, resilience and research around what to write and how to write it. Cue multiple drafts, edits and a lot of gumph consigned to the recycling bin. Effective and successful writing doesn't just 'happen'. It is a multifaceted beast that pulls upon both the subject knowledge domain and the literacy domain simultaneously.

When given a question, topic or task to write about, there is much that needs to be considered. What to write? And for what audience? What knowledge, concepts and skills? How to write it for this subject? What structure and conventions? What key vocabulary and jazzy grammatical techniques to use? Often the most terrifying part is 'how to start?' It has been likened to a complex game of chess due to the interplay of moves, how different pieces operate and the cognitive load (Kellogg & Whiteford, 2009) and so writing requires a lot of sweating the small stuff as 'writing involves deciding what to say, which words to use, how to spell them, perhaps how to form the letters, and what order to place the words in – and that's just at sentence level' (Hochman & Wexler, 2017). So how can we help to silence the cacophony of noise that writing can cause our students to experience, and how can we empower them to embrace writing for purpose powerfully? Effective scaffolding is central to achieving this.

The Simple View of Writing is a useful place to begin considering the many aspects that make up writing and how we can scaffold it. It provides all subjects with a clear way of knowing the key components of successful writing and identifies the importance of the working memory (reminding us of the importance of being mindful to not overload it).

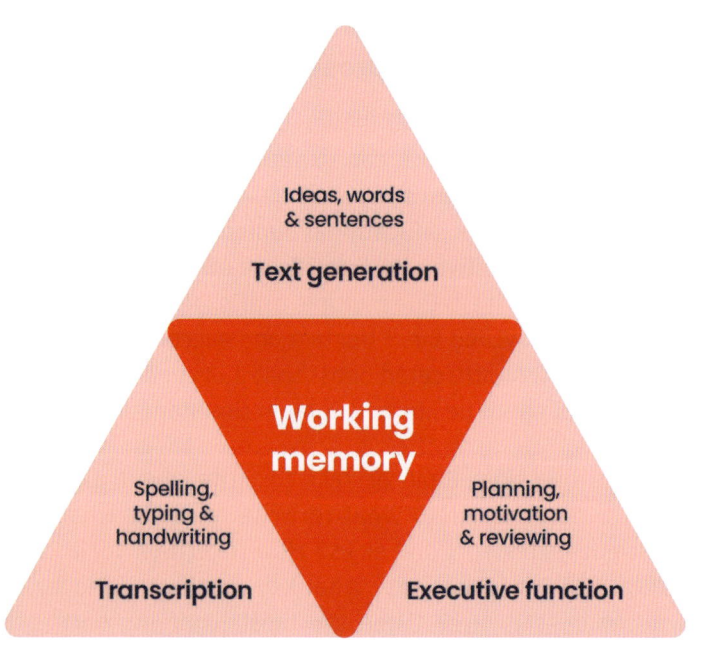

FIGURE 6A.1 The simple view of writing (EEF, 2021)

Scaffolding and writing 119

This overview helps us to see that there are three key features in the writing process:

- Executive function (planning the response, having the motivation and confidence to embark on the task and to sustain effort and have resilience, and to review and revise work)
- Composition (relevant substantive knowledge and concepts, disciplinary skills required for answering the question, organisation and categorisation, structure and conventions, tier 2–3 vocabulary)
- Transcription (the actual physical process of writing, spelling)

Linked to this, the Education Endowment Fund (EEF, 2021) has taken this to form a process of five sequenced chunks, which adaptive scaffolding underpins at each point:

> To develop pupils' ability to write at greater length, it can be helpful to think of writing as a task made up of five stages: planning, drafting, revising, editing, and publishing. Children can be taught, through modelling and scaffolding, strategies which support them to undertake each of these stages of the writing process.

This is useful as, similarly to the discussion in the reading chapter, secondary schools can have inaccurate expectations of how much and how effectively students can write when they cross the threshold into Year 7. Often, there is a misconception in secondary schools that students can arrive with the ability to know the writing process and that they can form mostly structured paragraphs and respond to answers in a logical format. This, more often than not, is not the case.

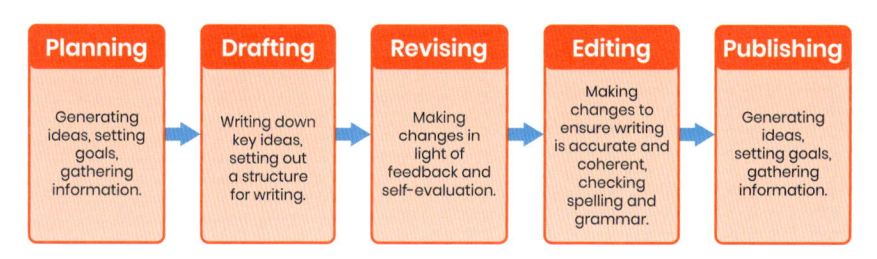

Planning	Drafting	Revising	Editing	Publishing
Generating ideas, setting goals, gathering information.	Writing down key ideas, setting out a structure for writing.	Making changes in light of feedback and self-evaluation.	Making changes to ensure writing is accurate and coherent, checking spelling and grammar.	Generating ideas, setting goals, gathering information.

FIGURE 6A.2 The writing process (EEF, 2021)

This is *not* because they have not been taught over many years what the writing process is and had significant amounts of curriculum time dedicated to modelling, scaffolding and carrying out much deliberate practice of writing. Primary practitioners dedicate *a lot* of curriculum time to supporting the process of writing including working with pupils to help them to 'learn specific strategies for writing' and also 'how a person thinks and acts when planning, executing and evaluating performance on a task and its outcomes' (DfE, 2012). An example of this is 'Talk for Writing' (talk4writing.com) where the format involves students moving through a writing process of a cold write (baseline), imitation phase, innovation phase, 'hot' write which is independent and focuses on invention, and the final assessment. Primary schools do also spend time threading in disciplinary writing within the subjects that form the primary curriculum, to drive understanding of how to 'write like an historian' or 'write like a linguist'.

However, at secondary school there are unique and different challenges that both teachers and students face which can act as barriers to the development of writing. At a secondary level, students instead have a range of teachers who may only see them once a week, within which they have a finite window to deliver content and skills, as well as find meaningful time to assess and develop writing in their subject area. This is particularly difficult given the dense content of current examination specifications.

For students, it can be a difficult transition for them to also make as, rather than having chunked mornings/afternoons focused on one particular subject and how to write in that subject (as well as having supporting writing development lessons too), they are instead expected to move between a suite of subjects hourly and adapt to the different writing demands and nuances that each subject has. Quigley (2022) highlights this by pointing out that writing is a 'moving target . . . at different phases and key stages' and that in

> Year 9 [pupils will be] moving from note-taking in science, to essay writing in history, then onto annotation in art, and finally some

narrative writing in English. Each act of writing proves subtly different, with different generic features and stylistic devices, along with often radically different approaches to how writing is taught, planned, drafted, edited and revised.

As such, this means within a school day, students are increasingly tasked with needing to broaden and develop their 'writing frameworks in specialised ways so that they can 'write like a . . .[historian, scientist, artist]' (Quigley, 2022).

What scaffolds can therefore support the development of writing and disciplinary writing throughout the course of a child's journey through primary and secondary school? And how do we ensure that we are 'developing their [students] frameworks of thought and coping mechanisms to overcome the difficulties of writing' (Hough, 2023).

The scaffolding of writing at primary

In Chapter 6b, we have curated a range of key stage specific writing scaffolding strategies written by primary experts. These case studies are useful in helping to understand the phase specific development milestones that children should meet and exceed.

The scaffolding of writing at secondary

Within secondary schools, the disciplinary focus of the writing deepens, and there is less holistic focus on 'writing lessons' and 'handwriting lessons'. As a result, this means that disciplines must consider how to meaningfully plan to build upon prior writing development in disciplinary ways.

For Secondary Literacy Leads, it can be tempting to introduce whole school approaches to developing writing in order to support a consistent approach. Arguments for this would be that if consistent and uniform approaches are adopted on a mass scale, then writing skills will improve holistically across all subjects. Some may instead advocate increasing English lesson curriculum time where a lesson is focused on developing writing skills, which then students are expected to apply in other subjects. There is a danger that such whole school approaches could result in writing being seen as the main responsibility of the English department (and not the responsibility of others) and generate misconceptions or assumptions that the improvements in writing in one subject will automatically result in improvements in the others. That is not to say that there can't be whole school principles, but that these principles must celebrate, elevate and create space for disciplinary writing and empower the teacher to know what scaffolds to use and when in order to develop writing in their subject. The EEF (2018) further this by stating that

> this does not mean that schools should stop whole-school approaches to literacy, but it does suggest a need to think carefully about how whole-school approaches . . . will be implemented and balanced with more subject specific support. It also suggests that schools should consider the quality of the professional development aimed at supporting teachers to develop the disciplinary literacy of their students.

Conclusively, at the heart of writing development must be focused disciplinary writing with appropriate scaffolding that focuses on the unique ways in which subjects communicate:

> As students progress through an increasingly specialised secondary curriculum, we need to ensure that students are trained to access academic language and conventions of different subjects. Strategies grounded in disciplinary literacy aim to meet this need, building on the premise that each subject has its own unique language, ways of knowing, doing communicating.
>
> (EEF, 2018)

Therefore, we must afford time for this in our subject curricula and make sure that we are planning for the scaffolding, modelling and deliberate practice of writing across our subject progression models. Webb (2020) states this is important as slowing down is crucial for better knowledge acquisition and development. It is better for students to write one to two very high quality, crafted pieces over a scheme of work, than to have to write six or seven pieces with no time to concentrate on quality or improve their work.

As a Senior Leader, time must be given to Middle Leaders and teams to find out about the unique ways that their subject communicates and understand the barriers that students might encounter as they tread the path of the writing process. If we take History as an example, Hough (2023) has summarised what Counsell (1997) has identified that a student is expected to grapple with each time they produce a structured response:

- **Memory and concentration**: struggling to avoid new information, ideas and/or instructions crowding out previous thoughts during the writing process.
- **Relevance and selection:** struggling to form criteria on which to select or reject information in order to keep their writing relevant to the topic (hard), question (harder) or argument (hardest).
- **Sorting**: struggling to shape information to give it meaning. History requires categorisation, and this can be substantive (political, social) or linked to disciplinary concepts (cause, change).
- **General and the particular**: struggling to understand the differing status between general points (big ideas) and supporting points (small ideas). Without this appreciation, answers can often lack structure and seem chaotic.
- **Language of Discourse**: struggling with their confidence and understanding of how to build a sustained argument, often lacking clever sentence starters, connectives and understanding of analytical prose.

Extending this level of subject disciplinary writing nuance and challenge across the curriculum, we can understand why students find it challenging to grapple with writing effectively and in-depth. And resultantly, this is why adaptive scaffolding (planned in advance, adapted live in the moment, and then reflected on afterwards to inform future planning) is vital so that we can equip students with the strategies and techniques to be able to remove those scaffolds over time so that they can write effectively and independently to a greater degree. Writing development can falter or flourish at various points, which is why the subject content must sit centrally at the heart of writing and why we must see writing as a 'continuum. It could be that for different tasks, or where pupils' background knowledge is uniquely strong, pupils may subtly slide along the continuum' (Quigley, 2021).

Retrieval: activating prior knowledge of content and writing

The first element of Counsell's (1997) overview pinpoints the issue of memory and concentration, which all subjects must consider in the writing process. When planning a lesson, how can a practitioner plan for writing in their subject so that they can avoid cognitive overload? Anecdotally beyond the subject of English and MFL, secondary practitioners will plan for how to avoid cognitive overload in terms of subject content, concepts or skills, yet not also for the demands of writing. This is something that must be planned so that we can support the broad range of our students who have different levels of writing readiness in our classrooms. For students with low working memories, writing can prove challenging at the very outset as they are simultaneously trying to process new content being learnt whilst trying to assimilate this with their memory of how to write for different purposes and using different structures.

Retrieval (as discussed in Chapter 2), is an important scaffold when writing, as you can not only plan activities which secure the recall of prior knowledge of content, but also prior knowledge of writing structures. Including writing techniques in your retrieval diet will mean that students have greater opportunities to strengthen their recall of writing, helping to avoid a pregnant gap between when certain writing structures were last used. For example, in GCSE History students are expected to write a response arguing how useful a source is. During the course of the paper that they are studying, practising the source utility question will be threaded into lessons across the sequence of learning. But how, in the gaps between those lessons that focus on this particular skill and written response, do we ensure that too much time does not pass between them recalling what the success criteria for this question is. To aid retrieval of writing structures, we can use common retrieval techniques such as:

- Question type brain dump
- Multiple choice questions focusing on writing and questions
- True/false focusing on writing and questions
- Writing down a writing success criteria from memory
- Find and fix – spotting errors in a response, explaining why they are incorrect and suggesting improvements

All of these strategies will help to activate their prior knowledge of writing within disciplines, warming up the foundations upon which the further development of writing can securely build upon. Moreover, 'writing and content knowledge are intimately related. You can't write well about something you don't know well' (Hochman & Wexler, 2017), which is particularly true for novice writers who 'benefit from pre-writing activities that build background knowledge to support a given writing task' (Quigley, 2021). We therefore have to ensure that we have planned to check the readiness of our students' content and writing knowledge in order to support effective writing, and that we use these checks to adapt our scaffolding of this process live in lessons.

The further strategies below will require being looked at through the lens of the discipline, as some strategies will align themselves more with some subjects and not be required to support writing in others.

Getting to the crux of the question

Linking to our reading chapter, another barrier that we must plan scaffolds to overcome is the accurate reading of the question or challenge given. Looking at any question, there can be a multitude of demands contained within what looks like even a seemingly simple question. For example, a GCSE History question asks:

> How useful are Sources B and C for an enquiry into the attitudes of young people towards the Hitler Youth movement? Explain your answer, using Sources B and C and your knowledge of the historical context. (8 marks)
>
> (Pearson Edexcel, 2016)

Within this question, students are expected to remember that to answer it successfully they must:

- Remember the structure
- Remember the content (attitudes towards the Hitler Youth movement)
- Use extracts from the sources
- Apply relevant own knowledge that relates to the sources and the content
- Explain why the content and provenance of the source is useful using a range of criteria
- Form a judgement as to how useful the sources are

This is no small feat, and it is not surprising that at times students can feel cognitively overloaded. Whilst developing the reading skills of students will contribute towards greater success in understanding a question, we must also scaffold and model how to actively break down a question into its composite parts, chunking it so that it becomes more accessible. This could take the form of:

- Using a procedure reinforced by a mnemonic like RUSS the question (see reading chapter, Figure 6.4) – Read, Underline [the key composite parts]
- Summarise [what is the question demanding overall], Solve [the question by now planning the response]

- Using a visualiser to model identifying and annotating the key components of the question
- Using arrows and key word prompts to pinpoint key features of the question
- Using mini-whiteboards for students to note down their initial summary of the question; this can be used alongside strategies such as 'turn and talk' prior to noting down the summary or after in order to tweak it in light of peer discussions
- Discuss in pairs then as a class how someone might start the question
- Identifying which parts of the question can be understood and which parts cannot be understood, and outlining what to do in those scenarios
- 'Ensuring that students understand the subject specific connotations of Tier 2 vocabulary used in writing questions' (EEF, 2021) such as confidently knowing what 'describe' or 'explain' means within the context of the subject

Planning: relevance and selection (Counsell, 1997)

Once the students are secure on what the question is demanding of them, they will then have to work out what content and skills are relevant to answering the question followed by then deciding from that content what they will finally select to use. Given the wealth of content knowledge that students are expected to know within each discipline, it can be hard for them (especially within timed or examination conditions) to sift through all that they know in order to identify the content before zooming in on the best content. Scaffolding can support with this filtering process through managing cognitive load if we use scaffolds such as:

- Mini-whiteboards to write down what content students think should be included

- Giving an overview of core knowledge and students highlighting and choosing which content would be the best for the given question
- Go big, then distil. A brain dump or thought shower followed by students then highlighting their final chosen content when reviewing their initial ideas
- Think, pair, share or turn and talk – building up content and discussing which is the better content; amending initial responses and building in alternatives
- 'I say, you say' (Quigley, 2021) where pupils share responses in a backwards and forwards knowledge exchange

Planning: organisation

Following students being able to identify the relevant content that needs to be included in a response, they will need support in shaping this knowledge into chunks – 'shapes that give it meaning' (Counsell, 2004). Hochman and Wexler (2017) argue that the two most important parts of the writing process are planning ('where the "lion's share" of the work of writing occurs') and revising, and that we must scaffold the planning process as 'although experienced writers may be able to turn out a well-developed paragraph or essay on the fly, most students will find it overwhelming to organise their thoughts at the same time that they're choosing words and figuring out the best way to structure their sentences'.

Once students have retrieved prior understanding of the content and question format then identified relevant content, students will then need to be supported in how to structure it. Various scaffolding strategies can be used to develop organising selected content, all of which can have further visual, verbal and written scaffolds woven into them:

Writing organisation strategy overview (Fairlamb, 2024), unpublished

Organisation Strategy	Detail
Card Sort	Content chunks which are then placed either in order, sequence or prioritised. Used within pair or group work, this can help argument formation alongside organisation and students articulate and justify their organisational choices. Hints and cues can be provided as a way to provide further scaffolding. Hough (2023) says this can scaffold writing as 'being able to move the post-it notes or cards around allows students the chance to change their headings to explore different categories and ways of organising their argument'. This formative approach can mean that students who are hesitant about making mistakes instead have the opportunity to 'give it a go' without it being a 'permanent' commitment to their writing being set in stone; they can move, erase and revise.
Graphic Organisers or Semantic Organisers	Caviglioli (2019) has identified four different types of graphic organisers which practitioners can select according to the disciplinary demands of the writing task at hand: 1. Chunk: tree diagram, mind map, concept map 2. Compare: Venn diagram, double spray, crossed continua 3. Sequence: flow chart, cycle, flow spray 4. Cause and effect: input-output diagram, fishbone diagram, relations diagram To support accessibility when developing student confidence with graphic organisers, further scaffolding can include guided practice (I do, we do, you do and the use of a visualiser), verbal/written/visual cues and prompts and partially completed examples.

(Continued)

(Continued)

Organisation Strategy	Detail
Logical Division	Working in pairs or groups to divide the content into determined categories.
Concept Maps	Attaching the relevant content to appropriate titles (big ideas). This enables students to group ideas but also to identify links between the big ideas which enables students to work towards creating fluent and logical responses.
Multiple Paragraph Outline (Hochman & Wexler, 2017)	Grids with big idea titles in one column which students then add relevant related content to in the supporting points column.
Essay Plan Templates	Supported by cues, prompts and sentence starters.
Think Sheets	To 'plan, organise, write, edit and revise two types of expository texts. Teachers modelled aloud how to use the think sheets and accompanying strategies such as brainstorming, and students were provided with assistance until they could apply them independently. During modelling and guided practice, teacher-student dialogue about writing performance and strategy use was encouraged, and students supported each other by sharing and talking about their work with classmates. Over the course of a year, this instruction led to improved writing' (Englert et al., 1991).
Mnemonic Devices	Using mnemonic devices for planning which helps students to regulate their planning process. For example, STOP&LIST - 'Stop, Think of Purposes, and List Ideas and Sequence Them' (Troia & Graham, 2002).

Drafting: seeing the big picture using modelling and metacognitive oracy

With relevant content selected and organised, focus can be turned to scaffolding pupils in being able to 'understand the differing status between general points (big ideas) and supporting points (small ideas)' (Counsell, 2004). Hochman and Wexler (2017) argue that this process is often too hurried and therefore flawed as students 'don't learn how to construct interesting and grammatically correct sentences first, and they aren't encouraged to plan or outline before they write'. To avoid this common pitfall and to outline how we can scaffold effective writing, the DfE (Department for Education) (2012) has stated that as part of this we need to break down and chunk the paragraph process; in essence, we need to sweat the small stuff to make sure that the outcome is successful:

> Struggling writers can benefit from explicit and targeted instruction in word-, sentence-, and paragraph-level skills. . . . Cognitive strategy instruction which addresses how a pupil is taught, in addition to what is taught. It includes explicit and systematic instruction, direct instruction, scaffolding and modelling. . . . Pupils learn specific strategies for writing and also how a person thinks and acts when planning, executing and evaluating performance and a task on outcomes. With cognitive instruction, pupils should be able to engage more fully in the writing process and be independent writers.
>
> (Santangelo & Olinghouse, 2009)

Clearly identified within this is the importance of the teacher articulating the stages of the writing process – what, how and why – whilst modelling and ensuring that students carry out guided and deliberate practice. Targeted questioning, using methods such as cold calling (whole class questioning whereby anyone can be called upon to answer), will enable a teacher to check for understanding during this process and therefore know if steps need to be repeated or modelled further for some students. Modelling, as outlined in an earlier chapter, can be teacher led to the whole class, in groups or 1:1; and modelling can also be carried out by peers

As part of this process, analysing how an answer should look can effectively scaffold responses.

Overview of different strategies to analyse writing (Fairlamb, 2024), unpublished

Analysing Strategy	Detail
Worked Examples and Model Answers	Using examples (pre-made or written live under a visualiser) and non-examples. Using a visualiser or smartboard, the teacher can focus on the structure, key features of the response/structure, and identify where writing has been effective or could be improved. Anonymised student responses can also be used. Some students may require multiple walk-throughs.
Success Criteria	Equipping students with a checklist of key features of an effective response. By explaining the why of this technique and modelling using them through metacognitive oracy (discussing your process; how you are using it), this will help students to also be able to do the same over time. This may be initially heavily scaffolded, then over time (using formative assessment) the teacher can then reduce this scaffold so that students can create and use their own from memory. Linking back to the earlier discussion of retrieval, this success criteria can be then recalled.
Authentic Texts	Using authentic texts where students can see further examples of the given style of writing in context through exposure 'to a rich range of genres and identification of key features' (EEF, 2018) as 'reading high quality texts in every subject, for example those that effectively illustrate the conventions of particular types of writing, gives students an opportunity to observe the discipline-specific aspects of writing that relate to particular subjects' (EEF, 2021).

(Continued)

(Continued)

Analysing Strategy	Detail
Oral Discussions	Oral discussions of the response which include how to start sentences: 'model for the class and then have students practise it orally as a group' (Hochman & Wexler, 2017).
Visualisers	During the drafting process, student work can be placed under the visualiser for peer assessment and/or discussion about the effective features and what the next steps should be. This can help other students to re-calibrate their own writing live in the lesson.
Matching Points or 'Topic Sentences'	Matching points/topic sentences with supporting details and/or arguments, followed by an explanation of why they connect as pairs.
Reverse Engineering	Reverse engineer a paragraph so that students pull out the key components and create the plan that would have enabled the person to write the response.
Target Setting and Feed-Forward	Setting a tangible goal for development for this piece of writing, building upon prior targets and examples of their own improvements of this target in previous corrections.

Putting pen to paper: writing the response

With the growing understanding of what effective responses to the given question look like, we can then employ differing structures as scaffolds for transforming big ideas supported by smaller points into coherent, powerful paragraphs. The first three of the below scaffolding strategies are all taken from the 'The Writing Revolution' (Hochman & Wexler, 2017) and are effective ways to chunk the process of writing. It is worth noting that they state that for them to be successful that these strategies rely on explicit instruction and repeated, deliberate practice which ensures that they experience 'a series of exercises that specifically target the skills they haven't yet mastered, while building on the skills they already have, in a gradual, step-by-step process'. There are, of course, other scaffolding strategies that teachers can deploy.

Strategy 1: Kernel sentences (Hochman & Wexler, 2017)

Using a choice of cues which students provide simple responses to: who, what, when, where, how and why. This acts then as a success criteria of content that must all be included in an 'expanded sentence'. An example of this would be: Describe Nightingale's role in the development of pavilion plan hospitals.

Who: Nightingale
When: 1848
How: Notes on Nursing (book)
What: large windows, tiles, separate wards
Why: improve sanitation in hospitals to reduce infection and number of deaths

Expanded sentence: From **1858**, **Nightingale** was massively influential in the development of pavilion plan hospitals as she suggested in her **Notes on Nursing book** that having **larger windows, using tiles as internal materials and having separate wards** would lead to **improved sanitation in hospitals and lower death rates.**

The Writing Revolution (Hochman & Wexler, 2017) outlines that the process of expanding the sentence using the responses should initially be modelled, then gradually faded to the point of independence. Using this approach helps students to chunk the key features of a sentence before they then have to write it, moving them from word level to sentence level writing. Additional scaffolding can be provided with the teacher carrying out class or small group feedback of the responses to the cues to build them up a complete set, before moving onto expanded sentence work.

Strategy 2: Because, But, So

This acts as a scaffold to support students to see arguments from different perspectives and expand sentences as well as use 'complex sentences and conjunctions' (Hochman & Wexler, 2017) as part of language structure development. Varying which number of conjunctions to use, modelling, worked examples and partial examples and class discussions can be used as part of the further scaffolding of this strategy. This supports students in being able to think deeper about their response as it requires them to respond in a multifaceted way, through which teachers can elicit greater understanding of the extent of the child's knowledge.

An example of this might be:

	'In 1861, Louis Pasteur developed the Germ Theory . . .'
Because	'. . . of his experiments whilst working as brewer and his work on pasteurisation'
But	'. . . failed to prove that germs cause disease and thus many continued to believe in Miasma theory until the work of Koch in the 1880s.'
So	'. . . this led to the challenge to Miasma theory . . .'

The sentence cues provide prompts to start sentences, helping to not only reduce the cognitive load of the writing process but by also mitigating against the fear of how to begin and then extend answers, acting almost like cat eyes to help the student to navigate their way. With deliberate practice, students can begin to use conjunctions to expand sentences more independently, adding to the fluency of their use in future writing (further reducing the cognitive load of the writing domain on working memory). Thornton (2020) further suggests that it is also a method to promote the use of tier 2-3 vocabulary as they can be woven into the open sentence or added onto the cue of because, but and so, signalling and encouraging students to incorporate them in their written responses.

Single Paragraph Outline (SPO) (for a single paragraph; multiple paragraph outline can be used for multiple paragraphs)

This template includes a topic sentence (created by the teacher), supporting details (which can be teacher-led through class discussion and feedback or students can complete this with peers or independently), and a concluding sentence. This format breaks down the formation of a paragraph into three key chunks, of which varying teachers can employ various levels of instruction and modelling for each part based on the readiness of students. This strategy links well with the earlier process of determining the relevance and selection of content as well as the categorisation of it. This is because it helps to then sequence the organised, relevant content into a coherent paragraph structure. Over time, scaffolds can be removed such as the teacher creating the topic sentence (and instead pupils generating their own) or providing less support in the selection of relevant content as supporting details. When appropriate, teachers can progress to getting students to write multiple paragraphs.

Strategy 3: DARE

This simple mnemonic helps students to remember the process of writing. DARE stands for 'Develop your topic sentences, Add supporting details, Reject arguments from the other side, End with a strong conclusion' (Troia & Graham, 2002). This could be useful for subjects such as RE, where countering opinions have to be given before forming a logical judgement.

Strategy 4: Writing frames

This is a commonly used approach! This mainly includes using varying levels and intensity of structure supports (like structure strips) or sentence starters to help give students nudges as to how to transform the plan into a coherent structure. A danger with this can be that we sometimes place these down in front of students and expect them to know how to access or use them. Additionally, we can make the mistake of leaving this scaffold in place for too long, leading to it becoming a crutch which students become dependent on, or it can stifle students being more independent in using their own phrasing.

Modelling the use of the writing frame and structure strips is therefore important, as is knowing the intensity with which to use this scaffold for the different students in the class. For example, do some need the full sentence starters, do some need cues and prompts, do some need none of those? Should sentence starters be given pre-prepared, or might it be better to carry out whole class recall/discussion of effective sentence starters as part of co-construction which enables conversations of why key phrases might be effective (especially when weighed against the purpose and success criteria of the writing task).

Of importance is how, over time, can we reduce this scaffolding using repetition and deliberate practice to achieve this.

Elevating written responses at word, sentence and paragraph level – 'The Language of Discourse' (Counsell, 2003) and creativity

Phrasing, vocabulary and grammar can add richness and depth to a written response, as well as support with the flow of sentences and paragraphs. Within subject disciplines, there are subtle and unique ways that people use certain techniques to communicate their ideas. An example of this is in History, historians commonly use fronted adverbials such as 'arguably' and 'admittedly'. It is worth time exploring which phrases and pieces of vocabulary can elevate your student's writing in your own discipline, so that students 'write like a . . . [historian]'.

Strategy 1: Key word, grammar and/or sentence signpost mats, banks or displays

These could contain any combination of key words, subordinating conjunctions, correlative conjunctions, conclusion transitions, illustrative transitions, and further subject-specific writing prompts. This could include categories such as grammar (e.g. fronted adverbials, emphasis and connectives/transition words) or key phrases (e.g. explanation: this therefore, consequently). This could be pre-prepared, or as scaffolding is reduced, it can be co-created as a class or in pairs, or independently created; 'what key words and phrases should I include?' The teacher can also provide further scaffolding through teacher-student dialogue about which words are the better ones to use for the given task.

Explain Why...

12 marks | 15 minutes (5 minutes per paragraph)

Structure: 3 x PEE chains

Paragraph 1:
The most important reason why...
Evidence to support this is... (2-3 pieces of SPED ev)
This therefore led to/ caused/ resulted in...

Link the factors

Paragraph 2:
The second important reason why...
Evidence to support this is... (2-3 pieces of SPED ev)
This therefore led to/ caused/ resulted in...

Link the factors

Paragraph 3:
The third important reason why...
Evidence to support this is... (2-3 pieces of SPED ev)
This therefore led to/ caused/ resulted in...

Example Question

'May' - you can replace a bullet point with a different, relevant factor, if you think it would work better. However, it must be accurate and relevant.

Explain why religion caused so much division in sixteenth century England. You may use the following in your answer:
- The English Reformation
- The impact of Mary I's reign (12 marks) 15 mins

You should use information from your own knowledge (12 marks)

Focus of the question - what your evidence and explanation must focus on. You must use words from the question. Check the timeframe!

Own knowledge - this means 2-3 pieces of SPED evidence per factor.
It also means that you must write an additional factor (bullet point)

FIGURE 6A.3 Writing frame (unpublished) (Fairlamb, 2020)

Strategy 2: Deliberate practice of appositives

To extend the pupil's factual knowledge and explanation of a topic being written about, students can incorporate appositives. To scaffold students to use these, activities such as matching the statement to the correct appositive can prove useful in demonstrating what effective appositives look like followed by discussions of when, how and why to use them. This could take the form of an explicit part of a focused writing activity followed by deliberate practice through starter activities which also weave in content to be retrieved.

Adding Appositives

Read through each incomplete statement carefully.
- Choose the correct **appositive** for each statement then rewrite the sentence in the table.
- Add capital letters in the right places.

(The first example has been completed for you)

(If you are stuck, the phrase bank is below – try to work from memory first).

1. Tension between the two biggest superpowers, **the USA and USSR**, increased after WWII.
2. Britain, France, and the US, _____, wanted to rebuild Germany.
3. On the other hand Stalin, _____, favoured a weak Germany that would not be able to attack.
4. Stalin's communist armies, _____ _ , quickly took control.
5. The USSR, _____, soon gained control of over twenty million people in Eastern Europe.
6. Bulgaria, Hungary, and Poland, _____, joined the USSR.
7. Churchill, _____, described Europe as being divided by an 'Iron Curtain'.

Appositive Phrase Bank
after expanding five hundred kilometres west
britain's wartime prime minister
the leader of the communist ussr
quickly falling to communism after world war two
~~the usa and ussr~~
ordered to remain in eastern european countries
wishing to resume trade as quickly as possible

FIGURE 6A.4 Adding appositives (Thornton, 2020), unpublished

Strategy 3: Word triplets

Quigley (2021) recommends the use of 'word triplets' 'to scaffold vocabulary selection, we can supply pupils with a triple of words to choose for their writing, thereby cultivating the crucial revision strategy of choosing the most apt vocabulary item'. This scaffold involves presenting students with three options of similar words that they could use or synonyms. Students then discuss and decide which of the words is the word that they want to use and why, which could involve them holding up their choices on mini whiteboards. An example would be with fronted adverbials. You would give students the option to choose between 'admittedly', 'arguably' and 'contestably'.

Strategy 4: Fragments

To develop the use of subject-specific vocabulary and to promote the use of grammar such as appositives and subordinating conjunctions, students are given a 'bank' of fragments that they must thread into their written response (Hochman & Wexler, 2017). This provides students with a checklist of words and grammar to use to elevate their responses and practice identifying where they are best used within a sentence. Doing so provides the students with opportunities to practise weaving them in and discuss why certain fragments have been used and how they have helped to create a stronger response, from which they can then be further prompted using scaffolds to use them in future writing. These fragments can either be pre-prepared, co-created as a class or pairs, or (when the student is at that point of readiness) can be created independently. As part of this, the process can be reversed with students identifying or correcting the key fragments within a model answer to help them to also see 'how to incorporate transitions into their writing [and not] overuse them or deploy them inappropriately . . . to help students to use them judiciously' (Hochman & Wexler, 2017). Hochman and Wexler (2017) further argue the importance of oracy when first modelling fragments as:

> When you give examples of fragments, it's best to present them orally, rather than in writing. For example, you might say to the class: 'ate a great meal.' To guide them to supply a subject, you

could follow that up with 'Does that tell us who ate a great meal? How can we make these words into a complete sentence?'

They suggest further scaffolding can include considering the complexity of the examples and fragments chosen with existing or new content.

Review and revision

A part that students sometimes want to skip over as it adds to the effort and time spent on a task is the review and revision aspect – or re-drafting essays. Having students review their own and other's work helps them to better understand how their work meets a given success criteria as they are practising applying it to their own and other works, which builds their competence and confidence with being secure on what success looks like. This itself acts as a scaffold, as does the opportunity to be able to see differing arguments which they can then use to enhance their own writing in the immediate or long-term future. Feedback given to the student by a teacher or peer, or self-assessment empowers the students to be able to hone and improve the work.

To ensure that self and peer review and revision happens successfully, we must ensure that we model and outwardly articulate the process alongside providing scaffolded, guided practice. We cannot assume that students will be experts at self and peer assessment within our disciplines and so must dedicate time to providing training and thinking of the misconceptions students might have when carrying out the review and editing process for a given question.

The following scaffolds can be applied to supporting review and revision for either parts of written responses or the whole of the written response:

Strategy 1: Revise and edit

Revise and edit (Hochman & Wexler, 2017). This strategy works as an effective scaffold to support students in identifying where they have been successful and where they need to improve responses in the forthcoming draft; alongside seeking teacher and peer guidance as to what those improvements could look like. Their template can be adapted to meet subject-specific demands.

Strategy 2: Editing space

Webb and Giovanelli (2023) advocate ensuring students leave 1.8–2 cm margin space around their written responses. This will provide them with reflection space and areas to add in further thoughts, ideas and improvements during the editing process. Moreover, it can support with cognitive load when editing by having white space surrounding the chunk of words.

Strategy 3: Review against a range of model answers and/or success criteria

A teacher annotating a model answer or a student response and highlighting where and how improvements can be made, to then be applied to their own essays.

Strategy 4: Vocabulary and key term booster banks

These can be used to thread tier 2–3 vocabulary into responses.

Strategy 5: Review stage in 'slow essay writing'

Taylor (2020) outlines this metacognitive sequence for the review phase in 'slow essay writing':

i) Students submit a first draft essay in response to the question.

ii) Review stage 1: Students debate some of the key ideas in their essay with peers in a staged discussion [Academic Debate Cards to support]. Students might then reflect on how these discussions have refined and shaped their analysis.

iii) More challenge. Students are given a further draft of challenging questions which they might use to further develop their response. They write a second draft.

iv) Peer assessment – either have peers read their colleagues' essays and give feedback using some form or success criteria, or have them write a peer review letter [with a supporting template with written prompts].

v) Final draft followed by reflection. What were the most important questions during the process which guided my thinking? What did I change in my drafts which made the most difference? How might I improve my next essay task differently? Why?

As with all scaffolding, it is important to look at how the writing scaffolds will be removed over time as well as making sure that teachers are clear about how to identify when those scaffolds should be removed. As mentioned in prior chapters, Needham (2019) succinctly summarises this stating that:

> we should use backwards fading so that students are asked to complete applications independently as quickly as possible. If we keep presenting worked examples, then not only will this waste time, but it will also prevent students from developing the ability to complete tasks without support. How long students spend on each stage of the [I do-we do-you do] continuum is an empirical question and will largely be determined by the quality of examples and completion problems that you use as well as the proficiency ad prior knowledge of the students. Feedback to the teacher is key here: if students are performing successfully on a stage, then you can make the transition to a lower level of support.

Essentially, writing is difficult. But it's not impossible. And with effective scaffolding, we can help students to 'write right'.

Chapter 6 Self-Reflection Questions

Take a few minutes to reflect on the questions below and jot down your answers...

1. How do you currently scaffold writing?

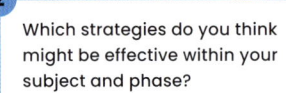

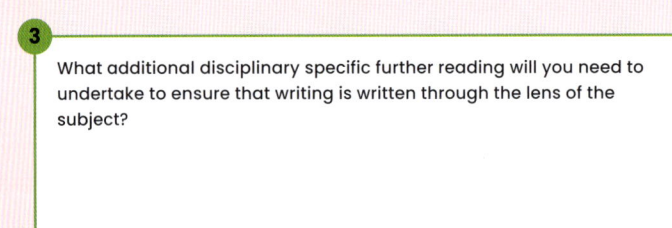

2. Which strategies do you think might be effective within your subject and phase?

3. What additional disciplinary specific further reading will you need to undertake to ensure that writing is written through the lens of the subject?

References

Caviglioli, O. (2019) *Dual Coding with Teachers*. Woodridge: John Catt Educational

Counsell, C. (1997) *Analytical and Discursive Writing at KS3, Historical Association*. Dorset: Blackmore Press (Online). Available at https://www.history.org.uk/secondary/resource/1948/analytic-and-discursive-writing-at-key-stage-3. Accessed 14th May 2024

Counsell, C. (2004) *History and Literacy in Y7: Building the Lesson Around the Text, History in Practice*. London: Hodder Murray (Online). Available at https://www.coursesidekick.com/arts-humanities/22892235. Accessed 7th June 2024. Quoted in Hough, J. (2023) *Writing Like a Historian, What Is History Teaching, Now?*. Woodbridge: John Catt Educational

Department for Education (2012) *The Research Evidence on "Writing" Education Standards Research team Education Standards Analysis & Research Division* (Online). Available at https://www.gov.uk/government/organisations/department-for-education. Accessed 14th May 2024

Education Endowment Foundation (EEF) (2018) *Improving Literacy in Secondary Schools* (Online). Available at https://educationendowmentfoundation.org.uk/education-evidence/guidance-reports/literacy-ks3-ks4. Accessed 16th April 2024

Englert, C. S., Raphael, T. E., Anderson Helene, M., Anthony, L. M. & Stevens, D. D. (1991) Making Strategies and Self-Talk Visible: Cognitive Strategy Instruction in Writing in Regular and Special Education Classrooms. *American Educational Research Journal*, 28, 337–373. Quoted in Troia, G. & Graham, S. (2002) The Effectiveness of a Highly Explicit, Teacher-Directed Strategy Instruction Routine. *Journal of Learning Disabilities*, 35, 290–305 (Online). Available at https://www.researchgate.net/publication/8224270_The_Effectiveness_of_a_Highly_Explicit_Teacher-Directed_Strategy_Instruction_Routine. Accessed 12 June 2024

Fairlamb, A. (2020) *Writing Frame*, unpublished

Hochman, J. C. & Wexler, N. (2017) *The Writing Revolution*. San Francisco: Jossey-Bass

Hough, J. (2023) *Writing Like a Historian, What Is History Teaching, Now?*. Woodbridge: John Catt Educational

Kellogg, R. & Whiteford, A. (2009) Training Advanced Writing Skills: The Case for Deliberate Practice. *Educational Psychologist*, 44(4), 250–266 (Online).

Available at https://hillkm.com/EDUC_715/Unit_6/kellogg_whiteford_2009.pdf. Accessed 12th June 2024

Needham, T. (2019) Writing Skills. In J. Murphy (Ed.), *The ResearchEd Guide to Literacy*. Woodbridge: John Catt Educational

Pearson Edexcel (2016) *Edexcel GCSE History (First Teaching from 2016) GCSE Networks 2016/17 Delegate Pack* (Online). Available at https://qualifications.pearson.com/content/dam/pdf/GCSE/History/2016/Teaching-and-learning-materials/GCSE%20Network%20event_Sources%20and%20Interpretations_delegate%20booklet.pdf. Accessed 12th June 2024

Quigley, A. (2022) *Closing the Writing Gap*. Abingdon, Oxon: Routledge

Santangelo, T. & Olinghouse, N. G. (2009) Effective Writing Instruction for Students Who Have Writing Difficulties. *Focus on Exceptional Children*, 42(4). https://doi.org/10.17161/foec.v42i4.6903

Talk for Writing (Online). Available at https://www.talk4writing.com/. Accessed 14th May 2024

Taylor, Dr. P. (2020) Write Like an Academic. In J. Webb (Ed.), *Teach Like a Writer*. Woodbridge: John Catt Educational

Thornton, G. (2020) *Breakfast Jam. Writing Revolution 1: Adding Rigour Using Because, but, so*. Unpublished

Troia, G. & Graham, S. (2002) The Effectiveness of a Highly Explicit, Teacher-Directed Strategy Instruction Routine. *Journal of Learning Disabilities*, 35, 290-305 (Online). Available at https://www.researchgate.net/publication/8224270_The_Effectiveness_of_a_Highly_Explicit_Teacher-Directed_Strategy_Instruction_Routine. Accessed 12th June 2024

Webb, J. (2020) *Teach Like a Writer*. Woodbridge: John Catt Educational

Webb, J. & Giovanelli, M. (2023) *Essential Grammar: The Resource Book Every Secondary English Teacher Will Need*. Routledge

6b Scaffolding and writing
Primary case studies

In this chapter, we have sought out the expertise of primary practitioners who have significant experience of scaffolding writing in KS1-2. We felt that the lived experience and knowledge of practitioners who live and breathe the scaffolding of the writing process at the primary phase was vital.

CASE STUDY 1: SCAFFOLDING BEFORE THE WRITING TASK IN KS1

Elliot Morgan (Curriculum Advisor for Primary Knowledge Curriculum) @MorgsEdu

As a Curriculum Advisor for the Primary Knowledge Curriculum, I work with over 300 schools, supporting nearly 100,000 pupils nationwide and internationally to learn through a knowledge-rich curriculum. In this work, I have noticed a common theme with writing tasks in Key Stage One (KS1). Children transition from the Early Years Foundation Stage (EYFS) into Year 1 with limited writing experience, typically having written only simple phrases and sentences, and still developing their fine motor skills.

The expectations for writing escalate drastically from EYFS (aged 4-5) to Year 2 (aged 6-7), where students are expected to produce coherent narratives and use coordination and subordination. This significant

DOI: 10.4324/9781003467069-8

gap necessitates substantial writing instruction and practice to bridge it effectively during Year 1.

To compound this further, children at this stage are not yet competent writers and are still learning phonics. Writing tasks can and should be integrated with phonics instruction to reinforce learning through application and retrieval practice.

Given these challenges, many teachers working with Year 1 students (aged 5–6) anticipate significant struggles when it comes to writing at length, leading to a well-intentioned yet counterproductive practice: over-scaffolding.

In an effort to support these learners, teachers may simplify tasks so much that students are not sufficiently challenged and engage in minimal independent thinking. This extensive scaffolding often involves breaking down tasks into overly simplistic steps, providing excessive prompts, or offering too much instruction, which hinders the development of the students' writing abilities.

However, many teachers may not know how to balance providing necessary support while fostering independence, leading to a counterproductive cycle of excessive scaffolding that hinders the development of writing competence.

In the Primary Knowledge Curriculum, we place great emphasis on disciplinary literacy. For children to be successful across the curriculum, they need to be able to communicate their understanding. Therefore, we not only need to write in phonics or English lessons, but across the curriculum. While writing is not the only way to communicate thinking, most disciplines lend themselves to writing to communicate ideas. We believe that writing tasks require students to structure their thoughts logically and coherently. Writing should therefore not be viewed just as a means of communication, but as a tool for organising thought.

A common conversation I have with teachers when supporting schools is how to scaffold writing in KS1. Teachers often say they want pupils to be able to write more independently but, in reality, find it rather challenging to achieve. Because of this challenge, a lot of writing can come in the form of tasks that are heavily scaffolded, such as gap-fill tasks. While this scaffold usually leads to pupils being able to complete the task, it leads to little writing on the part of the learner.

It is important to consider that task completion is a poor proxy for learning; while easily observable, it is not sufficient evidence to tell us that learning has occurred. This is especially true of gap-fill tasks where the first letter of a word is provided for pupils along with a word bank – if we do this, is the learner thinking deeply enough about the content we have taught them? More often than not, this scaffold results in the learner writing just four or five individual words for an entire task.

As an initial scaffold and when designed appropriately, gap-fill tasks can work well – the problem is when they are used for every task and not gradually faded out over time as a scaffold should be. The frequent use of these tasks may be borne out of a common misconception that exists around scaffolding: that scaffolding should make the task *easier*.

A scaffold is there to make the task more accessible, not to make it easier. Everything you do for the learner should have a scaffold, but a scaffold should not do everything for the learner. A scaffold makes the task possible for the learner to engage with. It should provide the necessary support so the learner can work through the task without reducing its inherent difficulty.

On the other hand, a scaffold that makes the task easier simplifies the task itself, reducing both the difficulty of the task and the demands placed on the learner.

We have high expectations; we want all learners to learn the same content and meet the same learning goals. A scaffold that makes the task easier lowers these expectations. Therefore, in order to retain our high expectations and ensure all pupils are challenged to think hard and work independently, we should keep the task outcome the same, but consider how the level of support needs to be different (i.e. considering necessary scaffolds and adaptations).

I believe that most of our thinking around scaffolds focuses on scaffolds for the task itself; overlooked is the scaffolding we can use *before* writing tasks to support all learners in accessing the writing task.

Scenario

Imagine children have just learnt about the United Kingdom and are tasked with writing an explanation of what flags the Union Jack includes.

For a pupil who can access this task independently, they can simply just start writing.

For a pupil who needs support in accessing the task, we must keep the task expectation the same, but provide a scaffold to help them answer. For example, a sentence starter:

E.g. The Union Jack flag includes_____.

As the teacher, I am looking for children to demonstrate their understanding of what the flag represents. This feeds directly into how a sentence stem will scaffold the task so that pupils can demonstrate that understanding.

We can then gradually remove the scaffold towards the end of a task by encouraging them to write a sentence (or sentences) by themselves. So for example, they may complete three sentence starters and then write one full sentence independently.

This final sentence can still be scaffolded by providing a question to prompt thinking:

'Which four countries are in the United Kingdom?'

The expectation for both pupils is the same.

Scaffolds are meant to be removed over time not only as the child becomes more independent, but to actually build that independence.

Wood et al. (1976) explain that scaffolding is about ensuring the learner can recognise the actions they have to take to access the task independently over time. In their own words, they say, 'Comprehension of the solution must precede production.'

The pupil has to recognise what the task requires of them before they are able to do so without a scaffold. They have to see the link between the mode of communication in the task (i.e. writing) and how it can be used to explain the content (i.e. information about the Union Jack). As such, we need to consider how scaffolding extends beyond the task itself.

In fact, I would argue that the most important scaffolding happens before the task takes place – scaffolding that enables the learner to think deeply about the content before they have to apply it in a task independently. This scaffolding helps pupils to reach the 'comprehension' stage (understanding the material and the task) before they have to engage in the 'production' stage (engaging in the task itself).

With writing tasks, we are trying to get pupils to organise and then communicate their understanding. There are many scaffolds we can use during the teaching part of the lesson that can facilitate this, but I will cover three in particular that I believe are often overlooked.

1. *Rehearsal*

Once children have been taught information pertinent to the task, provide them with opportunities to rehearse this information. Alongside choral response (where pupils repeat the learnt information aloud as a group), a simple and effective way to do this is through the use of partner talk. The principle behind this is that pupils get the opportunity to think about the content and then articulate it out loud.

Going back to our task from earlier, it may look something like this:

(a map of the UK is on the board)

Teacher: 'There are four countries that make up the United Kingdom. Those countries are England, Scotland, Wales and Northern Ireland. Turn to the person next to you, tell them the four countries that make up the United Kingdom. Partner A you start, then partner B.'

This ensures all pupils rehearse the information they have just heard and increases the likelihood of pupils being able to use this information in the task. Naturally, this could be rehearsed and questioned on more than once too.

2. Wait time

We know that as a profession we do not wait long enough after asking questions.

One study found that the average length of time that we wait is between 0.7 and 1.4 seconds (Stahl, 1994) – the length of time for a heartbeat or F1 pitstop.

Giving children time to think about what they are going to say or write about can again lift the success rate of 'comprehension' across the class.

Let's revisit that same scenario:

Teacher: 'There are four countries that make up the United Kingdom. Those countries are England, Scotland, Wales and Northern Ireland. In a moment, you are going to turn to the person next to you and tell them the four countries that make up the United Kingdom. I want you to think for a moment. What are those four countries that make up the United Kingdom? [*the teacher pauses for 10 seconds*] Partner A you start, then partner B.'

The phonics scheme you use in school will likely have a learning behaviour children are familiar with for writing sentences – for example, Essential Letters and Sounds models sentences for pupils which they then write independently with the model removed. This happens at

Scaffolding and writing: Primary case studies 153

least three times a week. As this would be a familiar behaviour to your pupils, consider using this same learning behaviour in lessons across the curriculum.

3. *Notetaking (cognitive offloading)*

When there is a lot of information to take in at once, it can overload working memory. Allowing pupils to take notes can act as a form of cognitive offloading – they can free up working memory by having the information written down, knowing they can refer back to it when needed.

However, it is not as simple as just getting pupils to write notes as you talk – this can lead to attention being split between listening and writing, which many pupils (especially novice writers) can find difficult. Instead, notetaking should be built into the instructional phase with plenty of time to think and write.

Let's revisit our scenario again:

Teacher: 'There are four countries that make up the United Kingdom. Those countries are England, Scotland, Wales and Northern Ireland. Write down the four countries on your whiteboard [*the teacher allows enough time until pupils have written them down*]. In a moment, you are going to turn to the person next to you and tell them the four countries that make up the United Kingdom. I want you to think for a moment. What are those four countries that make up the United Kingdom? [*the teacher pauses for 10 seconds*] Partner A you start, then partner B.'

The combination of these scaffolds before the task will significantly boost the 'comprehension' of pupils across the class and increase the chances that they can engage with writing independently.

While scaffolds for a task should be gradually removed over time to build competence, these three scaffolds before the task are beneficial throughout the writing process. They allocate mental resources effectively, reducing the strain on working memory. Rather than removing them, teachers should emphasise their consistent use to optimise students' working memory capacity and overall writing performance.

CASE STUDY 2: USING WRITING PACKS AS SCAFFOLDS FOR YEAR ONE

Faith Hearn, Year One Teacher and EYFS Lead

As students arrive into Year 1, they are often dependent on adult support and guidance, which is why, as they transition from a more play-based environment, they still require time to continue their learning through play and exploration. Understanding this developmental stage is crucial, and my approach incorporates strategies to support this gradual process of adapting to a more formal classroom situation through planned continuous provision.

In my Year 1 class, the foundation of all that we do is based on scaffolding, which is particularly crucial at the start of the year. Students need a nurturing environment where they feel secure and confident enough to explore new concepts in an ever-increasing formal manner. Setting high expectations and aspirations with my class with regards behaviour and attitude towards learning fosters a sense of responsibility and community amongst the students. Students need an environment with consistent rules and routines so that they can regulate their behaviour and develop a mindset to explore more formal learning. It is important to create opportunities where students can succeed in order to drive their motivation to continue to want to learn and explore, and scaffolding enables us to create these experiences for them. These scaffolds also include peers as scaffolds.

Through formative assessments, I noted that my lower prior attainers were only mark-making in literacy. To tackle this, I began a sequenced approach to support them by including modelling and other forms of scaffolding, so that the students were able to practise and learn the components of writing through chunking, before they use them together. Scaffolding must support students to manage the writing knowledge and skills that they have not yet securely acquired such as handwriting and spelling. During this process, their progress must result in enabling students to experience success.

At this time, as it was the transcriptional knowledge and skills along with the phonetic knowledge needed for spelling which needed support, I made packs containing visual aids, including an alphabet strip, our phonics Grapheme-Phoneme Correspondence (GPC) mats, Common Exception Word (CEW) mats as well as a manipulative finger space lollipop stick.

To begin with, I modelled how I would get the pack out when we were going to do some writing, and place all the mats out around me. To support their metacognition, I articulated what I was doing and why, over time encouraging the students to explain to others the purpose of their packs and the skills they were developing. This knowledge played a key role in their writing development but also their self-regulation; their developing ability to manage their own writing. Teacher-led modelling was followed by teacher verbal reminders, then peer reminders. With plentiful opportunity for deliberate practice, over a few weeks, the level of reminders reduced and the students independently accessed their packs.

The next step in the gradual removal of this scaffold was the verbal reminders to use our working walls. Everything that was in their pack, was also available in the same format as a visual reminder for all the students, on our working walls. The alphabet strip and phonics sounds encircle the classroom, with the GPC we are working on that week in phonics highlighted by a big arrow. We have a CEW wall, words always in the same order as the mat, so that they become familiar with their position. Scaffolding at this point supported students to realise that the information they needed was all around them, and to make the crucial move away from the pack; to be successful without it, whilst still supported and reassured with their transcriptional and spelling knowledge. Some students needed lighter scaffolding, with fewer cues and prompts to access the working walls whilst others needed medium scaffolding, involving me physically moving to the wall and pointing, as a visual reminder.

Peer modelling also worked well during this transition period so that by Spring term all but one student had moved away from their packs. Their confidence was high and they were writing independent sentences, with finger spaces, using their phonics knowledge to spell and recognising an increasing number of CEW in their reading and writing. This in turn fostered a sense of internal drive and purpose, building their intrinsic motivation, with students keen to write, their successes feeding into a love of writing.

One student needed some additional support to encode his words. He knew his GPCs and through daily flashcards reminders of his CEW, he was beginning to recognise and write some of them. For each written activity, I utilised the I do, we do, you do approach. I introduced the writing strategy – which was to spell each individual word – and I broke it down into small steps, explicitly linking it to what he already knew. I modelled how to orally break down each word, using his knowledge of GPCs, then wrote down each part, using his transcriptional knowledge of the GPCs, before reading it back. We repeated the process together – we do – then he became able to move towards independence with I do. This continuum moved backwards and forwards until he became more proficient in how to break down the words, build them back up and then read them back.

Over time, this process became more refined. The student would break down the word and write it, at first often missing out the last phoneme. But the repetition of the process through plentiful opportunities for deliberate practice embedded it further, which enabled him to achieve success each time and retain the motivation. One day, the student wrote a sentence without any support from me – this process, whilst protracted, allowed the student time to develop his literacy skills without full cognitive overload.

As the year progressed, all the children developed their independence and resilience. This was because the scaffolds were gradually removed when appropriate to do so and because metacognition was woven in so that they could better understand the process of writing. This meant that over time they moved towards greater independence and had the resilience to be able to do so.

CASE STUDY 3: SCAFFOLDING WRITING IN KS2
Ben Cooper, Primary Headteacher
@WAGOLLTeaching

The challenge with teaching writing in Primary is that it is a very complex process. When writing, we are asking multi-novice children to consider and utilise a vast array of skills and knowledge that we hope they can organise and construct into a cohesive set of ideas. Cognitive load will always be a challenge when we are asking students to knit together knowledge surrounding transcription, text structure, syntax alongside the craft of writing and idea generation. This challenge is enhanced when we add in the idea that many of our primary children are still developing the regulatory skills needed to manage a task like this, not to mention the physical development still taking place to sit, hold and use a pencil accurately.

While developing fluency in key areas of writing will reduce cognitive load, developing a toolkit to scaffold writing was a useful next step in ensuring teachers can manage working memory demands by outsourcing thinking to the environment around them, be it a staff member or resource.

Scaffold 1: Writing frames and sentence and word prompts

Writing frames work as a scaffold in two ways. Firstly, writing frames outsource the process of generating ideas by listing down the side of a page what events take place within a paragraph (e.g. First, the main character leaves their home. Next, the character notices something strange outside their house.). Secondly, writing frames free up working memory so that children can focus purely on the construction of sentences. These can be phased out as the child gains more ideas of what might happen next in their text; getting started is always the hardest part.

Where sentence construction and vocabulary choices can overload students' working memory, sentence and word prompts outsource this thinking so that students can consider the craft of writing and generate creative ideas or information to include. A small list of vocabulary choices or sentence starters is a simple way of prompting students with ways to add richness to their creative ideas on paper. Additionally, by orally rehearsing this language as a class or group, fluency can be built so that these prompts can be removed over time.

Sometimes, it is beneficial to combine the two by sharing a writing frame that prompts both paragraph structure and shared sentence and/or vocabulary prompts *(e.g. First, the main character leaves their home. Describe this using a simile.)*. This isolates thinking even further so that a child can simply focus on one sentence at a time.

We have also suggested that the toolkit should be child-led. By designing a great sequence of lessons, children can create their own prompt sheets and writing frames in the lessons that build up to the writing task. If students are familiar with the scaffolds they have created, they are more likely to use them and are on the journey to fluency. The student-designed scaffolds will be available within their books to refer back to and the very best are enlarged and displayed on the class working walls for all to access.

Part of the toolkit also focuses on the staff members within the classroom. Offloading thinking to adults within the classroom can be an alternative to resource-based scaffolds. Adults can respond much more instantly to the amount of support needed. They can prompt vocabulary, sentence structures and creative ideas just like a resource, but perhaps more beneficially, they can prompt and model the metacognitive thinking that is needed to construct writing. Here is an example script of what this might look like.

Scaffold 2: Scaffolded Teacher Talk

Teacher scaffolds idea generation: *'Now we want to describe our character leaving the house. Remind me, who is our character and how do we want them to feel leaving their home?'*

Child responds

Teacher scaffolds vocabulary choice: *'That's a great idea, I like that you want our character to be sleepy. How might they be leaving the house? On our working wall, we have some suggested vocabulary we can use to describe our sleepy character. Discuss in pairs which one we should use and why and write your choice on your whiteboard.'*

Gather responses

Teacher scaffolds sentence construction: *'I can see some great ideas for describing how sleepy our character is. Now we have all chosen our choice of vocabulary, I'm going to start my sentence and ask you to finish it using your word choice. I'm going to try and use an adverbial phrase to open my sentence.* **With the morning sun casting gentle hues upon the sleepy street, Maria . . .** *I am going to use the word* sluggishly, *but you need to now finish the sentence on your whiteboard using your vocabulary. See if you can adapt my adverbial phrase too.'*

Scaffold 3: Lesson Structure

Lesson structure can also scaffold thinking. Peeling off strategies can allow students who need fewer scaffolds to begin independent writing quicker than students who need more modelling and guided practice.

We also always recommend selecting students for a focus group to ensure that those who need further scaffolded discussion receive it. Sit down with your focus group at a table and continue shared writing. A misconception is that the focus group always ends up being the less able writers, but more able writers may be the ones that need scaffolded support to get that greater depth of writing. Indeed, even vocabulary prompt sheets can be utilised to extend thinking by suggesting complex and ambitious vocabulary. Writing frames can add complexity to paragraph structures that do not need sharing with the main cohort of children but perhaps are used to extend select students who really need challenge.

What we make clear to staff is that the toolkit has examples of the most successful and commonly used scaffolds but is not exhaustive. There will be many other strategies that teachers use to offload working memory that are helpful in their classroom context. As we are an international school with seven or eight classes per year group, having a bank of scaffolds that all teachers understand how to use, supports collaborative and effective planning. A teacher can share a writing frame with their team with little explanation and will know that it will be used effectively in each classroom because there is a common understanding of why Writing Frames are useful. Individual teachers can then choose which children would benefit from using it within their classroom context. Similarly, if the unit is designed well by the year groups team, all teachers know that the student-created scaffolds exist in books already, reducing the need to create additional resources and reducing workload. The toolkit provides a starting point for all staff members to begin to think about how they can support all students in being successful while also making planning more efficient.

CASE STUDY 4: REACHING THE END POINT: MASTERING INDEPENDENT AND FLUENT WRITING IN KS2

Emma McCauley, Lower KS2 teacher

As teachers, when it comes to writing we ought to consider what are the key aspects that need to be achieved so that independent writing can become the best it can be and so that we can provide children with the means to master the process of writing in full. The framework of Talk for Writing promotes and supports children's ability to write independently, successfully, and accurately. First, students are encouraged to **imitate** the language required for a specific text type by reading, analysing and unravelling a high-quality text, focusing on how specific effects have been achieved and their subsequent impact on the reader. Then, students begin to **innovate** the text through teacher modelling, all leading up to the endpoint, in which the children can **independently apply** everything they have learnt by creating their own piece(s) of writing. The following elements are essential when supporting children's independent writing:

- Identify critical concepts/literary features within a genre
- Understand the writer's toolkit and structure
- Practice writing using a boxed-up structure and toolkit
- Write a genre-appropriate text independently

Stage 1: Imitation

First and foremost, teachers must ensure that all students are interested and fully engaged when introducing a new unit of work, by selecting a text or by creating one which fits more accurately with the current learning. Such texts are designed by the teacher to be relevant, exciting and tantalising. Time needs to be taken to consider this carefully, as they should not simply be generic texts aimed at the children's general reading age.

When a new writing unit is introduced, students are shown several different examples of texts within the genre. This scaffolds their current learning as it enables them to use their own pre-existing knowledge and understanding of the genre to engage in a shared discussion, where common themes are identified, and vocabulary and structural patterns are explored. For example, when we were exploring features of 'rags-to-riches' stories, the children brought similarly themed films into the discussion, as well as books that they had read. They even mentioned personal experiences and real-life stories which deepened their understanding of such stories and established learning in their long-term memory.

Similarly, to support retention, it is important to illicit emotional responses from the children, by discovering how such writing makes them feel. They can then offer newly discovered vocabulary, which might be useful in their own writing, to the teacher. Following this exposure to several examples of a particular text type, students are asked to produce a 'Cold Write', to hook them into the literacy topic. This term is used to describe students' first, unsupported attempt at writing their own version of the text. This is essential as it helps the teacher to discern their understanding of the genre before any explicit, modelled guidance has been given. This, in turn, informs planning as it reveals any gaps in any necessary language and grammar skills.

After completing a 'Cold Write', students are then introduced to a model text, which shows what the finished written piece may look like. At this point, children are exposed to more sophisticated, aspirational vocabulary and creative literary devices that are fundamental to the genre. Additionally, the text's structure and themes are reinforced, and this is often complemented with further isolated reading lessons. When students begin to retell the text, they can explain and add more elements to it, by considering the range of examples that they have been exposed to.

Creating a toolkit

To foster strong writing skills in children, they must understand how to effectively use various literary techniques to achieve specific effects, such as developing characters or advancing the narrative. Teachers can support and scaffold this process by establishing a 'Writer's Toolkit': a collection of practical techniques that students use in order to analyse writing excerpts objectively. This way, they can appraise the writer's methods and assess the impact on the reader. These are then paired with focused grammar lessons, where children work on specific language features relative to the text type being investigated.

These sessions allow teachers to check the students' confidence and understanding, as well as providing additional scaffolding, before moving on to the innovation phase of writing. They also allow the students to delve deeper into the text, thus beginning the initial process of innovation, where the teacher can model writing whilst encouraging collaborative editing, leading up to independent writing, in short, following the 'I do, we do, you do' teaching approach.

Boxing-Up

Then, it's back to the model text where, in a 'boxing-up' activity, students explore the key purpose for each section, breaking the structure of the text down into its vital parts. For example, a suspense narrative may follow a structural pattern like so:

- Opening – where the author may set the scene and introduce a main character(s)
- Build-up – the writer may introduce a minor problem and develop the character further
- Problem – a complication, obstacle or challenge for the main character
- Resolution – a turning point in which the main character faces the biggest challenge
- Ending – a conclusion to wrap up events

The 'boxed-up' structure will inform the next series of lessons, guiding students through their writing of each section.

Stage 2: Innovation
I do-

In shared-writing sessions, teachers demonstrate writing using the boxed-up framework that students developed during modelled planning lessons. During these lessons, the internal thought processes necessary for planning and producing quality writing are shared out loud by the teacher. Through the use of this metacognitive oracy, students are taught how to approach writing, whilst attending to common misconceptions. Moreover, teachers can illustrate how to write well-organised texts, concise sentences (utilising the Writer's Toolkit) and ambitious vocabulary whilst highlighting the importance of the editing process, an aspect often undervalued by students.

By crafting and editing sentences out loud, in front of the class, the students are provided with a clear, structured process to follow which they can refer back to when constructing their own creative work. It provides another example of a finished short-burst piece of writing, in which children are shown what to aim for before co-constructing a collaborative piece.

We do- 'Shared Write'

At first, students can use the model text as a reliable guide but should start to modify it gradually until they have produced a more original piece of work. While some more confident students would be able to innovate the text further, and begin approaching independent applications, others may need to take longer, adapting the text little by little in order to build up their confidence.

It is essential to do this to build students' confidence for the final independent write ('Hot Write'). By working on the writing together a section at a time, the class will collaboratively produce a shared text under the teacher's expert supervision. The children can 'magpie' from this collaborative writing when they reach the final stage and work on their own piece. This shared writing practice encourages students to focus on their writing objectives so that they understand clearly how to produce high quality, independent work in the final stage of the process.

You do-

Once a 'Shared Write' has been created, each student can then work on this passage independently, using the available model texts and the 'Writers' Toolkit' as scaffolds. During this 'you do' phase, teachers can provide further scaffolding through the use of success criteria targets which are typically in the form of a list, showing what should be included. They can use these lists as forms of self or peer assessment.

Without support the student checklists do not always work; students may still tick off a requirement without including a necessary feature in an appropriate way. So students should be encouraged to evidence use on the checklist not just to tick elements off. For instance, if the teacher wants students to use a fronted adverbial in the introductory paragraph, they should highlight where this has been done and note this on their list. This approach helps the teacher, and student, to work together on omissions and address misconceptions. Where necessary the teacher can offer further phased scaffolding to target areas of need.

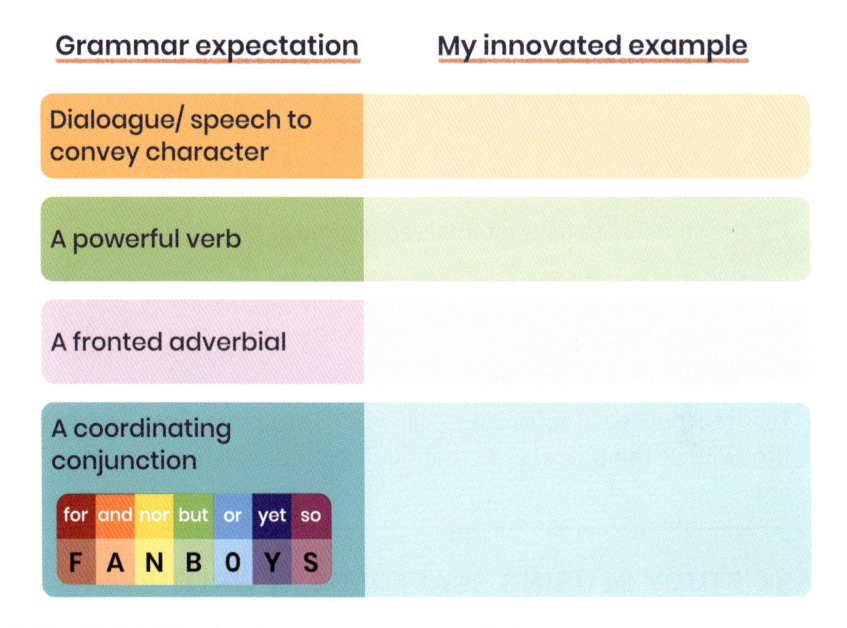

Grammar expectation	My innovated example
Dialoague/ speech to convey character	
A powerful verb	
A fronted adverbial	
A coordinating conjunction for and nor but or yet so F A N B O Y S	

FIGURE 6B.1 Laying down grammar expectations

Stage 3: Independent application

This final stage of the writing process should be where all scaffolds are removed. The children should be in a confident position to attempt total independent work. The odd verbal reminder may be offered to remind the students of common errors (e.g. capital letters and full stops).

However, primarily this is the opportunity for the students to shine and showcase all they have learnt. At this point, through the lengthy planning process, the students will be filled with creative ideas, which they have collected along the way.

Of course, teachers can facilitate further learning opportunities through peer or self-marking by providing success criteria linked to the year group writing expectations. This is all in aid of giving valuable summative assessments, in which teachers can judge the success of the unit, whereby future planning may be tweaked if certain misconceptions keep cropping up and can track the pupil progress by the progression quantity and quality of the written work.

Overall, what ought to go well for the independent 'Hot Write' to be a success is as follows:

- For the students to have internalised a stimulating, exciting model text
- For the students to have created an indispensable writer's toolkit
- For the students to understand the underlying structure of a written piece (through the boxing up activity)
- For teacher-led scaffolding, in which students are supported throughout the process to create quality, independent writing

CASE STUDY 5: USING SCAFFOLDS IN WRITING AT UPPER KEY STAGE 2 (UKS2)

Eve Morton, Primary Literacy Adviser for 'Education North Tyneside' @Eve_Morton17

By the time pupils reach UKS2, our aims are to help them reach the point of greater levels of independence, both compositionally and structurally.

There is an expectation that pupils can 'write effectively for a range of purposes and audiences, selecting language that shows good awareness of the reader' (Department for Education, 2022). This doesn't mean that scaffolds to support writing aren't valuable as part of this process; they may be less explicit, however, than strategies such as writing frames and prompts which may have been used in the earlier primary years.

As the National Curriculum states: 'Teachers should prepare pupils for secondary education by ensuring that they can consciously control sentence structure in their writing and understand why sentences are constructed as they are' (National Curriculum, 2014). Even by the end of KS2, pupils still need some guidance from teachers to achieve this, as well as some support to consider techniques and their impact on the reader. This might be scaffolded for pupils through thinking about text, refining this thinking, scaffolding and modelling to some application initially, and finally aiming to remove scaffolds to encourage independence. Without this crucial knowledge, pupils are less likely to make conscious decisions about what will make their writing effective.

One approach to providing appropriate scaffolding at UKS2 is to use it as an intrinsic part of the writing process, with a view to slowly removing it at an appropriate point to promote independence, which is, after all, our ultimate goal. In the approach outlined below, the teacher scaffolds pupils' thinking and response to text and helps to reframe this to support independent writing at a later stage. Aspects of such scaffolding form part of the Talk for Writing approach, devised by Pie Corbett (Corbett & Strong, 2016).

In the first stage, teachers scaffold pupils' thinking about which techniques a writer has used to have an impact on the reader. This should ideally be done through shared reading which involves good quality dialogic talk about the text. Having read and explored the text as a reader would, the focus should then move to analysing the writing as a writer might. This involves the teacher drawing pupils' awareness to the grammatical techniques and language that the writer has used. To support and scaffold writing later, these discussions are then refined down to a 'tool kit' from which pupils will be able to select which techniques they wish to use to create a specific effect. Such 'tool kits' should be generated *with* the pupils, not for the pupils. When created *with* the pupils, this contributes to key metacognitive thinking, allowing pupils to see how to monitor and refine thinking, and purposefully direct this learning.

Pupils at this point of KS2 may also still benefit from a focus on the underlying structure of the text being explored. By building this into a sequence of learning, awareness grows of the need to build cohesion within and across text, and the techniques used to do this. Scaffolding at this point often takes the form of 'boxing up' or the use of grids, which involves the teacher supporting the pupils to identify key aspects of the plot of a story or structural aspects of non-fiction. Once again, this scaffold should be constructed *with* the pupils to support deeper understanding of text structure.

The generation of tool kits and boxing up, form the basis of scaffolding which the teacher can then use in pupils' first attempts at writing for a particular purpose and audience. Pupils in upper key stage two still benefit from some support to begin to craft their sentences so they meet the needs of their intended reader. This should ideally be done through a combination of shared and modelled writing, built up across a few lessons, each with a clear focus of skills linked to the tool kit previously generated. Shared writing involves all the pupils, and the teacher helps to construct a shared piece of writing, using the tool kit to guide the crafting of sentences. During this teaching, there should be a focus on how the grammatical techniques used in sentences written are impacting the reader; the accuracy of sentence construction; and editing and improving text. Modelled writing involves the teacher demonstrating how they approach the crafting of writing, relating this back to the tool kit. Both methods are seen as useful scaffolds in the writing process for pupils, allowing them to be actively involved in the process of writing, as well as seeing how a more 'expert' writer approaches writing.

It is down to the teacher's professional judgement, having seen how successfully pupils' first attempts at writing have been, how and when these scaffolds are removed to help pupils reach greater levels of independence. If the teacher has observed, after the use of scaffolds, that pupils are ready to make their own conscious decisions about sentence and text construction with success, they may choose to remove some previous scaffolds. Some pupils may still require the support of some of these scaffolds, and as the year progresses and confidence grows, they may also slowly be removed.

References

Corbett, P. & Strong, S. (2016) *Creating Storytellers and Writers – an Introductory Guide to Talk for Writing 6-12 Year Olds*. Leicester: Roving Books

Department for Education (2022) *Teacher Assessment Frameworks at the End of Key Stage 2*. Standards and Testing Agency (Online). Available at https://www.gov.uk/government/publications/teacher-assessment-frameworks-at-the-end-of-key-stage-2. Accessed 28th July 2024

Department for Educational (2014) *National Curriculum* (Online). Available at https://www.researchgate.net/publication/8224270_The_Effectiveness_of_a_Highly_Explicit_Teacher-Directed_Strategy_Instruction_Routine. Accessed 28th July 2024

Stahl, R. J. (1994) *Using "Think-Time" and "Wait-Time" Skillfully in the Classroom*. ERIC Digest

Wood, D., Bruner, J. S. & Ross, G. (1976) The Role of Tutoring in Problem Solving. *Journal of Child Psychology and Psychiatry*, 17(2), 89-100

7a Scaffolding and oracy

[With oracy] Without exception, poor approximation to scaffolding is reported, together with considerable variation over what happens instead.

(Howe & Abedin, 2013)

In 1994, Bob Hoskins famously told us that 'it's good to talk'. He was right. It *IS* good to talk. Broadly speaking, 'talk is a powerful tool for learning and literacy. It can improve reading and writing outcomes, enhance communication skills, and increase students' understanding across the curriculum' (EEF, 2018). In short, oracy is essential for all students for lots of powerful reasons.

Exploring this deeper, Knight (2023) rightly frames effective oracy instruction as a pathway to transformation in two ways; 'personal transformation through "exploratory" forms of talk and societal transformation through the cultivation of agency and empowerment.' The pivotal role of oracy in a child's development is therefore key for us to appreciate and ensure that we embed into our curriculum, particularly for our disadvantaged students.

However, research suggests that this vital gateway to success in life and employment is currently hampered by language development barriers which mean that disadvantaged pupils start school 19 months behind their peers from more affluent backgrounds (Sutton Trust, 2012). Given that 'talk also appears to be particularly beneficial for low attaining students and those from disadvantaged backgrounds' (EEF, 2018), we educators must up the ante with our oracy provision. As Howe and Abedin (2013) surmised in their research, this may be a challenge in some educational institutions given the lack of teacher development time dedicated to oracy and the scaffolding of it.

This cannot be allowed to continue to happen. Oracy cannot be a luxury accessible to the few, but should instead be a fundamental part of *every* child's development in school.

Whilst the merits of talk for cognitive development and learning have long been researched, anecdotally the role of oracy as a discrete process and strategy within classrooms prior to 2020 was often absent or poorly defined in many educational settings (the poor relative of literacy). However, this seems to be changing, due in part to the focus of the DfE in 2024 under the Labour government and the inauguration of the Oracy Commission. Arguably, the pandemic has played a large part in this interest in oracy. During the Covid-19 pandemic from 2020, the world was reminded of the importance of talk and the value of human interactions for wellbeing, social development and for fostering emotional intelligence.

For educators, I feel that the pandemic was a turning point in the appreciation of oracy as a central, clearly defined tenet of the classroom that needed greater attention. Thinking back to 2020–21, teachers were trapped in a physical box at the front of a classroom of masked children with our and the student's ability to communicate verbally with one another impeded. Teachers were unable to circulate the classroom to communicate with small groups or students 1:1, and this context reduced opportunities for peers to engage in exploratory talk and 'interthinking' (collective thinking) (Littleton & Mercer, 2013). Moreover, the ripple effect of either being silent behind monitors or having narrowed opportunities for discussions during the initial stages of remote provision before the return to a physical classroom took their toll in terms of habit building and purposeful peer talk development. Resultantly, one of the C19 legacies has been that rebuilding the culture of talk in the classroom has been challenging. This is concerning as 'language skills play a key role in children's attainment and employment opportunities' (Law et al., 2017) and so time must be committed and work must be done to empower our teachers to be able restore the role of discussion in the classroom, using the scaffolding of talk to achieve this.

We must acknowledge therefore that there is much need for oracy to be given due focus in our classrooms and that in order to overcome sizeable barriers which limit the development of language and discussions, we are going to have to draw upon Herculean efforts. Aiding us in this challenge is scaffolding. One thing to note is that this is not a chapter that will capture all of the scaffolds within oracy; a whole book could be dedicated to this. Instead, this chapter will outline selected high impact strategies which lay the foundations for your further reading around the topic.

Some of the other chapters have already captured how oracy can be developed in retrieval and modelling. As mentioned in the reading and writing chapters, literacy and oracy are symbiotic and so cross-referencing does take place across the chapters. At various points, the scaffolding outlined will champion the importance of disciplinary oracy (see case study) as oracy can be developed within teaching and learning strategies, within literacy, but also be discipline specific so that we are creating students who can 'speak like a [discipline]'.

Your phase/stage and subject may play a role in how extensively and effectively practitioners in your educational setting are scaffolding talk. There will be varying levels of readiness for the implementation of oracy in some settings and some educators, particularly in secondary; many wrongly think that students arrive with a pre-existing ability to be able to talk in all contexts with confidence and expertise. Capturing this, Millard and Menzies (2016) found that

> primary teachers are significantly more likely to report using scaffolding and modelling in all or almost all of their lessons in comparison to teachers in secondary or FE settings . . . FE teachers in particular were significantly more likely than both primary and

secondary schools to feel scaffolding, modelling, setting expectations, and giving feedback on what pupils say and how they say it is 'not applicable' to them ... Differences in practice between phases are closely related to the fact that FE and secondary teachers are subject specialists. English and languages teachers are significantly more likely to scaffold oracy in most of their lessons.

This may mean that in secondary and FE settings, and in some subjects, that it may be more difficult to engage practitioners in understanding the importance of scaffolding talk. This should be considered by those leading on oracy in terms of factoring in the scaffolding of talk into CPD (Continuous Professional Development) programmes as well as giving time to middle leaders to plan to lead their team in researching disciplinary oracy and the unique scaffolds that relate to their subject. Therefore, preliminary audits should be carried out to determine the extent and efficacy of the scaffolding of talk before embarking on wider scale staff training.

So how can scaffolding the process of talk help those who are struggling to use their voice to develop the skills to engage in high-quality talk and therefore progressively speak more confidently and fluently? How can we scaffold our student's ability to generate, share and refine ideas through talk? And from this, how can we make talk accessible for all in order to support social mobility?

What are the different types of talk?

For us to unpick how to scaffold talk, it's useful to have an idea of what the different types of talk are, as this can guide which scaffolds you use and when. Before we do this, it's important to clarify that 'Oracy can be considered as both a process in which learning can take place and a measurable learning outcome' (Davies, 2022). Ambition Institute (2021) have echoed this and further suggest that Oracy is made up of the components shown in Figure 7A.1.

For the purpose of this book, we will be focusing on the scaffolding of the *process*. This means we will zoom in on how we can scaffold the development of their talk, including confidence and motivation to talk.

```
                    ┌─────────────────────────────┐
                    │ Spoken language development │
                    │    Reception & production    │
                    └─────────────────────────────┘
```

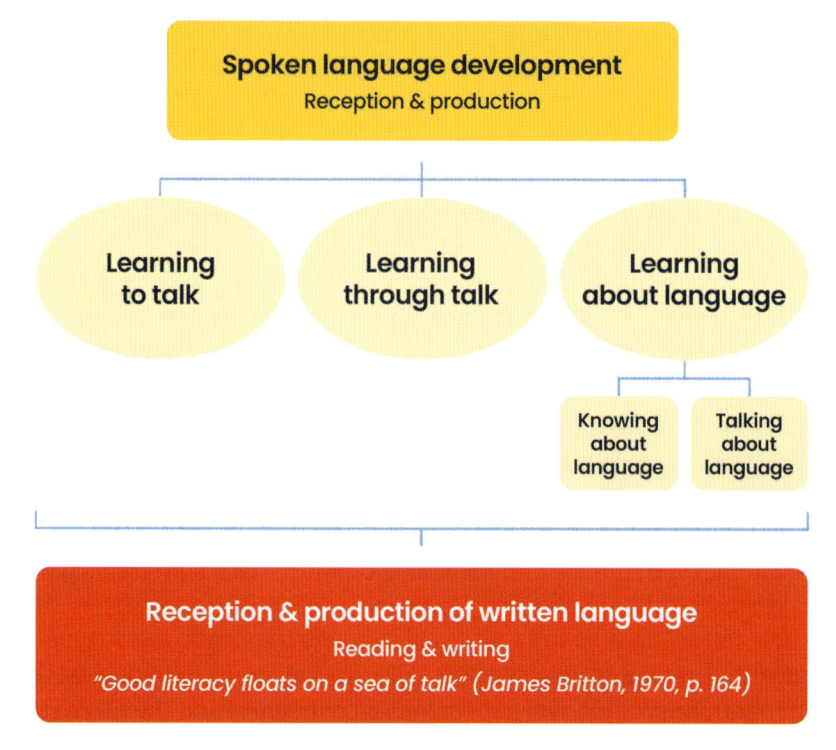

- Learning to talk
- Learning through talk
- Learning about language
  - Knowing about language
  - Talking about language

Reception & production of written language
Reading & writing
"Good literacy floats on a sea of talk" (James Britton, 1970, p. 164)

FIGURE 7A.1 The different types of spoken language development

Millard and Gaunt (2018) have surmised Alexander's (2018) definition of the different types of speaking that children will be exposed to in the classroom as:

1. Rote: imparting knowledge by getting students to repeat key pieces of information to impart facts, ideas and routines.
2. Recitation: using questions to test students' knowledge and understanding, to check students' progress and stimulate recall.
3. Instruction: telling students what to do and explaining key facts, principles or processes in order to transmit information.
4. Discussion*: encouraging the exchange of ideas within a class, to share information.

5. Dialogue: using structured questions and discussion, helping students deepen understanding of key knowledge, principles and processes.

*Discussion can be known as exploratory talk, where students share ideas and viewpoints between themselves, engaging in reasoned debate in order to reach a consensus.

For the students themselves, the type of talk that you want them to be engaged in is dialogic talk (between teacher and student), exploratory talk (between peers; the wilder relative of the three listed as talk is more 'in the moment', leading to organic questions and ideas) and presentational talk (student presenting ideas). Barnes (2008) defines this more eloquently stating that 'exploratory talk is typical at the early stages of approaching new ideas. It is hesitant and incomplete because it enables the speaker to try out ideas, to hear how they sound, to see what others make of them' and that the main difference between presentational and exploratory is that 'in presentational talk the speaker's attention is focused on adjusting the language, content, and manner to the needs of the audience, and in exploratory talk the speaker is more concerned with sorting out his or her own thoughts'.

Having a clear idea of the type of talk you are wanting the students to engage in will aid you in scaffolding the process of talk as well as support you in being adaptive with scaffolds, live in the lesson. But before we can consider the scaffolding of talk *content* and the process of talking, we need to explore how we can scaffold the *conditions* in which effective talk can take place.

Scaffolds to create an environment for talk

A key starting point in scaffolding talk is ensuring that there is a culture and environment which supports respectful listening and active participation in discussions and questioning.

Creating this culture is not simple and often is tied to the behaviour policy and classroom expectations of the school on a wider scale. With the support of a whole school ethos of calm, purposeful environments where students listen and respond sensitively and powerfully, supported by speaking frameworks, these conditions can be replicated at a practitioner level in the classroom more readily.

For those who are not in a school that has at this point fully achieved this culture, establishing clear, concise oracy ground rules are important to ensure that talk remains focused and purposeful. Creating this culture itself may require the scaffolding of learning behaviours over time in order to achieve this. However, the juice is worth the squeeze as having ground rules are fundamental to ensuring that high impact discussions can take place as well as reducing cognitive load through having clear routines and procedures in place. This is particularly the case for exploratory talk as it 'is less predictable than other types of talk such as scaffolded responses to teacher questions . . . Being explicit about how to engage in exploratory talk is essential to support effective dialogue' (Voice 21, 2023).

From an Equality, Inclusion and Diversity perspective, please do consider the demographic of your students and the different cultural conventions of talk within family and home environments. The rules of talk that you want for your classroom and what you perceive to be common conventions are only common conventions to some, and not all. Therefore, careful framing, sensitivity and implementation of the ground rules is vital, and it may require additional scaffolding for some. An example is that there is often a misconception that 'boys talk, and girls don't' and therefore only girls require oracy scaffolding. However, research has shown that it is far more complex than this and that it cannot be reduced to such a simple binary. For example, the 'extreme talkativeness of a sub-group [of high attaining boys]' was noted in Howe and Abedin's study, but lower attaining boys and boys from different cultural and socio-economic backgrounds did not exhibit the same behaviours. This tells us that research is needed into understanding the barriers that students additionally face as individuals which can mean looking at a range of barriers 'together with [their] gender' (Howe & Abedin, 2013).

It is important to create ground rules so that:

- There is a culture of high expectations for all
- Students develop an understanding of the process of talk – how to listen and when, as well as how, to speak. This will take time to develop into habit.
- Talk is inclusive. All voices are heard, elevated and celebrated
- Talk is efficient and purposeful. Students remain focused on the topic at hand and don't drift off topic, reducing the potential for lost learning time.

Contracts

One way to achieve establishing these ground rules is either through teacher generated ground rules or the co-creation of contracts with the students. William (2017) summarised by Clark (2024) states that contracts are a good idea for group work, whereby students are held to account by a 'signed agreement outlining what students are expected to achieve, the responsibilities and specific deadlines'. I would argue that this is also a useful idea that can be adapted for exploratory talk scenarios. As mentioned, you may already have routines in place in school such as Lemov's (2023) SLANT (Sit up, Listen, Ask and Answer, Nod, Track the Speaker) or STAR (Sit up, Track the Speaker, Ask Questions, Respect Those Around You), which can be deployed or used as part of building broader oracy ground rules. Therefore, the context of your school and classes will help you to determine which rules to put into place or which adaptations to make to existing policies. Potential ground rules could include:

- Respectful listening. No interrupting.
- All eyes on the speaker, bodies turned towards the speaker, pens down, no talking.
- Turn taking.

- Psychological safety; to take responsible risks with ideas, an atmosphere of trust, a culture of error.
- Active participation by contributing ideas and asking questions.
- Respect all contributions.
- Ideas can be challenged. However, the challenge is focused on the ideas, not the person.
- Talk remains focused on the topic at hand and our shared goals.
- Praise peers' responses.

Whichever approach is adopted (use of existing school strategies, teacher generated ground rules or co-created contracts), to embed the ground rules and to develop an environment conducive to purposeful talk, differing types of scaffolding to achieve this (using the EEF model, 2023) are:

- Visual: explicit modelling the ground rules in action using a group of students or other adults (film clips could be used), referring to posters or displays, symbols which represent a rule, modelling expected behaviour using role play or video clips (Voice 21 have a selection available online), photographs which reinforce particular rules in action, gestural cues (Fisher & Frey, 2010)
- Verbal: reminders, cues, prompts, narrating of positive behaviours, countdowns of when to end conversations or timers for the amount of time a person is expected to talk for
- Written: written rules for talk in books or laminated sheets in front of students, the aforementioned class charter for talk in front of them

This could take time to achieve, depending on your context, with varying levels of scaffolding intensity required and so perseverance and adherence to the rules is important. This can be frustrating at first, but McCrea (2024) suggests that automaticity can be achieved stating that:

Routines can be powerful tools for learning. However, they take time and effort to establish, and typically come with an initial dip in performance. . . . The amount of time it takes for a routine to automate depends on its complexity and how frequently we run it. Simple routines can take 20 repetitions. More complex sequences can take up to 200. It can be weeks or months before a teaching routine becomes automatic.

Whilst at times it may be more difficult to achieve (Year 9 Period 6 on a Friday when there's a wasp in the room), it is very important to scaffold and model the desired behaviour for talk so that all students are ready to listen respectfully and engage in talk with intent. Mercer and Hodgkinson (2008) also suggest that talk expectations should be revisited and reflected upon, arguing that whilst it 'may help to make these norms explicit' it is also valuable to 'consider if they need to be revised'.

Once ground rules are established, the next step would be to scaffold the students' ability to know what type of talk they are engaging in and how they should therefore adapt their discussions to meet this type of talk.

Scaffolding students ability to understand the type of talk

How often have you walked into a meeting and found out that instead of it being an informal chat about your subject/remit that actually you were meant to be formally presenting on your vision of it? I've had many sleepless nights re-thinking such scenarios recalling how I've sat with the cold sweat of the dawning realisation that I was not prepared for the type of talk in the meeting that I was expecting. Good leadership tells us that no one should arrive to a meeting without knowing what it is about, who the audience is and what the purpose is – all of this helps you to determine content to include, language to use, tone to strike, bodily gestures to rehearse and resultantly feel as confident as you can about the situation.

However, think back to the last talk task that you gave students. Were they fully clear on what the type of talk was, in what context and for which audience, and why they are doing it? Because the above meeting hell scenario is sometimes what we unintentionally do with students by immersing them into situations where we haven't made the purpose of a talk task clear. We might ask them to discuss things as a group, but we don't support them in recognising the type of talk task, and we don't clarify what we are expecting as part of that talk or show them examples of what that talk looks like.

Think about when you last asked students to give a presentation. How did you prepare them for this beyond knowing the content? I doubt very few students regularly give formal presentations in their home about topics such as the process of osmosis or why the role of the community in law enforcement in England declined from the 16th century. So we can't expect them to just know how to do this when in the classroom, or know how it differs from having a dialogic or exploratory discussion with peers and the teacher, without modelling and scaffolding this talk type to them.

A lack of knowledge of types of talk and how to identify them can lead to confusion, panic and dissociation from the process of talk, or them engaging in talk incorrectly. We must therefore equip our students to be able to know about different types of talk and how they function.

As part of understanding the type of talk, it is important that we develop the metacognitive skills of our students so that they are able to understand the process of talk. This will begin with identifying the talk task at hand and then carefully plan through the development of their ideas and then move onto the articulation of these ideas for the given intended purpose and audience. Gaunt and Stott (2019) succinctly outline Evans and Jones (2007) three stages of children understanding the process and the types of talk. They describe it as

> First, there is the moment that a child becomes conscious of a strategy or skill employed in the talk. This is termed aware use. When a child is able to choose the best strategy or deploy a skill appropriate to the task at hand, this is known as strategic use. The highest level of understanding is reached by reflective use, when

children are able to evaluate the effectiveness of the choices that they have made and set targets for future improvement.

As a result, the students need to be clear about the purpose and if it is exploratory, dialogic or presentational talk. Each purpose and audience will require students to code switch, to know which language to use, and with that what tone, content and what gestures to use. We must teach them to clearly identify the purpose and therefore format of the talk that they are about to engage in, so that they can activate their knowledge of how to process their thinking into appropriate speech that will meet this purpose. An example of this would be:

- Talk type 1: A presentation of a summary of Romeo and Juliet to the Headteacher

- Task type 2: An exploratory talk where students have to summarise Romeo and Juliet to then feedback to their peers

These are two very different types of talk. Therefore, we must model how we identify what type of talk format we need to use in order to inform how we will plan to approach discussions:

- What is the topic that you have been given?
- What content is most relevant to this topic?
- Who is the audience?
- What is the format?
- What language should be used?
- What tone and pitch?
- What body language, position or gestures might be most appropriate for this?

Talking is a process and we must help them to make sense of the talk-task at hand, make the process clear to them, and within that provide scaffolded opportunities for deliberate, guided then independent practice.

To achieve this, your scaffolding could include:

- Exposure to examples of different types of talk. This could include giving contrasting examples, like the aforementioned Romeo and Juliet tasks, and asking students to discuss what the approach to each would be and how they differ. This promotes metacognition in terms of them breaking down what the type of talk is and what the key elements of that type of talk typically look like. Intensity of this form of scaffolding can be shifted from providing additional hints and prompts, or modelling a first contrasting pair before giving a different example of contrasting pairs.

- Linked to the above, identifying different types of talk can be supported by using kernel sentences (Hochman & Wexler, 2017) to chunk and break it down into composite parts:

    Who: is the audience? *The Headteacher*

    What: is the context? *Formal, student to person in authority*

    Why: *to demonstrate knowledge of Romeo and Juliet*

    How: *presentation*

    Using this information, students can then go on to discuss what types of language are most appropriate for a formal setting, what tone would be the most appropriate for a presentation etc.

Once the type of talk is understood by the pupils, they can better prepare to sift through their growing knowledge of the topic at hand and determine which content should be used and why.

Scaffolding the content that is being discussed

I'm sure we've all been in a situation where we have in our minds what we want to say. Then when it comes to our turn to talk, our minds go utterly blank. This too will be the case for students in our classrooms. Voice 21 (2019) identifies within their skills framework the role of cognitive and linguistic understanding as two of the pillars of oracy, framing that for oracy to successfully take place, the students need to know what to say and provide reasoning for ideas as well as what words to use.

With this in mind, what scaffolding can help students to develop their cognitive and linguistic skills so that they can engage in discussions confidently with the knowledge they need readily to hand? That will depend on the type of talk they are engaging in. Barnes (2008) frames this as 'in presentational talk the speaker's attention is primarily on adjusting the language, content and manner to the needs of the audience and in exploratory talk the speaker is more concerned with sorting out his or her own thoughts'. This essentially means that content scaffolds might look different as live, responsive exploratory talk or dialogic talk with a teacher might require quick reference to facts and research to counter a point, whereas presentational is more the recalling of predetermined talk content. Therefore, I have bracketed where each scaffold is best utilised.

Retrieval (exploratory, dialogic)

Through frequent retrieval, students are able to recall information more readily and so be able to deploy this knowledge in their responses. This is also the case for verbal responses and discussions. Retrieval should be used as a scaffold for supporting the students in activating prior knowledge so that they can then formulate responses with increased fluency and confidence and with reduced cognitive load. This in turn will help to develop their motivation to want to take part in dialogic or exploratory talk in terms of sharing their ideas as they have the knowledge readily to hand to share.

That said, the willingness to participate in verbal retrieval may still be daunting for some. Scaffolds to help overcome this can include ways for students to formulate their responses in advance or write them down as an aide-memoire before contributing:

- Mini whiteboards – students articulate ideas first and have a cue/prompt when called upon to answer.
- Turn and talk. An opportunity to trial out initial thoughts and develop them using peer ideas, before feeding back in class discussions.
- Brain dump. Writing down key content points linked to the question posed.
- Thinking time. Considering the amount of thinking time that might be required based on the difficulty of the concept or their prior knowledge.

Aide-Memoires (all)

When immersed in presentational talk, having aide-memoires can help the speaker to be able to talk at length about a given topic without having to commit everything to memory. In less formal settings, in exploratory talk or dialogic talk, it can act as a prompt when thinking stumbles or provide a useful overview of knowledge that can be used as counter-points when agreeing or disagreeing with someone. These could include:

- Graphic organisers
- Knowledge organisers
- Flash cards (particularly in presentational talk or within MFL lessons when practising for the spoken assessment)
- Wall displays
- Cues and prompts on the board
- Photographs, sources or diagrams
- Script or bullet point notes (more suited to presentational)

Mini whiteboards (all)

Using mini whiteboards, students can write down initial ideas that they have in response to the stimulus or question/s posed. Having a whiteboard acts as a draft, allowing for the ability to erase ideas with ease and reformulate them. This can also provide useful opportunities to check for understanding to make sure that students really do understand what is being discussed.

Paired talk to share and develop ideas (all)

Using strategies such as turn and talk, students can vocalise first thoughts, using their peer as a soundboard to receive feedback on their chosen content and seek out further ideas. This will then enable students to trial their first thoughts and receive developmental feedback in a low stakes environment, helping to engender confidence and therefore the motivation to talk.

Mutual scaffolding (exploratory, dialogic)

Peers within groups can also act as a way for pupils to hone the content they're discussing, also termed as 'interthinking' (Littleton & Mercer, 2013). Knight (2020) argues that during exploratory talk the process of mutual scaffolding can take place as 'peers can exhibit as a group all the features of a scaffolding role usually attributed to an adult'. Knight, surmising Littleton and Mercer's (2013) 'interthinking', states that there are three processes involved:

1. Appropriation. Learning strategies from peers that can then be applied independently
2. Co-construction. Creating new ideas and strategies through collective reasoning that surpasses an individual's capability
3. Transformation. Developing transferable metacognitive understanding about individual reasoning

As discussed, knowing what to say is vital for talk and therefore having the scaffolds to be able to formulate, test, hone and develop ideas is a central part of effective oracy. However, sometimes despite having the ideas of what to talk about, what students then go on to say can still fall short of expectations in terms of rich vocabulary. How can we scaffold students' ability to use a broad range of powerful tier two and three vocabulary?

Scaffolding the vocabulary that is being used

Explicit teaching of tier two and three vocabulary is an essential part of teaching, in all subjects and phases. Gaunt and Stott (2019) rightly argue that 'we must create classrooms that are language rich and encourage children to interact with a wide-ranging, diverse, and complex spread of vocabulary, through both speaking and listening'.

Given the extensive research that demonstrates how disadvantaged children do not always live in a home environment where language development is supported (often unintentionally), Gaunt and Stott (2019) assert that school is therefore 'their second chance to acquire the rich and varied vocabulary that they will need for success both in life and academically'. The EEF (2018) highlight particularly the importance of disciplinary literacy including dedicated vocabulary instruction within the curriculum because as 'students progress through an increasingly specialised secondary school curriculum, there is a growing need to ensure that students are trained to access the academic language and conventions of different subjects' (EEF, 2018).

How can we scaffold student's ability to use tier two and three vocabulary correctly and powerfully? Please note that the below suggested scaffolds are equally applicable to reading and writing.

Frayer models

A Frayer model contains a student-friendly definition of a word, the key characteristics of the word and most typically examples and non-examples. This graphic organiser can be adapted to suit the needs of a subject, for example substituting in diagrams and formulas in science and mathematics. This is a powerful way for students to learn vocabulary as 'organising information visually can support pupils' understanding of content, making abstract learning more concrete and reducing reliance solely on the verbal' (Aubin, 2023). When using Frayer models, differing approaches can be used depending on the readiness of the pupils (prior knowledge of the topic, concept). They can either be given as completed models which students can annotate or transform, partially completed (completing it with the teacher, peers or independently) or completing all of it (either with the teacher, peers or independently).

Saying the word aloud

Students should be given the chance to verbalise vocabulary and practice using the word in varying contexts. Gaunt and Stott (2019) reinforce this saying that students must 'try out, revise and demonstrate their understanding of words . . . getting students to speak, to use new vocabulary, and to hear themselves say words out loud is a key step to truly learning a word'. A useful account called Sounds and Syllables (@SoundSyllable on X) breaks down root words into the syllables and creates opportunities for teachers to use the morphology as a further way to scaffold students' understanding of a range of words that include the root.

How you get the students to say the word aloud can vary according to your knowledge of your students. It might be that choral chanting is more appropriate. However, you may wish to get students to practise first in pairs or small groups so that you can circulate and hear if the word is being pronounced correctly.

Word banks

Providing students with a list of words that they must and could include provides them with a written reminder of how they can incorporate existing vocabulary or new vocabulary. This will require modelling to students, as merely placing the word bank in front of them will not mean that they know how to use it. Teacher modelling using strategies such as a visualiser or ticking words off on a word bank on a wall can demonstrate to students how the word bank should be used to elevate talk.

'Summary Bullseye'

Gaunt and Stott (2019) have adapted the word bank approach into a 'summary bullseye' so that when students are in scenarios where they have to verbally summarise their learning, they do so with ambitious vocabulary. The 'summary bullseye' is a resource where tier 2-3 vocabulary are given points in terms of sophistication (with one point words being in the outer ring and five word points being in the centre). The aim is to achieve a high score, with the peer keeping tally. This encourages students to weave in more complex and sophisticated vocabulary into their speech. This, they argue, adds challenge and drives motivation to want to use varying vocabulary. However, they do suggest that it's important to first of all clarify what an effective summary contains, as well as plan for ways to avoid students from 'shoehorning in vocabulary, but not necessarily using it correctly' (Gaunt & Stott, 2019).

Say it again, but say it better

During dialogic discussions, when students are responding and give overly-simplistic or unsatisfactory responses (for example, key tier 3 vocabulary not being used), 'say it again but say it better' (Sherrington, 2018) can provide a prompt for students to rethink their initial response and respond again with greater depth and/or breadth. When approaching this, using our knowledge of the students and checks for understanding, it's worth considering when asking them to say it better if they may require scaffolds to be able to achieve this. Examples of additional scaffolding might include pointing a student to word banks for missing vocabulary or encouraging students to use their graphic organiser to add greater detail to the response.

Scaffolding the process of talk

Area 1: Retrieval

As discussed in the writing chapter, retrieval shouldn't solely be focused on content. It should also include opportunities to recall the process of talk. This will help to develop routines and habits, as well as provide you with checks for understanding in terms of which students may require additional scaffolding when carrying out articulating their knowledge through a talk task. In short, the student may know the content, but still be uncertain with how to begin to verbalise it. This is particularly true when we consider disciplinary oracy, as exploratory talk may look different in geography compared to science. By securing a high success rate when carrying out this retrieval, this should help to improve motivation as they taste greater success with getting to know what the key components of talk are. Within your repertoire of retrieval, include the retrieval of aspects such as:

- What are the different types of talk?
- What key vocabulary would be useful for this discussion based on previous learning?
- What sentence stems can we recall?
- Remember when we did a presentation on X. How did we approach preparing for this?

Area 2: Scaffolding to develop respectful and active listening

Success criteria or a Listening Ladder

Using your oracy ground rules (discussed earlier) as a success criteria and as a pathway into diving deeper into defining what respectful and active listening looks like and sounds like. This could include a list of key characteristics of listening which could be used as a visual scaffold with a display on the wall to remind students or images which demonstrate active listening positioning. A version of this is Gaunt and Stott's (2019)

Listening Ladder, which is essentially a success criteria for listening that has at the bottom some easier to achieve actions such as 'giving 100% of their focus to the person speaking' and 'being calm and still' to then more challenging aspects of listening such as being able to ask 'questions that dig deeper' and summarise 'the speaker's ideas'. This is a useful scaffold in terms of carrying out modelling and deliberate practice of each of the steps, as well as providing a benchmark of readiness from which further scaffolding can be provided. It can also be used as part of metacognition and target setting, with students aiming to secure a rung of the ladder before moving onto the next, which is then aided by further scaffolding.

Model listening

William (2017) suggests that teachers should 'model effective communication and respectful language by actively listening to your students and demonstrating how to acknowledge other viewpoints'. This could be supported by providing examples and non-examples through role play or video clips, to reinforce what effective, respectful listening and turn taking looks like. Often asking the students to observe interactions at lunchtime will provide them with examples of how respectful listening does not always take place! Remember to plan for students who may find listening more challenging due to a disability or those who may struggle in group scenarios where there are many talking.

One to one or small group listening

Teachers could also partner pairs to carry out deliberate practice of turn taking and respectful listening. This should be supported by a success criteria. This will enable students to practise before engaging in wider group or whole class discussions and therefore build confidence as well as a stronger understanding of listening conventions.

Group sizes

Linked to sharing ideas and turn taking below, respectful listening can be scaffolded through the use of different sized groups. It may be that pairs or trios are used initially, so that students have the opportunity to practise ground rules and listen to one another, before scaling up to small group or whole class talk situations. Over time, it may be that you vary the group sizes depending on the development of listening skills by different students. One thing to remember is that McCrea (2024) sagely told us that it can take up to 200 repetitions for something to embed into routine so this may take greater time and more intensity for some students.

Area 3: Scaffolding sharing ideas and turn taking

Sentence starters or question stems

Sentence starters and question stems can provide nervous and/or reluctant students to know how to begin the sentence that they are trying to verbally form, therefore acting as an anchor in the storm of possible ways to start their speech which are thundering around in their head. Whilst there are more general oracy sentence starters which are discussed below, it would be beneficial to investigate what disciplinary specific sentence starters (and linked vocabulary) might be more appropriate within your subject area. Disciplinary oracy (how to speak like a historian or geographer) must be front and centre of talk within the curriculum, and so tailoring more generic oracy stems to subject-specific stems might be better suited to achieving purposeful disciplinary talk. As to how to deploy these sentence starters, this will depend on the intensity of scaffold needed for your identified students. For example, some students may require an individual copy which is stuck in their books, whereas some may need reminders from a display on the wall or board, whilst others can suggest their own sentence starters and vocabulary based on their growing skills and knowledge.

Wilkinson and Govier (2022) has created oracy sentence starter supports for each subject as part of her 'Speak Like A . . .' strategy across her Trust. For example, her Design Technology oracy sentence starters are:

- My product is fit for purpose because . . .
- My research has helped with this design because . . .

- I have selected these tools and/or materials because . . .
- My analysis and evaluation of this product is . . .
- I could improve my design by . . .

Voice 21 Talk tactics

The Voice 21 talk tactics (2022) of summarising, probing and clarifying are essential reading skills; through guided practice with using these talk tactics in oral discussions, students are able to write more considered responses. Having been taught the strands of the Oracy Framework, students are more aware of the linguistic and cognitive skills that they are using and how to apply them effectively (Schofield, 2023).

Habits of discussion

Habits of discussion (Lemov, 2022) is a process whereby respectful listening and turn taking is scaffolded through the process of talk being structured. This process involves defined roles with supporting sentence stems to help students to start their responses:

- Instigator. Starts the discussion. 'I think we should consider. . .'
- Builder. Develops the ideas. 'Building on that . . .'
- Challenger. Presents another idea. 'You said . . . but I think . . .'
- Summariser. Shares the key points. 'Overall, the main points were . . .'

Talk tokens or thumbs in (Gaunt & Stott, 2019)

The purpose of talk tokens is to make sure that all children contribute to discussions (by 'spending' their tokens) and that some students don't dominate the discussion (and therefore can't talk once they have spent their tokens). Whilst I'm uncertain of how talk tokens might be received by KS4 students, in primary settings and lower KS3 this can be a useful way to scaffold turn taking. What might be more appropriate for upper

KS3+ might be the use of 'thumbs in' (Gaunt & Stott, 2019) where a student signals that they want to add a contribution by having their thumb up. The speaker will then select a person with their thumb up to take over the role of speaking, and so on.

Over time, the need for talk tokens should be reduced as students develop the habit of turn taking and perhaps thumbs in is a way to slowly move from a more scaffolded and controlled approach to a strategy that moves responsibility for turn taking to the students' ability to acknowledge when another person wants to say something. Alternatively it may be that as you reduce the scaffolding of talk tokens, you introduce time limits for how long each person within a group talks for, and specify that each person must talk at some point.

Scaffold 3: Scaffolding voice, physical stance and body language

The way we use our body and face in talk is almost as powerful as the words that we are speaking. Voice 21 (2019) outline the physical aspects of oracy as being about the voice (pace, tone, clarity, intonation) and body language (gesture, posture, eyes). As mentioned, if students have had limited exposure to certain types of talk and formal scenarios, then they will need scaffolds to help them to develop their ability to match their words and talk type with their body language. With an EDI focus, it is important to be mindful of disabilities and also cultural sensitivities (such as eye contact).

Modelling

Either as a teacher modelling, a group of students role playing, photographs or diagrams or a video clip, modelling to pupils the different types of tone, volume and gestures that people use when carrying out different types of talk. For example, when someone gives a speech, they may benefit from watching clips of how famous speakers over time have used their body and face to add momentum and meaning to their words, or how they use a certain tone when they reach a phrase that they hope will galvanise their audience. Obvious examples of famous speeches such as Malala Yousafzai or Martin Luther King can help to provide cultural capital examples, or you may wish to demonstrate using students or yourself within a classroom setting.

Additionally, you might want to include subject-specific examples of great presentations and talk. It would be worth also including infamous non-examples of where a lack of gestures or a poor choice of gestures have impacted delivery, and get the students to identify what could have been done better; recent political televised debates provide a wealth of examples.

Bringing it back to Bob, he was *almost* right when he said 'it's good to talk'. Perhaps, what is a better way of succinctly capturing the value of talk is to instead say 'it's good to *continue to learn* to talk, *for different purposes, and this requires constant work and scaffolding*'. Admittedly, it's not as catchy as the original, but it does capture the more accurate understanding that talk is complex and multifaceted.

Whilst the desire to communicate through sound and then talk might be inherent in the majority of us from birth, we still do require the continued nurturing of those sounds and words, and how we use them, throughout our lifetime. So for me, Oracy is not a destination, it is instead a lifelong learning process. This is because we cannot say we have ever fully secured all the facets of oracy, as language and ways of talking and audiences are constantly evolving with each generation (Gen Z language and the arrival of TikTok are evidence enough of new vocabulary and types of talk). Instead, we would be better to see it as a skill which requires continuous reflection and fine tuning. Within the classroom, this means that we have to prepare our students for this lifelong endeavour using differing scaffolds in order to foster the metacognitive skills required to identify types of talk and therefore select their content, vocabulary and physicality with accuracy.

Chapter 7 Self-Reflection Questions

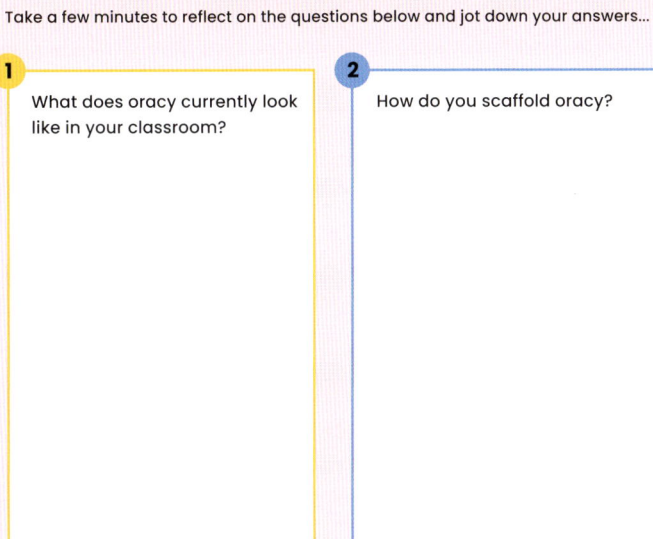

Take a few minutes to reflect on the questions below and jot down your answers...

1. What does oracy currently look like in your classroom?

2. How do you scaffold oracy?

3. What may be the barriers or pitfalls with oracy in your classroom that you need to plan for?

References

Alexander, R. (2018) Developing Dialogic Teaching: Genesis, Process, Trial. Routledge. Quoted in Millard, W. & Gaunt, A. (2018) Speaking Up: The Importance of Oracy in Teaching and Learning. *Impact*, 3

Ambition Institute (2021) National Professional Qualification for Leading Literacy: Course 2 Developing Language.

Aubin, G. (2023) *EEF Blog: Cognitive Strategies – Let's Have a Think. Using Cognitive Strategies to Support Pupils with Special Educational Needs.* EEF (Online). Available at https://educationendowmentfoundation.org.uk/news/eef-blog-cognitive-strategies-lets-have-a-think. Accessed 17th July 2024

Barnes, D. (2008) Exploratory Talk for Learning. In N. Mercer & S. Hogdkinson (Eds.), *Exploring Talk in School Inspired by the Work of Douglas Barnes*. London: Sage Publications

Clark, J. (2024) *Teaching One Pagers*. Woodbridge: John Catt Educational

Davies, S. (2022) *Developing Oracy Skills in the Classroom*. Teachit (Online). Available at https://www.teachit.co.uk/cpd/teaching-and-learning/developing-students-oracy-skills-effective-speaking-and-listening. Accessed 9th July 2024

Education Endowment Foundation (EEF) (2018) *Improving Literacy in Secondary Schools* (Online). Available at https://educationendowmentfoundation.org.uk/education-evidence/guidance-reports/literacy-ks3-ks4. Accessed 16th April 2024

Education Endowment Foundation (EEF) (2023) *The Five-A-Day Principle. Scaffolding* (Online). Available at https://d2tic4wvo1iusb.cloudfront.net/eef-guidance-reports/send/5-a-Day_Reflection_Tool_2023.pdf. Accessed 30th July 2024

Evans, R. & Jones, D. (2007) Perspectives on Oracy – Towards a Theory of Practice [Editorial]. *Early Child Development and Care*, 177(6–7), 557–567

Fisher, D. & Frey, N. (2010) *Guided Instruction: How to Develop Confident and Successful Learners*. Alexandria: ASCD

Gaunt, A. & Stott, A. (2019) *Transform Teaching and Learning Through Talk: The Oracy Imperative* (R&L).

Hochman, J. C. & Wexler, N. (2017) *The Writing Revolution*. San Francisco: Jossey-Bass

Howe, C. & Abedin, M. (2013) Classroom Dialogue: A Systematic Review Across Four Decades of Research. *Cambridge Journal of Education*, 43(3), 325–356

(Online). Available at https://doi.org/10.1080/0305764X.2013.786024. Accessed 19th July 2024

Knight, R. (2020) *Classroom Talk: Evidence-Based Teaching for Enquiring Teachers*. St Albans: Critical Publishing

Knight, R. (2023) *Oracy and Cultural Capital: The Transformative Potential of Spoken Language*. The United Kingdom Literacy Association (Online). Available at https://onlinelibrary.wiley.com/doi/full/10.1111/lit.12343. Accessed 9th July 2024

Law, Prof. J., Charlton, J. & Asmussen, K. (2017) *Language as a Child Wellbeing Indicator*. Early Intervention Foundation and Newcastle University (Online). Available at https://www.researchgate.net/publication/330292437_Language_as_a_child_wellbeing_indicator. Accessed 9th July 2024

Lemov, D. (2022) *"Rolling Out" Habits of Discussion with Ipswich Academy's Ben Hall, Teach Like a Champion* (Online). Available at https://teachlikeachampion.org/blog/rolling-out-habits-of-discussion-with-ipswich-academys-ben-hall/. Accessed 16th July 2024

Lemov, D., McCleary, S., Solomon, H. & Woolway, E. (2023) *Teach Like a Champion 3.0*. San Francisco: Jossey Bass

Littleton, K. & Mercer, N. (2013) *Interthinking: Putting Talk to Work*. Abingdon: Routledge. Quoted in Knight, R. (2020) *Classroom Talk. Evidence-Based Teaching for Enquiring Teachers*. St Albans: Critical Publishing

McCrea, P. (2024) The Valley of Potential: Managing Expectations Around Routines. *Evidence Snacks* (Online). Available at https://snacks.pepsmccrea.com/p/valley-of-potential. Accessed 18th July 2024

Mercer, N. & Hodgkinson, S. (2008) *Exploring Talk in School: Inspired by the Work of Douglas Barnes*. Sage Publications

Millard, W. & Gaunt, A. (2018) Speaking Up: The Importance of Oracy in Teaching and Learning. *Impact*, 3

Millard, W. & Menzies, L. (2016) *The State of Speaking in Our Schools, Oracy*. Voice 21 (Online). Available at https://cfey.org/wp-content/uploads/2016/11/Oracy-Report-Final.pdf. Accessed 19th July 2024

Schofield, A. (2023) Let's Talk About Disadvantage: The Fundamental Importance of Oracy in Closing the Gap. *Impact* (Online). Available at https://my.chartered.college/impact_article/lets-talk-about-disadvantage-the-fundamental-importance-of-oracy-in-closing-the-gap/. Accessed 9th July 2024

Sherrington, T. (2018) *Great Teaching: The Power of Questioning.* Teacherhead (Online). Available at https://teacherhead.com/2018/08/24/great-teaching-the-power-of-questioning/. Accessed 9th August 2024

Sutton Trust (2012) *Social Mobility and Education Gaps in the Four Major Anglophone Countries Research Findings for the Social Mobility Summit.* London (Online). Available at https://www.suttontrust.com/our-research/social-mobility-report-2012-summit/. Accessed 9th July 2024

Voice 21 (2019) *The Oracy Skills Framework and Glossary.* Available at /oracycambridge.org/wp-content/uploads/2020/06/The-Oracy-Skills-Framework-and-Glossary.pdf

Voice 21 (2022) *Talk Tactics* (Online). Available at https://uploads-ssl.webflow.com/61f98cbcb29084298b30965f/64b94eb0ac6dbe0dac8a99f7_Student_Talk_Tactics.pdf. Accessed 9th July 2024

Voice 21 (2023) *The Talking Point, Voice 21's Journal* (Online). Available at https://voice21.org/voice-21s-journal-2023/. Accessed 9th July 2024

Wilkinson, S. & Govier, J. (2022) *Speak Like a . . ., Leo Academy Trust* (Online). Available at https://g.co/kgs/N2FnRw9. Accessed 30th July 2024

William, D. (2017) *Embedded Formative Assessment: (Strategies for Classroom Assessment That Drives Student Engagement and Learning) (The New Art and Science of Teaching)* (Second edition). Bloomington: Solution Tree Press

7b Scaffolding and oracy
Case studies

Alongside the theory and examples offered in Chapter 7a, we felt it would be useful to include case studies which help to explore two of the strategies in greater depth. One of the strategies focuses on the thorny issue of dialect and 'standard English', and how we can encourage those with regional and diverse dialects to feel empowered to talk. The second strategy looks at how we can develop student agency and thought processes when they are asking and answering questions.

CASE STUDY 1: ORACY AND STUDENT AGENCY – 'EVERYTHING BUT THE ANSWER'

Elizabeth Brydon, Humanities Deputy Curriculum Team Leader, @misshistobry

Context and diagnosis

Ahead of launching our Oracy initiative, we assessed the existing understanding and practice of Oracy by collaborating with senior, curriculum and phase leadership, and also through conducting listening walks across all phases and key stages. During these walks, we identified much existing good practice; 'Oracy' was already happening. This included, but was not limited to: *think-pair-share, cold-calling, formative assessment through mini-whiteboards, Socratic questioning, reciprocal reading, choral chanting of words* etc.

However, as we were still in the infancy of our whole-school oracy initiative, we recognised that a greater depth of implementation needed adding. Teachers were demonstrating competence beyond just 'initiation, response', and were offering 'initiation, response, feedback and/or evaluation' (Knight, 2020), showing that there was a recognised awareness of the importance of offering feedback, ones which were largely teacher-led.

However, our ultimate long-term goal was for our students to hold more 'agency' in the classroom (Gaunt & Stott, 2019). This could only be achieved if classroom dialogue offered a continuous exchange of ideas which were probed, challenged and built upon in order to support the internal narrative of our students (metacognition). Ultimately, we recognised there was a need to empower our teachers to model and scaffold such exchanges in their facilitation of classroom talk, before we could expect the same of our students. Questioning needed to be 'a scaffolded interchange, geared towards guiding learning and developing students' metacognitive awareness' (Knight, 2020, p. 30).

There are countless scaffolds I could have picked to focus on. However, at the time of writing this case study there was one in particular which stood out as being our own next step in empowering staff to enhance the educational dialogic exchanges in their classroom. We named this, rather uncreatively, **'Everything but the answer . . .'**

'Everything but the answer . . .'

What is it?

During our initial diagnostic listening walk, we observed two teachers (both secondary – Mathematics, PE) employing a scaffold of this nature; something which directly targeted our aforementioned diagnosis of limitations to teacher-led talk.

Everything but the answer is a verbal scaffold used by staff through questioning and probing. This is implemented during the lesson and may be done at various points, but more than likely at key hinge points of the lesson to formatively assess student understanding or address misconceptions. Teachers must offer students everything *but* the answer. The example of the scaffold I unpick here is very loose, and that is intentional. Scaffolds cannot be used as cookie-cutters; one scaffold should not look the same across different contexts. Therefore, consider what adaptations you would need to make such as how you can ensure all pupils engage with and benefit from the implementation. For example, the use of mini-whiteboards and/or *Think-Pair-Share* may be beneficial in order to offer students a safe, supportive, exploratory environment to retrieve and corroborate their thoughts before they are probed and questioned.

How is it implemented?

Firstly, I will explain how I observed my colleague using this in a GCSE PE lesson on 'movement analysis'. The teacher had identified a misconception of their GCSE students regarding joint movements. So using a whiteboard-walled room, they identified four initial movements they wanted the class to dual-code in groups (flexion, extension, abduction and adduction) using the whiteboard walls to document their discussions. As the teacher circulated they were formatively assessing student understanding and making notes of their 'interthinking' (Littleton & Mercer, 2013).

Instead of responding to student questions simply with the correct answer, the teacher continued to probe and question so that the student engaged in deep thinking to sift through their own misconceptions they may have and use cues and prompts to deeply think their way to the correct answer. This was done through various means such as the use of antonyms, comparisons, body movements to represent the type of joint movements and a blend of open and closed questions. It is important that we model and engage the students in this deliberate practice of deep thinking and answer searching, as it dispels the myth that learning is easy and things are just 'on the tip of your tongue'.

It requires sustained effort, retrieval and application to achieve fluency of knowledge in areas being studied. Moreover, by verbalising the thinking process, the teacher is better equipped to see where misconceptions may have arisen and how they can scaffold future learning to calibrate and correct this faulty knowledge, as well as consider curriculum adaptations if the discussions unveil that more students also hold the same misconception.

As I observed these exchanges, I recognised the impact this could have in my own GCSE history classroom. For example:

Student   'Miss, was the Norman use of fines as punishment a continuation or change from the Anglo-Saxon period?'
Teacher   'Well, in Anglo-Saxon England fines were a common punishment. The amount of the fine would depend on . . . what? Would it be the same for all crimes?'
Student   'No, it would not be the same for all crimes.'
Teacher   'Why was it not the same for all crimes? What did the amount depend on?'
Student   'It would not be the same for all crimes as for example, if the suspect had committed a crime against the person such as assault or murder, the fine they paid would depend on the social status of the victim.'
Teacher   'Excellent. What was the purpose of this punishment? For example, who would the fine be paid to? Was it paid to the local community?'
Student   'No, it was not paid to the local community. It was paid to the victims or their families if the victim was no longer alive.'
Teacher   'Correct. Why would it be paid to them? What would this provide them with?'
Student   'I suppose it provided them with justice? They were being compensated for what they had endured as a victim of the crime.'
Teacher   'Fantastic. So in summary, in Anglo-Saxon England fines were a common punishment which were paid to the victim or their

	family to provide justice, and the amount would depend on the social status of the victim. So, in Norman England were fines still used?'
Student	'Yes, I think so . . .'
Teacher	'You are correct. They were. But, their purpose had changed. When William Duke of Normandy conquered England, how stable was his position? Was his power secure?'
Student	'Not really . . . The Normans were quite outnumbered. William was conscious of this which was why he made some changes to laws such as the murdrum for which punishments were more severe if the crime had been against a Norman.'
Teacher	'Correct. So if William was wanting to increase his power, and if he was making fines for crimes against Normans more substantial, who would he want to make the recipient of these fines? Would allowing victims and their families to receive these fines increase his power in any way?'
Student	'No. To increase his power it was more beneficial for the fines to go to him as this would increase his wealth and control.'
Teacher	'Excellent, so – let's answer your question – was the Norman use of fines as punishment a continuation or change from the Anglo-Saxon period?'
Student	'The Norman use of fines was a partial continuity from Anglo-Saxon England as it was the same punishment but in a different form. In Anglo-Saxon England fines were used to ensure justice for victims as the money was paid directly to them or their families, whilst in Norman England fines were paid directly to the king in order to increase his power.'

And there we have it. By offering everything but the answer, the teacher was able to guide the student to a position of confidence in answering their own question by getting them to filter through their knowledge using scaffolded questioning and discussion cues. The student is able to move from a place of uncertainty to a place of being able to correctly answer the question but also do so in a 'say it again, but say it better' form.

Rather than simply telling a student that the Norman use of fines as punishment was a partial continuity, the drive to offer the student everything but the answer allows us to co-construct the bridges between pockets of existing student knowledge so they are supported and empowered to make necessary links to build on and truly consolidate their understanding; as opposed to just parroting a fact.

Why?

This scaffold is in no way groundbreaking and is likely something you already do. But with oracy, less is truly more. As mentioned earlier in this chapter, refining the basics of talk is imperative to securing the crucial foundations for articulation of students in the current educational climate. Only once these skills are secured can students then develop and enhance their Oracy to 'talk like a X'. This scaffold ensures students 'feel the words [of the curriculum] in their mouth' (Turner, 2024) with meaning, as opposed to simply repeating words, thoughts or phrases they have heard.

Therefore by enhancing and refining an existing method of formative assessment, we can build our students' inherent confidence in applying disciplinary vocabulary with meaning in order to truly 'speak like a [X]'. We can only truly understand something if we have the ability to verbalise it with meaning and intent as opposed to simple repetition.

Next steps beyond the scaffold

Knowing when to remove the scaffolds depends entirely on your context. However, there are some impact measurement tools staff can use to determine the level of need for a scaffold. There are many I could discuss; however, one of the most pertinent is the accountability of teachers to appraise student progress in oracy, with this being one of the Voice 21 Teacher Benchmarks (Voice 21, 2019).

Teacher accountability of appraising oracy lies at the heart of ensuring scaffolding remains in place for the appropriate amount of time.

This can be achieved formatively through the age-old general classroom circulation, having the confidence to take a step back and simply listen to the talk that is present in your classroom amongst your students.

Realistically, however, we cannot appraise something that does not exist. Scaffolds cannot be removed until our curriculum and schemes of learning are planned with oracy as an integral pillar of learning; with students being given regular opportunities to trial talk in both exploratory and presentational contexts. Only then can the removal of such scaffolds be considered. In time another indicator should be reduced reliance on teacher-led facilitation, and you should feel yourself needing to speak less. Of course teacher facilitation remains crucial; Oracy is not just about getting our students to do more of the talking. However, our explicit modelling and scaffolding of teacher-to-student exchanges should enable students to champion the facilitation of peer-to-peer exchanges to enhance learning.

How often, when observing members of your department, does student voice indicate the class teacher as being the sole person to go to if unsure of something? Whilst of course the teacher should be viewed as a secure source of knowledge, is it not more desirable for our students to recognise how much they could also learn from one another? Even with the best will in the world, the ability to articulate ourselves in a range of contexts is difficult to master, even as adults. If teachers have embarked on relevant progressive planning of explicit opportunities for talk, students should in time become experts in the discipline themselves. Therefore, with the correct planning and coaching, one of the greatest scaffolds available for students who may still need it are the peers sitting around them.

Key takeaways and conclusions

- Less is truly more. Do not overcomplicate scaffolds, and ensure the basics have been addressed in order to allow student disciplinary competence to blossom.

- Ensure teachers recognise the accountability of appraising oracy in their classrooms. Only then can a true judgement of the removal of the scaffold be made.

- To empower students, we must first empower staff. You cannot be what you cannot see. Therefore if students do not see such probing and questioning taking place, they cannot themselves begin to model or replicate this. If we want them to hold true agency in the classroom, this is a non-negotiable.

CASE STUDY 2: ORACY – DIALECT AND STANDARD ENGLISH

Sarah Bagshaw-McCormick, Associate Dean at Ambition Institute, @BagshawMc_Ed

The problem at hand . . .

In my context, students often viewed speaking as something they *just do*. They didn't have the language to talk about their own (or other peoples') talk. And they did not understand that people use spoken language for different purposes and audiences.

Additionally, students were from a North West town and had a strong local dialect that was strongly tied to their identity. When teachers talked to them about standard English and talk, students often felt criticised, or like more formal varieties of talk were not for them.

I wanted students to know more about spoken language. I believed that if students understood more about the ways spoken language is used, they would understand the power of spoken language, without compromising their identity. And, from this, be able to use a repertoire of spoken language, be able to identify, use and discuss different ways that talk can be used. Including developing their metalanguage to talk about their language.

Across a scheme of learning students were introduced to examples of talk featuring a variety of dialects (The Apprentice is great for this). The examples of talk created the need for language to describe the things they were observing. Students were introduced to the vocabulary of linguistics, then supported to apply it to a variety of contexts followed by being supported to use it to comment meaningfully on the ways language is used to exert power.

There were two areas of focus in these lessons:

Students needed support to develop their metalanguage, which encompassed:

- Subject-specific vocabulary
- Subject-specific ways of talking about talk

Students needed support to talk in groups to apply, process and explore spoken language, this included:

- Turn-taking – speaking and listening.
- Building on one another's ideas.
- Respecting one another's contributions.

Scaffold

Before we asked students to apply their new knowledge, we spent sufficient time teaching it to them subject-specific vocabulary, ways of talking about talk, and the processes needed to work in groups. We used opportunities for retrieval, and formative assessment, which meant that we knew that students had secure knowledge that they were ready to apply to a variety of contexts.

However, it was important that we supported *all students* to develop their ability to use the metalanguage to comment on spoken language. In order to scaffold students' application of this relatively new knowledge, we used knowledge mats and 'I do-We do-You do' to support and backwards fade the support we were providing students with.

Knowledge mats

Because the vocabulary and ways of 'talking about talk' were so new to students, it was important to provide them with an aide-memoire. We provided them with knowledge maps that included key vocabulary, sentence stems and thinking prompts/questions related to their prior teaching.

This meant that all students were able to engage in the tasks to apply this knowledge to new contexts. It gave students somewhere to remind themselves of the language and approaches they had learnt. And it supported students to get started, without asking their teacher for these reminders which can be a struggle with our students.

I do, We do, You do

We wanted students to move from being supported to apply new knowledge, to being able to do this more independently, critically and drawing their own conclusions. So we supported students to apply their knowledge across three examples of spoken language. Our focus was on power, so we selected videos of situations that showed power imbalances; in particular, we wanted to focus on the use of regional dialects in spoken language. When we talk about regional dialects we mean the words and grammar used in particular parts of the country.

To support this, we used two clips from 'The Apprentice', before moving onto a video clip of a conversation between more local speakers in a variety of situations. Each clip was no longer than five minutes. Transcripts of videos were provided, because transcribing talk was not the focus of the activity. This sequence took place over two weeks of lessons, with four lessons per week (with some flexibility for teachers to respond to their own class' needs).

I do – teacher led

Step 1: students watch the video. The teacher models watching the video, pausing and describing how spoken language is used to help students notice interesting ways spoken language is used. Depending on confidence of students, the teacher may use questioning to draw out vocabulary and comments on the way language is used.

Step 2: Students use this information to annotate a short section of the transcript, with a focus on using vocabulary.

Step 3: Students use this information and their transcript to support a group discussion; they are aiming to articulate what they noticed about the language, for example finding patterns in language. They practice using the metalanguage they have been developing.

Step 4: The teacher supports students to explore how the things they have noticed about language can be linked to power relationships in the video clip.

We do – students work in groups to go through the same process with a different clip

Step 1: They watch the video, pause and comment together.

Step 2: They annotate the transcription focusing on using vocabulary to label.

Step 3: They undertake a discussion to articulate what they noticed about the language choices, the patterns they have found and use metalanguage.

Step 4: They use prompt questions to help them make links between language choices and power relationships.

You do – independent

Step1: Students work individually to go through the same process with a recording of a local person in a variety of power situations. This transcript contains similar features of spoken language in power situations.

Step 2: Students can use the other member of their pair as a support partner.

Step 3: They use the same prompts and scaffolds as in the 'we' stage.
Step 4: I prompt and support students to enable them to independently transfer the knowledge and skills to this new context.
Step 5: We use their work to discuss the transcript together as a whole class. Students are able to provide their insights more readily after thinking this through.

Impact

When we began this work, our students (and some of our staff) were unfamiliar with talking about spoken language in these ways. But this scheme, and subsequent schemes in the curriculum that built on it, had a variety of short and long term impacts on our students.

As a result of the careful scaffolding, even the most reticent of students were prepared to use specialist language independently. I taught a very mixed attainment class, and I realised the impact of these lessons when my least confident student with a range of learning needs volunteered a response that utilised some challenging linguistic vocabulary they were introduced to in this sequence of learning.

As well as equipping students with new tools to talk about spoken language, students genuinely understood that spoken language is used for different effects in different situations. This was evident in lessons as they increasingly brought examples from their own viewing, or life experience, to exemplify the ways they could see that power and language are linked.

Importantly, it became clear that students were considering how they could use spoken language intentionally for different effects. In particular, they became more willing to attempt and adopt different registers. This is something we built on in the next term when they explored speeches, persuasion and planned formal speaking.

References

Gaunt, A. & Stott, A. (2019) *Transforming Teaching and Learning Through Talk: The Oracy Imperative*. Lanham: Rowman & Littlefield

Knight, R. (2020) *Classroom Talk: Evidence-Based Teaching for Enquiring Teachers*. St Albans: Critical Publishing

Littleton, K. & Mercer, N. (2013) *Interthinking: Putting Talk to Work* (First edition). London: Routledge

Turner, E. (2024) *Feeling the Curriculum in your Mouth – Thinking Flexibly*. Available at https://thinkingflexibly.com/2024/02/04/feeling-the-curriculum-in-your-mouth/. Accessed 28th July 2024

Voice 21 (2019) *The Oracy Benchmarks* (Online). Available at https://voice21.org/wp-content/uploads/2020/06/Benchmarks-report-FINAL.pdf

8 Scaffolding in practical subjects

> Principles of teaching and learning are taken, grasped, probed and comprehended by the teacher with the aim of applying them to the subject in question . . . any teaching and learning CPD needs to give time to distilling the evidence and best practice into the subject and context.
>
> *(Foster, 2020)*

We have seen many scaffolding strategies already throughout this book, which move away from a limiting approach to that of high challenge and support. However many of these strategies are classroom based and revolve around students' writing. What happens in a practical classroom where different scaffolding approaches are needed? Obviously some strategies are transferable, such as modelling and chunking, but what does this look like in the Music, D&T, Art, PE or a Drama classroom?

As we are both History teachers, we wanted to ensure that the real experts shared the most effective scaffolding approaches in practical and creative subjects. Therefore, the rest of this chapter will include case studies of effective scaffolding strategies from expert practitioners in these subjects.

CASE STUDY 1: NIKKI SULLIVAN, DEPUTY HEADTEACHER @NIKKI__SULLIVAN AND LAUREN BANNON, ASSISTANT HEAD POST-16

Scaffolding in dance

Introduction

The dance curriculum can be broadly divided into three key elements: performance, choreography and theoretical understanding. In this case study, we will explore how we can scaffold in the performance elements of dance lessons.

Eaton (2022) discusses the importance of anticipating barriers, using assessment for learning to elicit understanding, and making in-the-moment adaptations. This structure (one which helps to scaffold the thinking process around scaffolding!) is equally effective in practical subjects.

When we are looking to teach students a new piece of extended performance material, we analyse to see which sections will prove most challenging and where we might need to employ the strategies detailed below. We utilise our knowledge of our students and their varying performance skills to add an additional layer to our planning, whilst recognising that although we can plan these adaptations and have a road map to students performing confidently and independently, we have to use our students' in-the-moment performances to determine when to remove (but also build-back-up) the scaffolding we put in place.

The tools we have at our disposal

There are core elements of scaffolding for dance performance that can be returned to time and time again. In the same way that in written lessons we might utilise a writing frame or metacognitive modelling or chunking larger tasks down into smaller components within which we can build fluency, we similarly return to a core set of strategies in performance lessons.

The following list is non-exhaustive but highlights some of these core strategies:

1) **Altering the movement content**
   By slowing down the speed of the music, we are giving students more time to retrieve what they know the next step is, or to follow the teacher without getting behind. Scaffolding is reduced over time by gradually speeding up the sequence until it reaches the required speed. Where sequences have particularly challenging actions, such as a double pirouette, we can simplify this, for example, to a single pirouette, until students have built up the necessary proficiency.

2) **Scaffolded modelling to illustrate WAGOLL**
   Although we need to demonstrate to our students WAGOLL (what a good one looks like), and enable them to see the whole so they get a sense of the piece in its entirety (imagine supporting students in Art by only showing them a section at a time, without them seeing the piece in its entirety at the beginning of the process!), we also need to show them where they need to get to incrementally. If we are altering the movement content, we have to model these adaptations. Our modelling needs to be scaffolded in the same way that what we ask of the students is scaffolded. We need to model the dance slowed down. We need to model the single pirouette. We need to model the balance adaptation.

3) **Linking movement material with words**
   Although most dances are to music, and one of the things that we assess students on is their musicality, when modelling and rehearsing with students, we will not always count and will often use our words and our voice to support students' understanding of the phrases they are learning. For example, if the phrase was simply 'Step, turn, step, hop, run backwards for four counts', rather than just counting '1, 2, 3, 4, 5, 6, 7, 8', the teacher is able to say the

actions in time with the performance, thereby also giving students a linguistic scaffold that they can use to rehearse and to strengthen their memory of the material.

Where students need additional scaffolding, as opposed to just saying the basic action words, the teacher can use simile and imagery to support students in gaining a clearer understanding of what the movement should look like, for example, 'reach to the top shelf', 'sweep the floor with your fingers', again, in time with the music.

Not only this, but how the teacher uses their voice enables the student to get a sense of the dynamics of the movement – saying 'hop' loudly reminds students that it is a hop full of energy where high elevation is needed; saying 'run, 6, 7, 8' with a gradually decreasing volume and in a low pitch reminds students of the scurrying quality of the movement. Over time, we are able to remove more and more of these linguistic cues, as students use their own movement memory to perform the sequence.

4) **Reducing teacher modelling**
Linked with the point above about reducing the word prompts we give our students, as the class become more confident with the phrases, we have to model less and stand still more (sometimes the hardest thing for a dance teacher!). If we don't create this desirable difficulty for students, we are not enabling that all-important retrieval, only rehearsal. Initially, this can result in increased errors, but we have to push through this phase to ultimately decrease errors and increase independence over time.

5) **Chunking to build fluency in smaller sections**
We don't get better at running marathons by running marathons (Christodoulou, 2017). When teaching students an extended piece of repertoire, much like how a musician might seek to learn a piece of music, rather than building their performance ability of the whole piece, every time, we look to isolate sections and build fluency, before accumulating these sections into the whole. This also enables us to spend more time on those sections which are more challenging.

6) **Proactive technical skill building, for example, strength or flexibility training**

As a practical subject, there are some things that will not be possible if we do not have the necessary strength, flexibility, or balance (among other skills). In the same way that a student might struggle to write an essay if they are yet to master all the individual ingredients which go into that much larger picture, so too will students struggle to complete a longer, more demanding dance piece if they do not yet possess the necessary physical skills. And if a moment in a dance piece requires, for example, a great deal of flexibility, we do not build that flexibility by just repeating that phrase. We design specific drills and sequences that build up students' flexibility in order that they are, further down the line, better prepared to tackle those moments within the piece which require that flexibility.

Assessment for learning and mirroring

Dance teachers will not always have mirrors in their classroom in order to be able to observe their students moving whilst they model. Without filming, dance is transient. Not only this, but we need to be able to observe and feed back in real-time before mistakes become embedded. If one of the three key areas of scaffolding is assessment for learning, then mirroring and observation are vital skills in the dance teacher toolkit. Whilst facing the class and travelling to the left, we have to say right, whilst also evaluating our class and determining next steps. A pivotal part of enabling effective scaffolding in dance.

Who needs a lot more, and who needs a lot less?

In all subjects, we need to think about those students at the extreme ends of our bell curve (Wiliam, 2018) – those who need even more support for even longer, but also those who grasp the material really quickly. In some circumstances, in dance performance, we are not able to make the material more challenging, or longer, as it has to be performed exactly as prescribed, for example, by the exam board. Where these opportunities are not available to us, and where a conducive classroom climate has been created, we can enable our stronger performers to act as rehearsal leads for others in the class. This increases not only their performance ability, but also builds those skills often beyond the formal curriculum which students can take into their futures – it has been great to see some of our most confident performers moving on to leading dance groups both within and outside of school.

For those students who continue to need stronger scaffolding for longer, we then have to determine, as teachers, whether it is better to have a performance which is performed less confidently but better reflects the material to be learnt, or whether significant adaptations to the material need to continue. As Tom Sherrington discusses, 'some of us will need more help, more guidance, more time' (2019) – there is no 'right' answer, and knowledge of both the course/curriculum and our students shapes this decision.

To close . . .

In dance performance, effective scaffolding absolutely involves *decreasing* support over time. However, a huge part of successful scaffolding is also making the task smaller, simpler, more accessible and gradually *increasing* the complexity. The 'go-to' tools in our toolkit may be the same, but these specifics of the adaptations are always shaped based on the curriculum (movement) content, and the students we have in front of us. There are very few places to hide in a practical dance lesson – your work, your ability, your skills are always on display for everyone to see. Creating a collaborative culture where students recognise that learning cannot be easy is key. Through careful planning, observation and adaptation, we are able to ensure all students can succeed and feel successful.

CASE STUDY 2: SARAH YOUNG (HEAD OF MUSIC/SLE, @MRS_Y_MUSIC)

Scaffolding in music

For the expert musician, it is easy to forget how cognitively overloading the process of learning a musical instrument is for a novice. In a mixed Key Stage 3 (KS3) setting most students are novices with only a small portion of the cohort having formal tuition on a musical instrument. The National Curriculum for Music (2013) states that students should 'use staff and other relative notations appropriately and accurately in a range of musical styles, genres and traditions'. This creates a barrier for students as many have the preconceived notion of 'I can't read music'. Just like any other skill, it has to be taught and then practised by students. To be a good musician you don't have to be able to read music, but if students understand how to interpret the symbols on the stave, then other forms of notation (for example, guitar tab) become easier to understand and interpret.

We scaffold the approach to mastery of notation reading by introducing Year 7 students to rhythmic notation and the basics of crotchets and quavers, using strategies developed by the composer and educator Zoltán Kodály. Kodály's teaching principles were centred on his belief that 'music belongs to everybody' (The Kodály Approach, 2021), and he developed a system of syllables that divide the rhythm into the beat accurately. Music is a universal language, and the Kodály method maintains this notion, as opposed to derivatives that use animals, foods or drinks. This is important as English as either an Additional or a Second Language is prevalent in most schools, and we run the risk of alienating these EAL students.

Students need to understand that when we read music, we are interpreting two pieces of information through the symbols:

1. Rhythm
2. Pitch

Scaffolding in practical subjects 219

Rhythmic notation is introduced through the medium of percussion to perform 'Dodge', composed for the classroom by Kaboom! Percussion[1] (2024). Students learn that the note head and stem/beam are how we recognise what rhythm we should play. In Music lessons, 'I Do, We Do, You Do' exercises take a more practical approach with the teacher modelling the rhythm through clapping and saying the syllables out loud with the class then responding by joining in. Sometimes, this is done bar by bar; other times it is done in phrases. This approach of *I Do, We Do* allows the class teacher to listen for any mistakes before setting the students off to practise either individually or in groups. The example below shows the rhythmic pattern for 'Dodge'.

'Dodge', Kaboom Percussion (2018)

$$\frac{4}{4} \, \, \, | \, \, | \, \, | \, \, \, | $$
Ta   Ta   Ta   Ta   Te-Te Ta   Te-Te Ta   Te-Te Te-Te Te-Te Te-Te   Te-Te Te-Te Ta   Za

As a reminder of the rhythmic syllables, students annotate their music as above so they have a point of reference when they move to individual practice or to support practice homework. Once students can clap the rhythm in time with a pulse, we then decode the positions on the stave. In the case of 'Dodge' this is the direction the performer moves in. Before we begin to add the movement into the rhythm we have already practised, we use a key to decode the position on the stave. In my classes, I check for understanding by instructing my classes to move in the correct direction based on the note I point at. This allows me to check that students are interpreting the notation correctly before they move onto performing the piece.

'Dodge', Kaboom Percussion (2018)

M R M L   M M R M M L   M M M R M M M L   M M M M R

Before we start to formally practise the piece, we watch a performance by Kaboom! Percussion (2024) so students can see and hear what a good performance should sound like. We follow the same strategy for adding the movement as we do for introducing the rhythm to the students to embed a practice routine built on breaking the music down into smaller chunks and use the 'I Do, We Do, You Do' (Killian, 2015) approach to practise again.

Once students have had the opportunity to develop their understanding of notation reading, we then introduce pitched notation. When students first see the notation on the stave, we spend time questioning students on what they can already comprehend.

Extract from 'Amazing Grace'

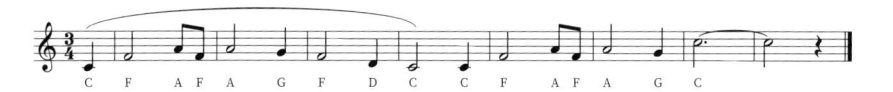

At first, responses are slow as students often feel daunted by the stave. However, using questions that link back to prior knowledge, for example 'What can we already read and interpret on the stave?', enables students to realise that they can already read most of the rhythms.

We then take the rhythm from the piece in isolation and identify how many beats we count in a bar. We do the same with any new rhythmic values and their syllable to ensure the correct division of the beat and then clap the rhythm, further embedding the chunking practice method that we had used when learning 'Dodge' (Kaboom! Percussion, 2024).

Rhythm only from 'Amazing Grace'

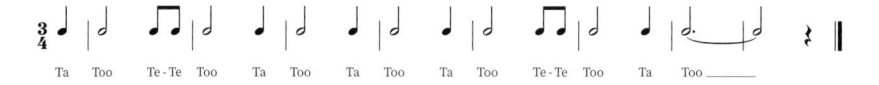

Once clapping accurately has been achieved, we then identify the position of the notes on the stave using the mnemonics FACE in the Space and Every Green Bus Drives Fast.

Mnemonics for reading treble clef notation

[Musical notation: F A C E — Every Green Bus Drives Fast]

The mnemonics start at the bottom of the stave and ascend from the bottom line/space to the top. Once students know these mnemonics, they can apply them to the notation to begin to work out the pitch names independently.

Emphasis is placed on the position of the note head rather than the stems and beams to enable students to comprehend that every time the note head is in a specific position on the stave, it is always that pitch in the Treble Clef regardless of the rhythm.

Skeleton of pitched notation for 'Amazing Grace'

[Musical notation: C F A F A G F D C C F A F A G C]

When students begin to play the melody on the keyboard, they are combining their prior knowledge of rhythm with the new learning of pitched notation and hand positions on the keyboard. Students are encouraged to annotate as much of the music as feel they need to. For those that already read notation, they might annotate any new pitches, usually those on/above the stave, but for most students they annotate everything. Above the music we also add numbers for which finger to use in order for the performance to be fluent, again reducing cognitive load for the student as using the correct hand position reduces the amount of movement needed on the instrument.

Fully annotated 'Amazing Grace'

[Musical notation with finger numbers: 1 3 5 3 5 4 3 2 1 1 3 5 3 5 3 5 and pitches: C F A F A G F D C C F A F A G C]

Before students begin any practical task, it is modelled by the teacher. We use our visualisers so students can watch what our hands do on the keyboard (or other instruments), so not only can they hear how the piece should sound but they can also see how to position their hands in order to give a musical and fluent performance.

Over time, students develop their competency in reading and interpreting music, and some students begin to annotate less in their booklets as they become more confident. Most students still choose to annotate everything onto the sheet music that they are given as a point of reference so they can focus more on their performances. Retrieval starters in lessons are often based on staff notation and require students to use the mnemonics to identify a series of notes on the stave. This is so they can continue to develop their independence and confidence when it comes to interpreting the notation on the stave. As students become more confident in interpreting the stave, they also begin to notice patterns in the music, for example, where melodic lines return, and often only choose to add annotations for finger technique as opposed to annotating each pitch.

By breaking the reading of staff notation down into the two component parts and establishing a clear practice routine in lessons, students build their confidence in accessing notation reading quite quickly, giving more time to developing their instrumental technique and accuracy and fluency in playing.

CASE STUDY 3: ELIZABETH JOHNSTON (CURRICULUM LEADER OF MUSIC, ART AND DT, @KPS_MUSIC)

Scaffolding in KS4 music composition

In 2016, the unit weighting of the GCSE Music exam across all exam boards saw the History and Listening exam unit increase from 20% to 40%. To accommodate this increase, the Composition and Performance

Units were reduced from 40% to 30% (Daubney, 2016). Alongside this change in weighting, fixed by Ofqual, all three units saw an increase in the skills and knowledge required to meet the assessment objectives and reach the top grades. Whilst I make no judgement here on the decisions to change the GCSE structure and specification, the result was that pupils were required to write more sophisticated compositions in less classroom time.

We observed that increasingly, lower prior attaining students, especially those whose performance element is either vocal (no requirement to read music) or drums (notation is rhythmic only) were struggling to access composition.

Although our initial teaching of compositional basics did not change (including rhythmic compositions, chord progressions and building texture and melody over a given chord progression amongst other skills), when the coursework element started and JCQ guidelines limiting individualised feedback kicked in, these students were struggling to know how to start their composition and felt overwhelmed by the 'blank' score and began to fall significantly behind their peers in this unit.

In November 2023, I attended a 'Composing with Schemata' Workshop at Newcastle University led by Dr Christopher Tarrant. His work on 'Schema Theory' draws on the work of Robert O. Gjerdingen's 2007 book, *Music in the Galant Style*, and starts with the premise that no single person can claim individual ownership of a simple chord progression: it is the metric, rhythmic, tonal, instrumental, tempo, textural, structure and melodic treatment applied to a chord progression that gives intellectual ownership. It was immediately clear that by offering a series of set scaffolded chord progressions would not only reduce the anxiety of how to start an effective composition, it could actually free pupils to apply greater individual creativity to their work by chunking the process into individual elements, starting with harmonic progressions.

224   The Scaffolding Effect

Dr Tarrant (2023) introduced students to a series of set chord progressions, each with variants and historical names:

E.g.:

Romanesca:

Prinner:

Fonte:

Monte

Ponte

Feneroli

Quiesecenza

Indugio

With each progression came a preferred structural placement. **Romanesca** typically comes first, **Prinner** typically sits second and leads towards a cadence whilst **Fonte** usually sits in the middle of a piece.

Monte is used for building tension, **Ponte** can be used to create a bridge: **Feneroli** is good for delaying an ending, **Quiesecenza** works well after a cadence and **Indugio** is great just before a **Ponte**!

Whilst this sounds initially complicated, in fact, what it is doing is scaffolding the compositional process by chunking the process into a series of building blocks for the students to create an effective composition with their own unique creative stamp.

Schematic pathways which students began to explore included:

i) Romanesca – Prinner (I) – Prinner (V):II: Fonte – Prinner (I) – Cadence

ii) Romanesca – Prinner (I) – Fonte – Indugio – Ponte:II: Romanesca – Prinner – Indugio – Cadence

iii) Meyer – Prinner (I) – Meyer – Prinner (I) Cadence:II: Quiescenza

iv) Meyer – Prinner – Indugio – Ponte:II: Monte – Indugio – Ponte – Cadence – Quiescenza

Ultimately, students can choose any order of schemata, any combination of instruments, any key, any metre, tempo and genre then decorate the structure rhythmically, ornamentally and melodically in any way they choose, giving individuality to each composition.

As part of the teaching process, modelling started with teacher-led demonstrations of schemata: I played different progressions and combinations of progressions on the piano. These were discussed, as a class, for efficacy, preferences and next steps.

This led to pupil improvisation in small groups (grouped according to instrumental combination not prior attainment) starting with a Romanesca followed by a Prinner before adding rhythmic, melodic and textural decoration. A model composition was shared with all pupils and collectively chunked by identifying schemata and uses of decoration.

Whilst the higher prior attainers were observed to be confident performing and improvising over schemata then notating, the lower prior attainers were initially supported with a combination of chunked teacher-led demonstrations both practical and notated: as pupils became more confident, they were asked to independently apply the newly learnt principles and processes to other schemata of their choice before linking the schemata together.

Compositing using schemata was introduced to all Year 10 pupils as a short, six-week project towards the end of 2023. Pupil voice at the end of the trial evidenced that 100% of pupils felt compositing using schemata made them more confident composers, 66% said they would be incorporating some elements of schemata into their compositions and 33% of the pupils (all lower prior attainers, singers and previously in the lowest third of the class) decided to use schemata as a foundation for their compositions.

Five months later, data suggests that in the Composition Unit, these lowest third pupils have improved their Forecast Grade by at least 1 Grade and 8% by 2 Grades.

CASE STUDY 4: DR JOVITA CASTELINO (HEAD OF SCIENCE, @DR_CASTELINO)

Scaffolding science practicals

Students expect to do practicals in Science, mostly having seen spectacular demonstrations at Open Evenings. Some might say it is the very essence of scientific study. In addition, secondary Science examinations assess investigative thinking and evaluation of required practicals.

There are two main purposes when we do practicals in Science:

- Students understand what is meant to happen during the practical, linking it to the theory they are currently learning
- Students have to know *how* to do the practical and correctly use the related equipment

And yet when a student hears it is time for a practical, they turn their attention to which group they will work in and how they can discuss the

Scaffolding in practical subjects 227

day's events with their peers. For some others, there is anxiety associated with having to use equipment they are unfamiliar with or glassware they may break. An additional issue around practicals is when one student does all the work while the others are excluded.

Adam Boxer's Slow Practical Method is the perfect scaffold for students, focusing their attention on the learning required to successfully complete a practical.

When I do a practical, the first thing I ensure is that the science behind the practical is absolutely secure. I explain the theory behind the practical and pose several questions to check that students know exactly what the practical hopes to achieve. This reduces the demand on student cognitive load during the actual practical so the main focus is on the mechanics of the practical itself, while the thinking occurs in the background.

On the day of the practical, I activate relevant knowledge using mini-whiteboards.

Students work in the pairs they are sitting in, which I think about when I work on my seating plan. Each member of the pair has a number, either one or two, so I can assign jobs easily.

For several practicals, students require the use of safety glasses so I usually pick a student to hand these out, while the rest stand up and clear their desks to make room for the practical.

The next step involves gathering equipment needed for the first step. For this, I model collecting the equipment needed and walk to my demonstration desk, usually at the front. I ask all the Ones to follow suit.

I model how to perform the first step, ensuring all students are watching carefully. I narrate what I am doing and why. Then, following a cue from me ('Your turn'), the students follow suit. When they complete the step, I call back attention to me using my school's cue for attention (3 . . . 2 . . .

1. . . STAR – Sit Up, Track the Speaker, Appreciate your classmates ideas, Rephrase the words of the person who has just spoken, Lemov, 2023).

This is repeated for each step of the practical and when recording observations and results. In each case, students work quietly, focused on the step.

If there are moments during the practical that require students waiting, for example when waiting for a reaction to end, I ask students to write down and explain their predictions for the practical on their mini-whiteboards. If the practical permits, I walk around and glance at these responses.

If the practical is straightforward or the set-up means mini-whiteboards cannot be used easily, I ask students to quiz each other on the current topic and the practical in their pairs.

When it comes to clearing away the practical, I ensure all students are listening carefully and then issue instructions whereby the Twos may bring forward used glassware and empty their contents into the waste bowl, and the Ones return equipment, in turn. In some classrooms, I have also used a one-way system to avoid crowding.

This way of doing practicals in the classroom has:

- Enabled students to focus on the purpose of the practical rather than using the time to think about unrelated matters.
- Focused attention on each step of a practical, allowing me to explain the need for the step and potential issues/improvements around it. This is incredibly useful as Science exams can include questions on a step within the practical method.
- Scaffolded the method behind practicals, ensuring all students can participate equally.
- Refined the whole process so practicals are purposeful and an important part of the curriculum.

As students gain in confidence with using equipment due to having used it several times, and when they have a greater understanding of the theory behind Scientific investigations, practical lessons can move closer towards independence. This is where, instead of modelling each step of a practical, students are given outcomes to achieve at strategic points of the practical method along with clear instructions to follow by themselves. This allows me to still move around the classroom, providing individual support if needed, or having discussions with students about the theory behind the practical.

Practicals have the power to demonstrate the theory of the curriculum and provide an insight into investigative Science. Using the Slow Practical Method (Boxer, 2018) to allow all students to participate and think about the methodology ensures the practical is purposeful and enhances the curriculum.

CASE STUDY 5: JO BLACKMAN (ASSISTANT HEAD AND DT TEACHER, @TEACHINGJB)

Scaffolding in DT

Student 1: 'Wow, this is cool!'
Student 2: 'Everything in here is terrifying!'

These are the two statements made by wide-eyed Year 7s when entering the Design Technology workshop for the first time. The first challenge is harnessing the enthusiasm to make everyone in the room feel happy and confident about working safely and producing a high-quality outcome.

Moving towards independence with a room full of students bearing saws can be a daunting and baffling concept, yet believe it or not, this is the best way to get them started in a practical setting. Our first project will be a small wooden box with comb joints. Now is your chance to demonstrate your own expert knowledge to a captive novice audience. Channel your inner Blue Peter presenter and show them one you made earlier.

I would start with an 'I do, we do, you do' demonstration.

I do: demonstrate to the whole class measuring, and marking out Part A of the comb joint, with the correct scribbled sections which act as the waste we cut away later. Throughout I will be checking for understanding with some choral response of key disciplinary terms, names of tools, specific materials, and measurements they need to use.

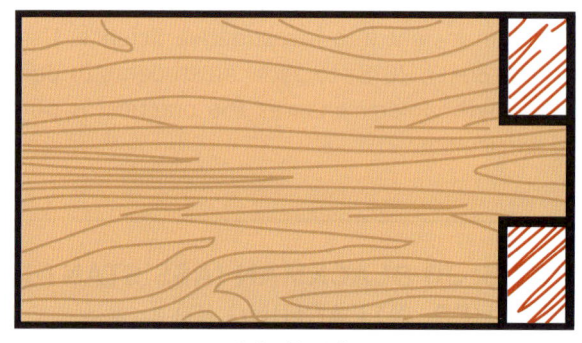

I do: Part A

We do: either the students make notes or complete a quick sketch on a mini whiteboard while we are still all together to check for understanding before they go onto the 'they do' task or we mark out Part B together noting the different waste section.

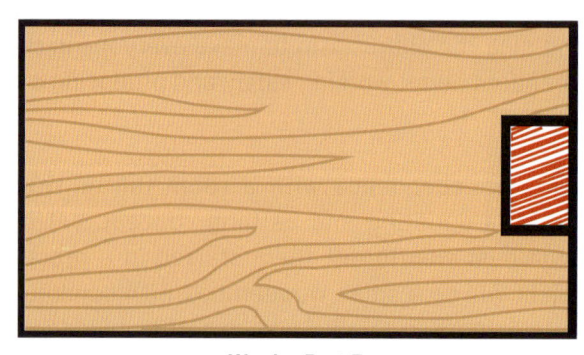

We do: Part B

They do: students then complete the marking out of the comb joint independently using their notes and I will ask them to use their classmates to quality control their work against the success criteria (displayed on the whiteboard).

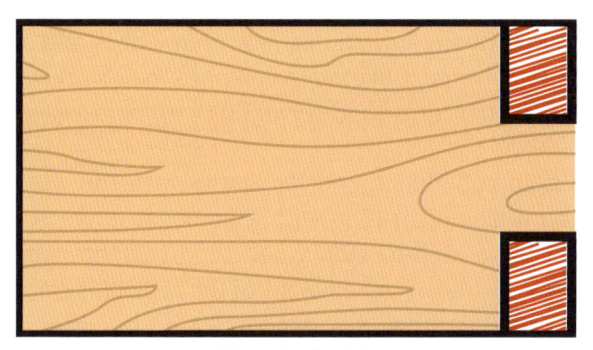

They do: Part A

The chunking of tasks is vital in DT. For a novice, the worst thing would be to model the measuring, marking out, and cutting of a wood joint in one go. I tend to break this down into one process at a time, returning the group to me to see the next stage. This means an active lesson with students ping-ponging between the teacher and their own work, but initially, it is essential to ensure what they're making is correct.

When it comes to sawing timber for the first time, it is essential to model the stance they need and ask them to mimic this before we cut anything, ensuring they use the whole blade to cut through the waste sections to ensure quality.

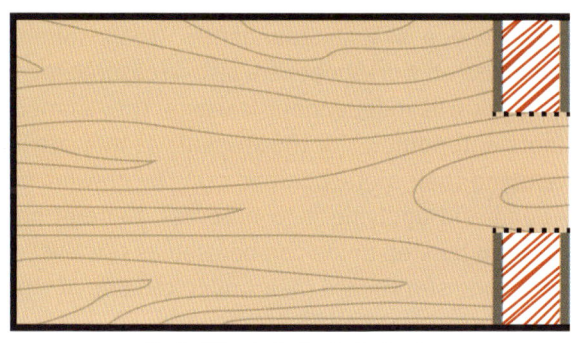

Dotted line to indicate first cuts

I keep every piece of material I use as a demonstration piece, so I have a set of tactile examples of each stage of a practical project. Students can use these if they struggle to master a skill, such as precision measuring of their comb joint. To avoid students using this as a crutch each time we complete tasks like this, after I have given them the piece to use once, I will direct them to the following example on my desk and suggest they take a photograph or quick sketch to compare their work with the practice piece to spot their error and correct it.

As students gain confidence and familiarity with the workshop tools, I can replace my demonstration with a demonstration from a further ahead student or a step-by-step video that students can watch and return to when required. If the element of the project is some CAD work, for example, engraving their wooden box lid on the laser cutter or 3D printing a small handle to assist with opening the box, I would flip this round and use the screen recording for all students first so they can work through it at their own pace and use myself or their peers to support if they hit an issue.

That said, in the workshop setting, with health and safety being such an important business, frequent verbal explanations and live modelling of using tools, machinery, and H&S rules need to feature with any level of experience to avoid complacency, these can be student-led with multiple-choice quizzes or Pictionary-like activities to help embed the information in long-term memory.

For any new design and make project I launch, I will always make short supporting videos as a way for students to catch up, develop an understanding, or practise a skill independently. Ikea-inspired instruction manuals or step-by-step worksheets are also a reasonable means to provide scaffolding towards independent learning; they immediately make the process more autonomous for the students as they are in the driving seat and developing their metacognitive skills by drawing out the information they need and applying it to progress. Generating an instruction manual or step-by-step guide can be used as retrieval exercises for students to recall and storyboard their understanding of a practical task for revision and as a formative assessment. How a retrieval task looks for students in Year 7, where I may provide word banks, partial drawings, and sentence starters, differs significantly from those in Key Stage 4, which may have one scaffold as a starting point. The outcomes can then help measure the understanding of the task; however, that is the easy answer for DT. Students describe their process and development of their project work either verbally or through writing. Then seeing the students independently translate these practical skills into their next project is the true measure of understanding.

CASE STUDY 6: KATE WALKER (HEAD OF PE/ ASSOCIATE ASSISTANT HEAD) @KATEWALKERPE

Scaffolding in PE

Throughout this case study, I will be referring to my subject as Physical Education and not simply 'PE'. This distinction will provide clarity regarding the inclusion of two specific elements of a practical Physical Education lesson that require scaffolding, both of which are equally important, yet one of them is often overlooked.

Physical Education differs from coaching because it emphasises not just the development of physical skills but also the holistic growth of students, including their social, emotional, and cognitive development. While coaching focuses primarily on improving performance in specific sports, Physical Education aims to instil lifelong habits of physical activity and promote overall wellbeing. To achieve this, teachers must develop students' declarative knowledge and procedural knowledge with equal emphasis.

In Physical Education, declarative knowledge is the understanding of the theoretical aspects of physical activity. This includes the rules of various sports, the principles of movement, the benefits of physical exercise, and the concepts of health and fitness. Students learn why physical activity is important and how it impacts their overall health and wellbeing. Procedural knowledge, on the other hand, involves the practical application of theoretical understanding. It encompasses the development of motor skills and the ability to perform techniques, strategies, and tactics correctly. This hands-on experience ensures that students can effectively apply their theoretical knowledge in real-life situations, fostering a more comprehensive and practical understanding of Physical Education. This approach significantly increases the likelihood of lifelong participation in physical activity or sports.

Both declarative and procedural knowledge are equally important in Physical Education, and therefore a scaffold for both elements need to be considered when planning a lesson. Here are some examples of how myself and my department scaffold for students, catering for a variety of physical and cognitive abilities.

Declarative knowledge:

Talking partners:

One effective strategy for scaffolding declarative knowledge in Physical Education is the use of talking partners. This technique encourages students to discuss key concepts and ideas with a peer, which not only reinforces their understanding but also helps them articulate their thoughts more clearly. By engaging in dialogue, students can explore different perspectives, clarify any misconceptions, and deepen their comprehension of the subject matter. This collaborative approach fosters a more inclusive learning environment where students feel supported in their learning journey, making it particularly beneficial for those who may struggle with the theoretical aspects of Physical Education. An important consideration here is who each student is partnered with. A mini-plenary/plenary runs smoothly when students speak to the same person throughout a scheme of learning. They can be paired with someone of a similar ability or mixed ability, both pairing provide challenge for each level of cognitive understanding.

Sentence starters aligned with the learning objective or learning question:

Using sentence starters that are closely aligned with the lesson's success criteria is an effective method for scaffolding declarative knowledge. These prompts help students structure their responses and reflections, keeping them focused on the key learning objectives. For example, when exploring the benefits of cardiovascular exercise, a sentence starter like 'One key benefit of cardiovascular exercise is . . .' enables students to organise their thoughts and ensures they address essential points. This approach is particularly valuable for helping students articulate complex ideas, especially those who may need additional support to fully express their understanding.

Incorporating the 'what', 'how', and 'why' questioning framework in a lesson can further deepen students' engagement. For example: *What skill have you learnt today? How did you perform it? Why is it important?* Students often require scaffolding at the 'how' and 'why' stages, as these questions demand deeper reflection. Providing sentence starters is crucial to ensure all students engage with these levels of questioning. Depending on your experience, these prompts can either be pre-prepared or written spontaneously on a mini-whiteboard during the lesson.

For instance, when teaching the straight drive in cricket and asking students 'how' they performed the technique, you might write the following on a mini-whiteboard:

- 'When performing the straight drive, my feet were . . .'
- 'When holding the bat, my hands were . . .'
- 'When I made contact with the ball, I . . .'

Allowing students time to discuss these sentence starters with their talking partners ensures that everyone can engage with the questions, preventing them from opting out due to a lack of understanding or confidence. This strategy helps all students to think critically about their learning, ensuring a more inclusive and reflective classroom environment.

Using the TA effectively:

The effective utilisation of Teaching Assistants (TAs) is vital in scaffolding both declarative and procedural knowledge in Physical Education. TAs can offer targeted support to individual students or small groups, helping to address gaps in understanding or skill execution. For example, while the teacher leads the class, a TA might work with students who require additional guidance, reinforcing key concepts or demonstrating specific techniques. This personalised support ensures that all students, regardless of their starting point, can make meaningful progress in their Physical Education journey.

It may seem straightforward, but I have observed many Physical Education teachers neglect to fully engage with their TAs, leaving them without clear instructions and often standing on the sidelines, feeling redundant. Building a strong working relationship with your TAs is crucial. Encourage them to change into active wear and empower them to actively participate in the lesson. As TAs may feel uncomfortable in a Physical Education setting, it is important to make them feel at ease. Share your scheme of learning with them, and communicate in advance – whether in person or via email – the key elements of the lesson where you would like their support.

Remember, as the Physical Education specialist, you are the expert in identifying and correcting technique. TAs may not have the expertise to do this, so it's essential to use their support effectively. Once you've set the group off on a task, ask the TA to oversee the class, ensuring everyone stays on task, while you provide verbal, visual, or manual guidance to those who need it based on your observations. This approach not only enhances the effectiveness of your lessons but also ensures that your TAs feel valued and integrated into the teaching process.

Procedural knowledge:

One careful consideration for PE teachers is the strategic use of competition. Introducing students to competitive scenarios before they've fully mastered a physical skill can be detrimental; their technique may deteriorate, leading to the formation of bad habits. This can significantly hinder progress and negatively impact the entire learning trajectory you're aiming to deliver.

When teaching physical skills, particularly in invasion games or team sports, it is often more effective to group students by similar ability levels rather than mixing abilities. This approach facilitates the application of scaffolds, which I'll discuss further below. These scaffolds align with the widely recognised STEP principle, commonly employed in Physical Education and Coaching.

Space: Adjusting the working space can either increase or decrease the challenge of a task. For instance, reducing the space typically raises the level of difficulty, while expanding it provides students with more time and room to practise the skill.

Task: Modifying the task based on ability levels ensures that students remain challenged yet successful, which is crucial for maintaining their motivation and effort. For example, when teaching the shot put, lower-ability students might start by throwing from their knees, focusing solely on upper body movement, while more advanced students incorporate footwork from a standing position. In football, some students might practise dribbling with their dominant foot while walking, whereas others work on using their non-dominant foot while jogging.

Equipment:

Adjusting the equipment to match students' abilities can also provide an appropriate level of challenge. For instance, in badminton, experienced students might use a standard shuttlecock, while less experienced students could use a balloon, giving them more time to focus on correct body positioning. Similarly, in basketball, a more advanced student might have specific spots marked on the floor to guide their foot placement for a lay-up, while a less experienced student could use a bench to step onto before aiming for the backboard and releasing the ball.

People:

Grouping students by similar ability allows for the application of scaffolds with greater ease. Within these groups, further adjustments can be made to ensure effective learning. This is especially useful in team sports or invasion games. For example, in netball, when practising a chest pass, a more advanced group might engage in a 2v2 or 3v3 scenario, while a lower ability group might play 3v1 or 4v2. It's important to overload the team performing the skill you want to develop. For instance, if you're focusing on defensive strategies, you might overload the defenders. In rugby union, when teaching rucking, this could involve having more attackers than defenders. Similarly, in handball, teaching zone defence might involve having more defenders than attackers in a conditioned game. This approach allows students at all levels to experience success while reinforcing correct procedural knowledge.

CASE STUDY 7: STEVEN KEARY (TEACHER OF PE, ECT MENTOR AND ITT MENTOR) @BIRKDALEHS_PE

Scaffolding in PE

Teaching students a skill effectively in PE can be a challenge because students have vastly differing prior knowledge coupled with very little experience of running on a curve. Some students can also find the bespoke tier two vocabulary a challenge. However, we isolate these elements, we model them, we practise them and we master them. Teachers are able to be responsive in when to introduce the next layer and can give really purposeful, live feedback that will not overload students' working memory.

One example of this chunked scaffolding approach can be seen in our teaching of athletics, specifically the 200m. In the summer term, students are taught how to run the 200m in a way that is consciously scaffolded to ensure that all students improve and achieve success. Modelling is also central to scaffolding students' learning because students need to have a clear mental picture of what success for each stage looks like, and it supports students' working memories. Students have previously learnt sprint and crouch starts, 100m and sprint technique on the straight. Therefore, they need to learn bend running to access the relay, 200m and 400m. This sequence outlines how we break the 200m run down to accelerate progress.

- Step one = outside to inside of the lane
- Step two = running to the apex
- Step three = increasing to the middle of the bend
- Step four = leaning to the left
- Step five = arm across the body
- Step six = full bend and accelerate out of the bend
- Step seven = full race

The changing room, an often neglected use of time, is where we firstly use video to give students detailed models through narrated videos. We do this to show what success looks like, but we also use this as an opportunity to front-load deliberate vocabulary instruction. We do not want key terms, either tier two or tier three to be a barrier to success, so we teach these explicitly, often using choral response to embed these prior to their application. Students are shown a looped video of Usain Bolt's 200m world record, which generates discussion points and questions. The demonstration video provides examples for the students to recall during the performance aspect of the lesson and allows us to front-load deliberate vocabulary instruction of key tier two terms such as apex, curve, bend, lean, acceleration and reacceleration. This allows us to pause and have discussions, tackle misconceptions and to ensure that all students understand and can use these terms accurately during performance.

> This scaffolded discussion leads on to students recalling prior knowledge of sprint technique and sprint start from previous lessons. We can then start to consider the similarities and differences between previous athletics lessons which allows students to realise the need to focus on how to run the curve. We then watch a second video which deconstructs the model for students, with narration at each stage. Using video here enables pausing to allow for interrogation and questioning about why the athlete is making choices at key moments: why do we use a staggered start? Why do we run from the outside to the inside of the lane? Why do we lean and bring our right arm across our body? This also allows for common misconceptions to be tackled before starting.

We then discuss the similarities and differences between the 100m and 200m. Since we are starting on a curve, we need to teach students how to navigate the curves of the track effectively. This involves leaning into the curve, maintaining speed and controlling the body's position to minimise lateral movement. We discuss why a staggered start is used; if you all start from the same place, then runners on outside lanes are running a further distance. We also discuss why we move from the middle/outside to inside to the apex of the corner; tight if you start inside of the lane, minimising distance and maximising speed.

Verbal scaffolding is fully exploited here as questions are posed and then students discuss with a strategically chosen partner having been encouraged to use the tier two vocabulary from earlier. Cold calling is then used to check for understanding and see where students need more support. In addition, choral response is often used here to allow the group to respond simultaneously, building belonging and embedding core knowledge.

Each stage is modelled before practice through teacher and student demonstration as the lesson progresses. This is done to ensure we can

Scaffolding in practical subjects 241

start the activity as soon as we reach the starting line. It is important to utilise this scaffold at this point so that students are aware of the high expectations and are supported to achieve them: they have now seen and discussed a professional on video, and seen a teacher and a student model to understand what success looks like.

Initially, students line up in group lines, positioned in the middle to the outside of the lane, angled in towards the start of the bend. They sprint fast towards a cone placed ten metres away on the inside of the lane where the bend starts. We repeat the activity numerous times to attempt to embed in long term memory and to build confidence.

For the next stage we increase the distance to about 20 metres towards another coloured cone at the top of the bend. We introduce a lean to the left between the first and second cones to assist with manoeuvring the bend. Before attempting this, we revisit the earlier model and discuss why a lean is important. We discuss how different lanes have different curve angles as lane one has one of the tightest turns, while lanes seven and eight have wider turns.

The next stage includes running to the apex - one of the tier two words introduced in the changing room - of the corner from the outside to the inside of the lane, leaning to the left as you manoeuvre the bend. It's important here that students bring their right arm across the body and keep the left arm straight whilst hugging the inside of the lane so this is something which is emphasised again. Once out of the curve and into the straight, the upper body should be back until it is straight and upright.

Students then practise running round the bend sticking to the inside of the lane and aggressively leaning to the inside of the lane, hugging the inside of the lane to maximise acceleration. In the early runs, we scaffold students by laying down small markers in the middle of the lane to cut off the outside part of the lane to ensure the students stick to the inside. As we increase the distance, the next step is to run round the bend further, 30m with the right arm coming across the body to assist with balance and running the bend more easily. We often spend time contrasting this technique with students' prior experience of the 100m sprint technique to show the difference between the arm movements and to remind the students that they must return to that technique after they have completed the bend.

The next stage is to model the same process as students learn to accelerate out of the bend. We encourage the students to exit the bend and kick start rapid arm and leg movements that they produced during the first 40m. They should feel a re-acceleration after gliding the bend which should be continued for the next 30 metres.

The final stage is to put all of the previous practice together (Outside to inside of lane – run to apex – increase to middle of bend – lean to left – right arm across body – full bend and accelerate out of bend – maintain acceleration down the home straight). The students will feel their efforts diminishing with about 50/60 metres to go. We encourage the students to focus on efficient sprinting form, keeping a tight core, and maintaining a comfortable stride and allowing recall on straight line sprinting technique from previous athletics lessons.

Throughout the lesson, as well as teacher assessment, peer assessment is also used to increase live feedback, maximise participation and to encourage every student to fully engage with the task. This sheet includes model photographs of each stage of the sprint to further scaffold for students and provide chunked feedback for each student at each stage.

Finally, we always follow up practice with further feedback in the changing room. For example, we use video analysis to provide athletes with visual feedback on their technique which helps identify areas for improvement and track progress over time whilst comparing their technique to professional athletes. This, combined with peer and teacher feedback, allows students to discuss and devise race strategies including pacing, when to accelerate, and how to maintain speed through the finish line.

CASE STUDY 8: FIONA LEADBEATER (PRINCIPAL TEACHER; EXPRESSIVE ARTS) @FIONALEADBEATER

Scaffolding in art

As an Art and Design teacher, I am very used to hearing from students (and sometimes even adults!) the ingrained notion that they 'can't draw'. Perhaps as a result of this, I think Art and Design teachers are particularly skilled in seamlessly scaffolding within lessons to allow even the self-perceived 'worst artists' to flourish. In this case study I will explore how demonstrations and the use of exemplars are particularly useful strategies to support reluctant artists as well as those genuinely struggling in the subject.

I'm unsure if the fact that Art and Design is such a visual subject makes scaffolding more difficult or in fact easier. However, the fact that student's work is often instantly recognised by peers from across the classroom, or publicly displayed in a way very different to a more personal written response in a jotter, means that it requires a certain bravery from students to create artwork. Instead it is often easier for pupils to self-deprecate. As a result, this means that teachers of Art and Design must use scaffolding as a tool to motivate and build confidence as well as skills and techniques.

Exemplars are an excellent way to inspire art students and are my go-to strategy in the scaffolding toolkit. The beauty of exemplars in Art and Design is that they are easily accessed by the majority of learners, because fortunately in a visual subject, they require very little literacy input. I've been using a WAGOLL (What A Good One Looks Like) at the start of lessons for a number of years now, and I find it really helps learners to visualise the goal we are working towards and the steps we need to take to get there. In creating the exemplar in advance, I am forced to work through the same process as learners. This is useful helping me to be more confident on the aspects which I need absolute clarity in my explanations and the area which might prove challenging. I usually use WAGOLL to prompt a discussion around success criteria and together, we unpick the aspects which make it successful. Another variation of this is creating a handout which breaks down the stages of the process providing photographs of the work in various stages of completion. This allows students to see the work in progress and the individual steps in the learning journey. This can be useful for those who might feel intimidated by the WAGOLL creating a more realistic and manageable task.

Personally, I think Art and Design teachers are the kings and queens of the Demonstration. Quite simply, we could not successfully facilitate learning without the skilled modelling process. Art teachers have always demonstrated techniques and material handing but over the course of the past few years this has changed significantly. Gathering students around a physical space and allowing them to see the staged process of drawing or watercolour painting is a hugely useful scaffolding tool. Pupils watch as the teacher draws, paints or creates. But it's not that simple. Effective demonstrations in Art and Design feature skilled narration by the expert, talking the children through the challenges of the technique and the thought process underpinning the creativity. I often verbalise where my eyes are looking and discuss how I am measuring to help students to think like an artist. The narration will also feature tips and tricks whilst all the time engaging the students through questioning and checking for understanding. Throughout my narration, I often give pupils choices and explain how different artists work in different ways. This provides further scaffolding to learners and another element of support which is tailored to their own learning needs and widens access for learners. During the Covid 19 pandemic, lockdown forced many Art and Design teachers to transfer their demonstrations to video, allowing every single pupil access to their own personalised learning instruction. The beauty of video demos is that students can pause and rewind as often as they need, providing invaluable, personalised support. Despite the initial time outlay in creating the video, these provide a legacy of learning which can be used again and again, year after year. Another result of lockdown was discovering my trusty visualiser, which is another way in which I demonstrate to learners in real-time. The overhead camera allows me to work on an art piece which is then projected onto the screen to allow the whole class to see close up details of my work, as I work. This is particularly useful for intricate details which can be magnified to help learners see more closely.

Great teachers use scaffolding without even thinking. But it is often these small, supportive adaptions which can make a world of a difference to learners. By scaffolding, we can allow everyone to achieve high standards, even if they insist they 'can't draw!'

CASE STUDY 9: LAURA SOLLY (ART TEACHER, @SOLLYLAURA)

Scaffolding in art

An array of challenges exist that hinder student learning and personal growth in art within secondary education. Upon entering Year 7, it is often noticeable that there remains a disparity in the level of pre-existing exposure to artistic content among students. The degree of familiarity that students possess with art history, materials, and techniques also varies significantly, resulting in hurdles in self-assurance as the subject is heavily visual in nature.

In my role as an art educator, I implement a three-tiered system of support to scaffold for students through the curriculum.

Layer 1 - Curriculum design and sequence mapping.
Layer 2 - Strategic lesson planning that incorporates techniques such as modelling, breaking down content into smaller chunks, and providing step-by-step guidance through tools like annotation writing frames and learning logs.
Layer 3 - Supplementary support for students needing additional assistance, including peer mentoring sessions outside of regular class time and a mix of blended learning. This entails peer feedback

and self-reflection, development of oral communication skills for expressing and refining ideas, and peer demonstration of successful problem-solving strategies.

Layer 1 – Curriculum and sequencing

Similar to other non-core subjects, our subject is only taught once a week necessitating a strategic approach to our content delivery. The Year 7 content is designed to cater to students with limited prior knowledge, focusing on fundamental skills such as shape and form. To further scaffold the curriculum we:

- Utilise easier-to-manipulate materials like pencils and coloured pencils initially.

- We gradually increase the complexity of tasks, materials, and techniques through scaffolding and incremental skill development (increased sophistication of skills over time).

ART – KS3 Key Concept Overview

	Autumn 1	Autumn 2	Spring 1	Spring 2	Summer 1	Summer 2
Year 9	Colour Theory Emotion Expressionism	Painting and Brushwork Cubism	Visual language Perspective and Surrealism	Interpretation and Visual language Composition and collage/ Pop Art	Sculpture 3D Pop Art	Perspective Architecture
Year 8	Painting and Brushwork Romanticism		Portraiture and Proportion Pre-Raphaelite		Colour Theory Impressionism and Post-Impressionism	
Year 7	Colour Pre-Historic	Line Egyptian	Shape and Tone Roman	Pattern Medieval	Materials and Gradients Renaissance	Materials and Textures Renaissance

FIGURE 8.1 KS3 Art Curriculum Map, Brunts Academy 2024, unpublished

- Incorporate frequent retrieval practice.
- Align our curriculum with the art history timeline, establishing connections between each period and note differences in visual language and spot themes centred on symbolism and concept.
- Assessments which test knowledge (multiple-choice questions) and skill, to inform future planning including scaffolding.
- Inspired by the 'Austin's Butterfly' technique of iteration, students are encouraged to refine and improve their work by re-drafting when necessary (Anser Chartered School, 2016).

Layer 2 – Strategic lesson planning: Practical tips on scaffolding within the art lesson

In my observation, a common challenge arises in the balance between skill versus outcome. While striving for aesthetically pleasing creations, it is imperative to prioritise the imparting of technical proficiency. Scaffolding methodologies should facilitate students in attaining equivalent levels of skill, rather than uniform outcomes. There are numerous effective strategies that can be utilised within the lesson to support student learning and enhance student confidence and competency. Below are some examples

- **Live modelling**. I have found that the inclusion of a variety of illustrative examples has proven to be invaluable. By breaking down the tasks during live demonstrations within the lesson using tools such as a visualiser, I am able to demonstrate the process of creating a piece of work. Using metacognitive oracy, I can then explain what I am doing and why, eliciting questions and responses throughout this modelling. Additionally, I capture the process through photography or recorded demonstrations as this can aid in creating step-by-step guides or a continuous reference scaffold for those needing extra assistance or absent students (as art is created over a sustained period of lessons). This means that as well as presenting a finished piece as a model of a desired result, students have been taken through the process to get there.

- **I do, you do, we do.** I have found that this model is effective in assisting students to achieve mastery of the subject matter. Furthermore, it fosters self-efficacy and minimises task anxiety, thereby promoting the development of student confidence.

  The 'I Do, We Do, You Do' instructional framework is founded upon the principle of incrementally transferring accountability from educator to learner. Again, a visualiser can be useful to demonstrate the 'I do, we do' parts of the instruction so that students can apply what is being modelled to their own art work.

- **Learning Logs.** I find these to be a valuable scaffolding tool as it can assist students in maintaining their attention on a central focus within their learning. A piece of art is produced over a sustained period of lessons and so in between lessons it can be that students forget the point of where they finished, what skill they were refining and how, and where to next take their piece of work. Students are able to use the logs to record their planning, their progress and their growth with a piece of work and across a broad range of pieces of work across the year, as well as set personal targets for development (teacher led in a tutorial format at the start of a lesson or self-determined targets). Feedback from my classes have shown that 75% of the sample population were positive about the impact of learning logs. The feedback highlighted the positive impact of the learning logs in aiding the students to effectively plan and achieve their targets. One student specifically cited the value of the learning logs in aiding memory retention of their academic goals, saying, 'It helped me plan my targets on paper and meet them at the end.' Another student said, 'It helps me remember what I am aiming for.'

Layer 3 – Supplementary support: Assertive mentoring

'The Education of Very Able Children in Mainstream Schools' HMI review 1992, identified several factors associated with high standards of work. Whilst we have moved away from the idea of 'this is what an able child does' and instead 'teaching to the top', their recommendations of what

Scaffolding in practical subjects 249

success looks like in art can be applied to the outcomes of all. These recommendations included careful monitoring and appropriate choice of resources, as well as encouraging students to think independently and take responsibility for their own learning using metacognition. One of the ways to apply these recommendations is to use 'assertive mentoring', a strategy which places the child at the centre of learning, based on a one-to-one dialogue between a student and mentor. Mentoring acts as a method of scaffolding because it provides mentees with additional tailored feedback and one-to-one guidance from a knowledgeable individual operating at a higher competency level. This feedback is provided by a relatable role model, enhancing the mentee's development. It is a way of working that enables us to focus on each child's strengths and areas of development and scaffold individual support relevant to that pupil. Assertive mentoring has the potential to effectively enhance students' academic performance, self-directed study abilities, and learning mindsets and ensure we teach to the top and ultimately empower students to take ownership of their progress.

I have incorporated assertive mentoring as a scaffolding tool (particularly at KS4) due to the limitation of time during lessons to offer personalised demonstrations and in-depth feedback, particularly at the GCSE level where students may be working on widely diverse projects within various specialisations. The process involves:

- Scaffolding mentor-mentee match ups. Matching KS4 students with KS5 students, based on their specialism or concept. This helps to ensure 'buy in' from students.

- Weekly mentor sessions. Mentors gave feedback on progress, modelled techniques and guided practice. They also pinpointed areas for improvement and agreed actions, with deadlines.

- Training. Prior to mentoring, I provided mentors with training which included a modelled mentor scenario and WAGOLL sketchbook examples of what a Grade 7,8,9 looks like. Pupils were shown an example of effective targeted feedback required on the mentoring record sheet. Mentors were provided with a variety of open and closed questions to use throughout their meetings. I also encouraged mentors to bring their own work to share their methods and experiences.

- Quality Assurance. I ensured the quality of mentor meetings through regular check-ins every half term. Additionally, I monitored data and the quality of books by documenting progress through photographing their work.

- Phasing the scaffolding support systems out systematically. In the initial stage, assertive mentoring would entail regular weekly meetings with a peer mentor, as well as extra assistance during lessons. This level of support could then be gradually scaled back to just in-class support. Subsequently, the mentor could be gradually phased out entirely, with the mentee instead being provided with a personalised learning log containing specific targets for each lesson by the classroom teacher.

With the implementation of this scaffolding method, we aim to foster autonomy and self-reliance in students by the end of Year 13. By this stage, it is expected that students will take ownership of their learning process and demonstrate proactive decision-making skills, with the guidance of the educator limited to assisting with relevant contextual cues.

Pupil voice was highly complementary of the assertive mentoring process as a scaffold. One hundred percent of students thought that being assigned a sixth form mentor was useful. One student said that it allowed them to 'get additional advice from a person who has already done their GCSE. Another student said that it helped them "process ideas" and support them with "new idea's"'. One student expressed that the peer mentoring 'Gave me good tips to help me achieve a higher grade as they are experienced'. Another student said 'I get inspired and I get help on how to develop my specific skills in more advanced ways'.

One thing to note is that mentoring's efficacy can be limited or even detrimental if the mentor withdraws from the process. It is important to be vigilant in selecting dependable mentors when utilising interventions to assist disadvantaged students.

Chapter 8 Self-Reflection Questions

Take a few minutes to reflect on the questions below and jot down your answers...

1 What does scaffolding look like currently in your disciplinary practice?

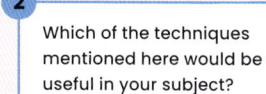

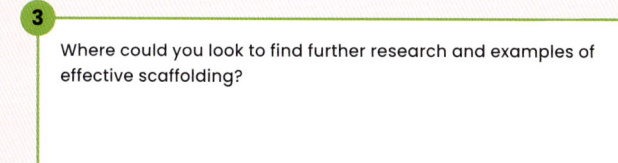

2 Which of the techniques mentioned here would be useful in your subject?

3 Where could you look to find further research and examples of effective scaffolding?

Note

1 Kaboom! Percussion are an Australian Percussion Duo whose principles are similar to that of the Kod·ly approach. 'At its core, Kaboom are passionate about harnessing the fun side of music, showing the world that music can be played with even the simplest of objects' (Kaboom! Percussion, 2024).

References

Boxer, A. (2018) The Slow Practical. *A Chemical Orthodoxy* (Online). Available at https://achemicalorthodoxy.co.uk/2018/12/06/the-slow-practical/. Accessed 27th July 2024

Christodoulou, D. (2017) *Making Good Progress? The Future of Assessment for Learning*. Oxford: Oxford University Press

Daubney, Dr. A. (2016) *Incorporated Society of Musicians*, March (Online). Available at https://www.ism.org/images/files/GCSE-music-comparison-chart-2016.pdf

Eaton, J. (2022) *EEF Blog: Moving from Differentiation to Adaptive Teaching* (Online). Available at https://educationendowmentfoundation.org.uk/news/moving-from-differentiation-to-adaptive-teaching. Accessed 3rd April 2024

Foster, P. (2020) *What Do Teachers Need to Know – Part 2- Pedagogical Content Knowledge* (Online). Available at https://curriculumteamleader.wordpress.com/2020/09/06/what-do-teachers-need-to-know-part-2-pedagogical-content-knowledge/. Accessed 15th July 2024

Gjerdingen, R. O. (2007) *Music in the Galant Style*. Oxford University Press

H.M.S.O. (1992) *The Education of Very Able Children in Maintained Schools: A Review*. London: H.M.S.O

Kaboom! Percussion (2018) *Tables*. Digital Score

Kaboom! Percussion (2024) *Team*. Kaboom Percussion (Online). Available at https://www.kaboompercussion.com/team. Accessed 8th May 2024

Killian, S. (2015) *The I Do, We Do, You Do Model Explained* (Online). Available at https://www.evidencebasedteaching.org.au/the-i-do-we-do-you-do-model-explained/. Accessed 8th May 2024

The Kodály Approach (2021) The British Kodály Academy, 8th December (Online). Available at https://www.kodaly.org.uk/the-kodaly-approach. Accessed 8th May 2024

Lemov, D. (2023) *Tracking in Classrooms: What I Really Think (and Wrote), Teach Like a Champion* (Online). Available at https://teachlikeachampion.org/blog/tracking-in-classrooms-what-i-really-think-and-wrote/. Accessed 27th July 2024

Models of Excellence EL Education-Austin's Butterfly: Building Excellence in Student Work (2016) (Online). Available at https://www.bing.com/videos/riverview/relatedvideo?adlt=strict&q=austins%20butterfly&mid=E3EA8A429DA76CA06035E3EA8A429DA76CA06035&ajaxhist=0

National Curriculum for Music (2013) (Online). National Curriculum for Music. Available at https://assets.publishing.service.gov.uk/media/5a7c869440f0b62aff6c2499/SECONDARY_national_curriculum_-_Music.pdf. Accessed 21st January 2025

Sherrington, T. (2019) *Rescuing Differentiation from the Checklist of Bad Practice* (Online). Available at https://teacherhead.com/2019/01/24/rescuing-differentiation-from-the-checklist-of-bad-practice/

Wiliam, D. (2018) *Creating The Schools Our Children Need: Why What We're Doing Now Won't Help Much (And What We Can Do Instead)*. West Palm Beach, FL: Learning Sciences International

9 Scaffolding at KS1/KS5

> Meeting children where they are is essential, but no good teacher simply leaves them there.
> *(NAEYC (National Association for the Education of Young Children), 2009)*

As the quote above suggests, a teacher's consideration of student ages and starting points is important.

Although many of the approaches to scaffolding are applicable at any Key Stage or age range, there is good argument to say that KS1 and KS5 have unique contexts which require the adaptation of more commonly used scaffolds as well as the use of additional other scaffolds.

Indeed in the seminal scaffolding paper, Wood, Bruner and Ross found that there were differences in the behaviour of the different age children in the study, and in what scaffolding was needed even between 3–5 year olds; 'Clearly, different age groups required different levels of assistance' (Kirschner & Hendrick, 2024).

Therefore, we felt case studies of specific scaffolding at KS1 and KS5 would be important and useful to include in this book.

EYFS/KS1 CASE STUDY 1: KIERAN MACKLE (DIRECTOR, ALTA EDUCATION, @KIERAN_M_ED) SCAFFOLDING: EARLY NUMBER (COUNTING)

Situated in the expanse between our evolutionarily advantageous sense of quantity and a more advanced understanding of mathematics, learning to count marks an important milestone in the lives of most humans. It is a transformational event and, if we are to accept the conditions described by Meyer and Land (2003), it follows that crossing this threshold, in addition to irrevocably altering our self-perception, should be very difficult indeed.

Children find learning to count troublesome because, beyond the surface of this seemingly rudimentary process lies the skilful weaving of several disparate elements of knowledge into a unified understanding upon which much else depends.

Anyone who hopes to teach a child to count must be cognisant of the existence of these elements (the principles of counting) and what to do when a child needs to develop one or more to count accurately and efficiently. When securely in place, these principles combine to form the process we recognise as counting. When one or more are missing, the results can range anywhere from miscounts to reluctance or total refusal to engage with the process of learning to count.

For the purposes of this case study, we're going to focus on what is traditionally considered the second of these principles, one-to-one correspondence. The idea that a value of one can be assigned to an item (object, sound, concept) and that each item in a given count has a value of one, and only one.

To ascertain where specific difficulties lie, we must begin by watching the child(ren) count. If one-to-one correspondence is yet to be developed, then we are likely to see children assigning a value of one to multiple items, arriving at a cardinal value less than they should have. For example, when counting four marbles, assigning a value of just one to two of the marbles will result in a count of three and an improper evaluation of the sum.

When teaching children to count, there is no greater scaffold than clear and concise modelling in a range of different contexts, over an extended period. However, when focusing on one-to-one correspondence, there are several additional layers we can add to our modelling. These layers are predicated on the continua which exist within counting and which, effectively, signpost the road towards proficiency.

The first continuum is a matter of abstraction and distance. Quite often, the development of sensory concrete knowledge is prioritised over the utilisation of integrated concrete knowledge (Clements, 2000), but in the case of developing one-to-one correspondence, having something to manipulate is highly beneficial and should in fact be prioritised. Children will benefit from physically moving each item as they assign a number name to it. For when they do, it is much more difficult to assign a value of one to multiple items. When counting three multi-link cubes, this may look and sound like this:

Adult takes cube and moves it to a predetermined place

Adult: One

Adult takes cube and moves it to join those already counted

Adult: Two

Adult takes cube and moves it to join those already counted

Adult: Three

Adult: Now it is your turn. Move the cubes and count them.

Child takes cube and moves it to a predetermined place

Child: One

Child takes cube and moves it to join those already counted

Child: Two

Child takes and moves it to join those already counted

Child: Three

Although they may not yet have developed a sense of cardinality, the trained observer can see that they have accurately assigned a value of one to each cube, and the scaffold has been effective in allowing the child to rehearse this principle in that moment. More adult-guided rehearsal will, likely, be needed, but success has been achieved and an accurate model provided.

The second continuum is a matter of presentation. Some of the ways we can group items are, quite simply, easier to count than others. The arrangement considered to be the least difficult to count is, perhaps unsurprisingly, a straight-line arrangement. It makes sense that an arrangement with a clearly demarcated start and end should be the easiest for novice counters to navigate and so, when scaffolding, we should consider this our first port of call when supporting children in developing a sense of one-to-one correspondence.

As children move towards greater proficiency and autonomy, we should then seek to introduce (and model counting at) the different milestones across the continua of distance and presentation. Each represents a step closer to independent and perpetual counting upon which the child(ren) can rely on as they engage with the rest of mathematics.

In order of complexity, beginning with the least complex, children should learn to assign one-to-one correspondence when touching, pointing and, finally, looking. Each time the distance between them and the items being counted increases until they reach the point where they can count anything their eyesight will allow. It sounds simple but at each juncture we should be modelling, correcting, discussing and developing alongside the child(ren).

The same is true of presentation. Once a child can count items presented in a straight line, we should then provide opportunities for them to count those arranged in a tightly controlled group (an array, for example), a dispersed group with little 'formal' arrangement and, eventually, a circle. The boss level of all counting arrangements.

If a child can accurately count items arranged in a circular formation just by looking at them, it is very likely that they have a fully formed conception of the one-to-one correspondence principle. In fact, they have likely developed a sense of all five principles, but this serves to demonstrate the nature of learning to count. Five elements woven together to create the foundations of number, calculation, algebraic reasoning and indescribably much more.

It is next to, if not entirely, impossible to isolate individual principles but accurate, explicit modelling, with an awareness of the continua, the gradients of difficulty and potential challenge, at the heart of the principles of counting are almost guaranteed to ensure that every child in receipt of such instruction not only learns to count but thrives throughout their time in school and learns to love mathematics for the beautiful, complex body of knowledge that it is.

CASE STUDY 2: SOPHIE MORRIS (DEPUTY HEADTEACHER) SCAFFOLDING: EARLY WRITING

Scaffolding student work in Key Stage 1 (ages 5-7) significantly differs from the scaffolding you may use for older students. This is largely due to the student's developmental stages, cognitive abilities and the learning needs that are specific to younger learners. At this early stage in their education, students are very much still developing their basic tools of communication; they are at the inception of learning to express themselves verbally, to record their ideas on paper and to read in the most basic sense of the term (still sounding out and decoding the phonic code rather than using reading to enhance their learning as they will in later years). Very much in the earliest stages of authorship, students in Year 1 and 2 are often still developing the physical muscles required to sit up, hold a pencil and write. Once the initial dynamic tripod grip is fully mastered, the art of handwriting then requires fluidity, speed, accuracy and the ability to maintain all of these over longer periods of time. Not to mention, pupils need to have a grasp of and think about grapheme correspondence, ideas for their own writing content and an understanding of basic grammar rules. Therefore, when teachers are designing writing opportunities for pupils in younger years, they need to consider that just the physical processes of trying to write can, in themselves, create cognitive overload. There is just so much for a young student to factor in and consider when learning to write. This is where careful, well-considered scaffolding can really unlock the complexities of writing for young students, enabling them to access the world of written words and experience success from the very beginning.

Caveat: For ease, I am going to link my scaffolding description to a specific example, a Year 1 Writing Unit linked to Little Red Riding Hood which used the traditional text alongside modern retellings. One of the written outcomes was a character description of the Big Bad Wolf.

The process of scaffolding a piece of writing in an English unit will often begin before the student ever picks up a pencil to write. Having started with a simple writing stimulus (more often than not this is a picture book, in this case 'Little Red Riding Hood'), we immerse the students in its language, themes and characters across a few days, ensuring that the students have an in-depth understanding of the story. You cannot write about that which you do not know, and this is especially true of younger students who are not yet capable of abstract thinking. Next, students will begin to orally rehearse the language, using drama or puppets to verbally engage with and explore the story, experimenting with the new vocabulary in context. At this stage we heavily model the process of how to use the resources, the structure of the story and the language to use. We scaffold this process using picture prompts of what to talk about (e.g. pictures from the story or of the character). The talk itself is also scaffolded with guidance as to what they might say, using key vocabulary symbol prompts and oral sentence stems to support, structure and develop student thinking as they rehearse the language that they will need for writing.

Next, we begin the process of recording their ideas, starting to plan out what they will write. We use a variety of basic scaffolds to support this planning depending on what they are writing about. These include story maps, sensory grids and mind-maps. In the case of the Big Bad Wolf, we gathered vocabulary around a character outline, considering, in turn, the different parts of his body and how best to describe these, adding adjectives around the body shape. At this point in the writing process, the recording is kept to a minimum with the focus being on the thinking process rather than the physicality of writing. Therefore, the layout of the planning scaffolds is always simplistic and easy to use. We regularly use the same planning proformas across the year so that as the year progresses, students become confident in how to use them to scaffold their ideas. To minimise cognitive load and to scaffold any writing opportunity, the students always have handwriting guides and phonic mats available to them.

When approaching the writing task itself, modelling is essential to ensure that students have real clarity around what they are being asked to do and how to go about approaching a task. With young students it is important to not only model how to write and what to write but also, how to physically use the scaffolds provided. For the Big Bad Wolf writing lesson, the students had access to a variety of sentence stems alongside their planning sheet. In modelling this lesson, I carefully demonstrated the process of choosing a sentence stem to start a sentence, then choosing an area of the body to describe and orally merging these ideas into a cohesive sentence out loud before modelling the recording process. For those that needed it, there was also a partially started character description allowing the students to start the writing process as a cloze task and then gradually, through a faded scaffolding approach, lessening so that they were more independently writing. Students also had the option to record their ideas on a whiteboard, allowing them to easily experiment with both word order and spelling without the pressure or finality of having recorded it in a book yet. Once satisfied with the sentence on their whiteboard, students can then transfer it to their books and begin the process again. It is important to note that effective scaffolding with younger students often needs to be highly adaptive to their immediate needs and frequently adjusted based on their responses and understanding. Much of the scaffolding that happens within a Key Stage 1 classroom is verbal or on whiteboards, where an adult may help to orally structure an idea or a sentence aloud with a student.

This 'paint-by-numbers' scaffolded approach to early writing enables emerging writers to build and play with sentence content and structure without the fear of a blank page or not knowing how to start or what to write about. As the year has progressed, students have become more and more independent and able to structure their own descriptive writing work, mentally referring back to previous sentence scaffolding put in place at the start of the year as they consider how and what to write in each sentence. In a recent piece of writing using our senses to describe a storm, students demonstrated a sound understanding of how to begin their sentences and describe aspects of the rain, lightning etc., applying their learning without the heavy sentence scaffolding.

CASE STUDY 3: SARAH DENNIS (RE LEAD, @SARAHDENNIS_RE) SCAFFOLDING: KS1 RELIGION AND WORLDVIEWS

There are several barriers which students at KS1 face when starting to understand Religion and Worldviews, also known as RE (Religious Education). Barrier one is the transition from EYFS to KS1. In EYFS, most things are concrete (objects to touch and see) and RE is also not taught as a discrete subject on its own, rather it is part of a wider area of learning titled 'understanding the world'. Moving into KS1, RE is then taught as a discrete foundation subject which means firstly establishing what we mean by the term 'religion' (the idea of worldviews and that it can be organised into a religion or a personal belief), alongside introducing abstract concepts and unfamiliar words (which are often hard to pronounce and tricky to read), can be difficult for students to grasp.

Barrier two is that for students to then develop their understanding of RE, they need to gain more substantive knowledge, form links across differing religions, and develop their own worldview. This in itself is a simple thesis of what students need to do. However, a complexity in knowing how to craft and create a sequential RE curriculum that puts that into action is that there is no National Curriculum for RE. However, the recent RE Ofsted research report (2024) has stated the characteristics of a good RE curriculum means 'pupils can build an informed conception of the place of 'religion' and 'non-religion' in the world. They [teachers] make thoughtful decisions about which narratives, texts, case studies and traditions pupils will explore in depth. They enable pupils to discern between different types of claims that different thinkers have about religion and non-religion. They plan carefully for how pupils can use the content of the RE curriculum to reflect on their own position, including their personal beliefs and attitudes'.

Barrier three is that alongside the growing knowledge of RS is the need for them to be able to communicate in a disciplinary way. In KS1, students are emerging writers, and so expressing their knowledge in a written format often does not do their RS knowledge justice. They can often articulate impressive growing knowledge verbally, but the mechanics of writing (such as the physicality of holding a pencil or pen, letter formation etc.) means that the process of producing print results in knowledge getting lost in translation. We know that we have two competing domains when writing; the literacy domain and the knowledge domain. Overtime, we scaffold student's writing and knowledge development so that they can harness both and put both to work simultaneously. So in the long term process of achieving this, how do we create opportunities for students to articulate their growing religious and worldview knowledge when they are novice/developing writers?

Whilst these are significant barriers, there are a range of scaffolds that will ensure that KS1 students can access RE content, remember and link knowledge over time and communicate in a disciplinary way. Within this case study, the role of physical objects as scaffolds will be outlined in terms of how they can be powerful in supporting the students to recall and connect growing knowledge, as well as provide scaffolding prompts during oracy based activities.

Scaffold 1: Suitcases of religious tools and stories

To support the students' learning I have three suitcases with persona dolls, 'Belonging and Believing' books by Gill Vaisey and artefacts or objects used in religious worldviews. Each suitcase and their contents function as a tangible scaffold, helping to scaffold the EYFS to KS1 leap. Touch is still very important in KS1, and so having the objects for them to touch, inspect and hold (and sometimes smell!) means that not only are they developing episodic memory, haptic memory (supporting later retrieval) but that they are also able to view the object in different ways than a simple visual could, such as the spice pot in the Judaism suitcase which is held by the students, they remove the lid and smell the clove and nutmeg inside. When I first use the suitcases, I use a task called 'I know, I think, I wonder', which incorporates modelling and oracy scaffolds into it. I begin by modelling the process of exploring and investigating an object where I talk through what parts of the objects or things that I notice which might give me clues about the worldview. Once this is modelled and the readiness is there, scaffolded discussions between peers then take place using the sentence stems where they hypothesise what they think the object will tell them about a worldview. Having oracy scaffolds that include formative wording ('I think, I wonder') means that the initial discussions of the contents of the suitcase are accessible to all students as there is less fear of 'getting it wrong' and instead being open to 'having a go. Additionally, having talk partners means that they are able to discuss their initial thoughts with their peers and refine them before feeding back to the class. This task is effective in supporting students to extend their oracy skills as they think, listen, and talk with the concrete objects there to scaffold their thinking and questioning. By approaching it in this way, the students are developing deeper knowledge of the worldview and have haptic memory to help scaffold the written work which comes later.

As we progress through the curriculum and learn more about differing worldviews, the suitcases act as a scaffold for retrieval and for comparing and contrasting religions. When carrying out knowledge recall, the students have to remember what objects were in the suitcase for the religion we have just been studying. They then have to discuss the links between the objects, persona doll and the real child in the Belonging and Believing book. Having the objects there to hold helps to tap into the episodic and haptic memory, and prompt prior knowledge during retrieval, aiding the transition of information into long term memory overtime. When knowledge of each religion and worldview is secured, I then introduce the links between the religious worldviews once the students have a good sense of each religion. We are able to hold objects up side by side and see similarities and differences between Judaism, Christianity and Islam. Students are able to take part in matching activities, matching the correct object to the correct religion or take part in 'find and fix' where they have to move the incorrect object to the correct suitcase.

Scaffold 2: Student choice of written and visual scaffolds

When progressing to a written RE disciplinary task, students draw upon the knowledge built up through the suitcases and the linked discussions. To support the students to then transform their knowledge into a written form, written scaffolds such as sentence starters (given out as word mats) can be used and/or visual ones such as wordbanks (created on InPrint) which students then annotate. It may be the case that additional scaffolding is needed for some weaker writers, and so it can be that they can first draw items and keywords which I then annotate for them with their spoken ideas. This then creates a crib sheet of their ideas which they can then use alongside sentence starters to help build their writing. The writing process that I use begins with me using a visualiser to model how to use the written and visual scaffolds. Students next use their whiteboards to formulate their ideas, and following this, talk partners then verbally construct their knowledge into sentences using the written and verbal scaffolds to aid this. They then can begin to write their sentences or annotate the images. As students write, I circulate the room and live mark their work, providing cues and prompts to those students who need it.

To help support disciplinary writing fluency, I keep the sentence structure similar each lesson and thread recalling writing structures into our retrieval process. It's perhaps obvious to say, but it's important to use words that can be decoded by KS1 students, but that this is balanced against being ambitious and the tier 2-3 RS vocabulary. Therefore, having a key word and sentence starter mat to hand out means that you can further support students who are struggling.

The impact of using the suitcase of objects and scaffolding the disciplinary writing process is that students are remembering more over time and communicating this growing knowledge in a disciplinary way, verbally and in extended writing. Something to consider is that when students are progressing from KS1 to KS2, the use of physical objects can be reduced as the use of visuals can be further incorporated into lessons in their place.

KS5 CASE STUDY 4: PAUL CLINE (DIRECTOR OF TEACHING AND LEARNING, @PAULCLINE_PSY) SCAFFOLDING: SUPPORTING STUDENTS WITH MATHS IN KS5 PSYCHOLOGY

One of the things a lot of students in Psychology find tricky is mathematical calculations such as for inferential statistical tests. However, it's the kind of question that fairly reliably comes up on the exam papers each year, and it's one of the few areas in Psychology where there actually are definitely correct answers. The calculations themselves really aren't that difficult (fiddly, yes, but not hard) and therefore worth investing the time in teaching students how to deal with these sorts of questions confidently. This requires scaffolding in a number of different ways.

The Scaffolding Effect

First, students would be presented with the formula (in this example it's for the Mann-Whitney U test of difference):

$$U_a = n_a n_b \frac{n_a(n_a + 1)}{2} - \Sigma R_a$$

$$U_b = n_a n_b \frac{n_b(n_b + 1)}{2} - \Sigma R_b$$

This can look quite intimidating at first! While students don't have to memorise this formula (it is provided in the exam paper), they do have to know what all of the bits mean, and how to apply it correctly. Therefore the first step is to explain what each term refers to, and have this highlighted and annotated on the board – with students having their own copy to annotate too (Cline, unpublished).

$U_a = n_a n_b \frac{n_a(n_a + 1)}{2} - \Sigma R_a$ $U_b = n_a n_b \frac{n_b(n_b + 1)}{2} - \Sigma R_b$	U_a = calculated value for condition **a**
	U_b = calculated value for condition **b**
	n_a = no. scores/PPs in condition **a**
	n_b = no. scores/PPs in condition **b**
	ΣR_a = sum of ranks for condition **a**
	ΣR_b = sum of ranks for condition **b**

The next step is to transfer the n values (no. participants in each group) onto the data table they are going to be working from (*italicised* in the example below). This acts as a scaffold as they are not continually flicking from one resource to another, which would otherwise increase cognitive load (via the split attention effect). A further way to reduce cognitive load is that for the purpose of learning how to do the calculations, data are presented entirely in the absence of any context (i.e. it doesn't matter at all what the scores actually represent) (Cline, unpublished).

PP	Group A ($n_a = 5$)	Rank A	Group B ($n_b = 5$)	Rank B
1	7	7.5	4	3
2	6	5.5	3	2
3	8	9	6	5.5
4	9	10	7	7.5
5	5	4	2	1
		$\Sigma R_a =$		$\Sigma R_b =$

I would then model how to complete the calculations for the first part of the formula (calculating U_a), breaking it down into chunks, making sure everyone is following along with me, and questioning as I go. I'd also make sure I was using gestures and clear instructions to explicitly direct attention to different bits of information as needed. For example, for the first step:

> 'How many pps in group A? (point to where this is labelled on the table) How many in group B? Okay, so that's 5 in both so the first part of our formula (point to the formula) is just 5 x 5. Which is...?'

This would continue until we have the three different elements of the calculations for U_a (which in this instance leads to a simple sum: 25 + 15-35 = 5)

We would then repeat the process for the calculation of U_b, but this time with students taking more of a lead in the process (moving from I to We in terms of modelling):

> 'Ok, what's the first thing we need to do? Right, N_a times N_b - everyone do that and hold up answers on your whiteboards... Great. What next... show me the next bit...' and so on.

Now we move onto the 'You' phase of modelling where students need some independent practice to build their fluency. However, experience tells me that just setting them off on their own inevitably leads to all kinds of problems, and so there is still a level of scaffolding required. First, they get another example dataset to work on, with a written set of instructions that match the process we've just been through together (Cline, unpublished):

Example 2

PP	Condition A	Rank A	Condition B	Rank B
1	12	10.5	9	4
2	10	6.5	8	2
3	12	10.5	6	1
4	13	12	11	8.5
5	14	13.5	14	13.5
6	16	15	10	6.5
7	11	8.5	9	4
8	18	16	9	4
		$\Sigma R_a =$		$\Sigma R_b =$

1. Add up the ranks for condition A to give you ΣR_a and for condition B to give you ΣR_b
   For U_a:
2. Multiply n_a by n_b
3. Multiply n_a by $(n_a + 1)$
4. Add the results of step 2 and 3
5. Subtract ΣR_a from the result of step 4
6. The result is your calculated value of U_a

7. Repeat steps 2–6 for U_b (you will need to use n_b x (n_b +1) at step 3)
8. Choose the smaller of two values (U_a or U_b) – this is your calculated value

For some students, writing their workings next to each step will also be a helpful scaffold, whereas those who are more confident can just write it all out in one go at the bottom. I offer a further level of scaffolding by circulating as they work, spotting any problems either with the process (e.g. they've missed a step) or calculation (e.g. they've made an error adding something up). Having taught this subject for a long time, I'm conscious of the likely misconceptions and errors they'll make and can pre-empt these. During these checks for understanding, if I see several students making errors, then I might pause the whole class to give corrective feedback. This may also involve using whole class questioning and peer responses to correct the thinking of the several who are struggling (*'Everyone show me on your whiteboards what you got for step 5. . . Ok some of you have different answers . . . who can talk me through how you got there . . .'*).

Following this, the students then work through a further set of examples during which the scaffolding is gradually withdrawn by shortening and then removing the written instructions for how to follow the formula. This also includes varying the difficulty of their calculations (e.g. presenting them a dataset with unequal group sizes which makes the calculations a little more complicated). Eventually, they should get to a point where they can complete the calculations with only the original formula plus a data table in front of them. Once this is secured, the final stage is to present them with an example set in the context of an actual study so that they are considering what the data means in real terms, rather than just an abstract set of calculations.

In the past I would have done some of the steps outlined here but in a far less scaffolded way. I tended to assume that if I simply showed them the whole process once, then gave them clear instructions to follow that they'd all be fine. Some of them were! But a lot of them got lost somewhere along the way, either during the initial demonstration or working independently. Quite often this led to them simply leaving out these kinds of questions on the exam, throwing away valuable marks. By carefully scaffolding throughout the process and breaking down the process into discrete steps, I've seen students grow in confidence. This includes saying things such as 'Oh, it's not that hard really once you've got the hang of it!' On internal assessments and public examinations, I have found that more students are completing these questions, often performing above national average on them. Obviously this is great for student outcomes, but I also think increasing young people's mathematical literacy and confidence is not a bad thing either!

CASE STUDY 5: DR DAVID PREECE (HEAD OF GEOGRAPHY, TEACH FIRST) @DOCTORPREECE

Scaffolding: Teaching synopticity in A Level Geography

In common with most specifications, the opportunities for extended essay writing are not really present in GCSE Geography for most students. As a former examiner, whilst a few really talented geographers might write something unusual and different for a 9 mark question, the majority are fairly predictable. They may not have a single common structure to all questions (pro/con/conclusion) or to all paragraphs (Point-Evidence-Explanation, What-How-Why), or have consistent use of examples or case study materials, but students can often confidently build on the thinking they have done at KS3 to generate success in these essay questions. Success in a GCSE Geography paper does not rely on mastery of essay technique, but rather the consistent delivery of effective question response against the clock, on a diverse range of topics, skills and question types.

But as the Assessment Objectives shift dramatically at A Level, to achieve the highest grades the variety of knowledge is taken for granted. Candidates are expected to show mastery of their knowledge, and write for a professional geographer audience. Simple structures like defining terms and key terminology, are far less relevant to the answer and marking unless it's important to your essay (e.g. 'weather' versus 'climate' as part of the exam question). Describing and narrating the 'geography' of what happens (process, explanation, description of a case study) will get you to the top of Level 2.

Far more important is the role of 'evaluation' and assessment, and the ability to recognise and construct a viable thesis argument in response to a stimulus (photograph, source, data) or essay question. This needs careful thought and scaffolding, both in terms of teaching, and in terms of getting student practice to write the essays effectively. There are two key skills that need to be considered and taught separately.

Essay plans, not writing essays

For both, I think one of the key scaffolding strategies for student success is practising essay *planning* rather than writing essays. In terms of cost-benefit of time and motivation, it is a quicker and higher-leverage strategy for students to get a sense of what they need to be doing. There is – of course – valid reason to practise writing a long-form essay, and to get used to constructing paragraphs and flow, particularly against the clock, and to get feedback on it. In the early stages of an A Level course, however, I believe that writing solid and detailed essay plans (and building up a bank of them, to use as revision) is a far more valuable way to spend time.

Scaffold one: know the box

Modelling this planning and decision-making process and offering insight into expert thinking is the first key scaffolding technique that teachers need to explore. Essay questions are often framed in the sense of 'this statement' – do you agree?, or 'to what extent is X important for Y'. At GCSE, this was usually an explicit comparison, and early Year 12 students will often just write an essay on the pros and cons of the stimulus only. But at A Level, it's important that students recognise this for what it is – an **implicit** opportunity to compare this thing against others in a similar area of the specification and come up with a discussion. It's important that we teach ways to identify 'What else could it be?', as part of the synoptic journey of learning.

In my A level teaching, we called this 'knowing the box' – the area of the specification that the question was drawn from, and being confident that we could pivot between each of the lines of it, depending on which factor was named in the question. Here's an example from my A Level booklet on rivers, looking at causes of flooding (Preece, unpublished):

> **Normally asked as a 'to what extent', they tend to pick one factor, and ask you to assess it compared to others.**
>
> 1. Flash floods (pluvial) are caused when there's simply too much water – these can overwhelm any conditions. Focus on physical volume of rain or antecedent conditions.
> 2. For most fluvial events we should look at the scale of human vs physical.
> 3. Human factors – same as hydrograph, drainage basin: modifications, stores, land use changes, urbanisation AND the extent to which it's managed well.
> 4. Physical factors – same as hydrograph, drainage basin: size, shape, soil/permeability, rock type, slopes, vegetation, land use and antecedent moisture (already full?).
>
> e.g. Assess the extent to which floods are caused by human activity.

We can see that there are two key themes – human causes and physical causes. Each has a number of factors that must have been taught first, and we will have discussed ways that case studies and examples can be used to illustrate each of these points. The aim of this is a prompt to scaffold 'box thinking' rather than to give all the answers. I could ask students to write three essays: one on 'To what extent is it human?', one on 'To what extent is it physical?' and 'To what extent are pluvial and fluvial floods similar?'. Instead, we're supporting them to learn and know the box. Their job is to respond to the question prompt first, and then talk about the rest of the box. If they were asked about physical instead, they write that block first, and then say 'But it could also be, and might be linked to . . .'

As part of the teaching, each 'box' on the specification would have an essay plan template like this in our booklet. For the first one, I will model it first on the board, or on a visualiser. By the second or third, I'm handing over that box thinking to the students to lead, and then discuss together. Judging the rate of progress is partly about a curriculum expectation: the first has full scaffolding for everyone, and the second a little less, but formative assessment is also critical here. As a Geographer, many of the students who also studied History or RE would be more confident in their essay writing skills more quickly; whereas some of our Mathematics and Science students might need a little more support. Working together with flexible grouping, or perhaps offering more direct support to particular students whose first attempts were less successful enables your curricular approach to be adapted individually.

By the end of the unit of work, we'd have completed and marked all of the essay plans and shared them together. In lockdown teaching, we also co-constructed these via Teams – and all could then share in the document we'd constructed as part of our A Level course.

Scaffold two: scaffolds for evaluation

In the first example, the scaffold gets the student one step further – they are able to acknowledge the multiple implicit dimensions of the question, and talk about them. But they have not addressed the 'evaluative' element yet. 'To what extent' is an implicit evaluation. Sometimes, the question might be more explicit, 'Evaluate X in the process of Y', but students needed to know how to make judgements and critically reflect on the different parts of the box.

It's important to identify what it could depend on. As part of the teaching and discussion, A Level students need to be shown the factors, and accept and recognise the complexity of the subject: it isn't the case that there are universal 'right answers'. Everything has a context. Often, it's about development – high-income vs low-income and the relative impact of money on what can be done for management approaches and who chooses to spend the money. Sometimes the factors are physical – it might work one way for fluvial floods but very differently for pluvial, or for hard rock versus soft, or constructive versus destructive boundaries etc. In teaching the material, these factors need to be explicitly drawn out for the relative novice learners: while they are obvious to expert graduate teachers, they need to be signposted.

This can be done in different ways. For some, it will be about how you layout comparisons in your teaching – perhaps constructing pre-labelled tables, or coding diagrams and parts of the lesson. You may have groupings of topic that help students to connect their schema like yours. For example, in the Rivers unit, the 'change with distance downstream' is an important framework. There is a theoretical long profile, and some models which predict behaviour. There are some landforms that occur at different parts of that long profile. You can teach these all as discrete units. Alternatively, you can join them up. Here is our long profile, and we can split the river into upper/middle/lower course. Our model predicts what characteristics each of these areas – let's call them 'landscapes' – will share. Now let's teach the different landforms of the upper course, and reflect on what they all have in common. Let's then move down to the lower course – what do *they* all have in common, and how are they *different* to the ones we've seen some lessons ago in the upper course? This spaced and retrieved schematic connection helps to build the complexity and mental model at the same time. Later, we'll sketch the long profile as the prompt for revision activities – and students can annotate the theory, changes, and landforms they expect at each stage, because we've explicitly set out to model and build the connections as we taught.

Then, the second part of scaffolding is to help students to come to some judgement structure. They have identified 'the box', and recognised that there are three aspects to talk about – how do they judge which is most important, or evaluate the extent to which one is more critical than another? Let's look at two comparative scaffolds that might help, with an example from the Hot Arid Environments booklet:

> **Evaluate the importance of the role of Pleistocene pluvials in the development of desert landforms. [20] (Cambridge, 2018)**
>
> Question typically phrased as the extent to which landforms of deserts are the result of one of the three things: you are expected to evaluate that with reference to the others, and make a conclusion.
>
> 1. Aeolian – small/constant, limited by height. Show examples & landforms.
>
> 2. Fluvial – small/intermittent, ephemeral water limits. Depends on aridity levels.
>
> 3. OR – fluvial at a large scale likely to have needed lots more water, i.e. past conditions to be wetter, pluvial periods, last example was in the Pleistocene. Depends on time and location.
>
> 4. Evaluation could be on effectiveness (how many landforms), scale (how widespread are those landforms) or rate (how powerful is the force for shaping an individual landscape). Always need to consider RELATIVE power/magnitude/frequency – water has a big impact on relatively weak land, but not very often. Wind has weak power, but quite a lot of it!

Here, the first three lines of the essay planning prompt show the box. There's a set of aeolian processes (wind) that students can describe, explain and say how they help. There's a set of modern fluvial processes (water that flows every now and then), and there's a set of past processes that occurred a long time ago (in the Pleistocene period) when it was much wetter (pluvials). Describing and explaining all of that is a significant skill. But to really master this, we need to be able to judge which we think is most important.

There are a few ways of stimulating that conversation. If it's a binary 'this or that', a 'washing line' debate can be helpful. You define the two ends of the line as the extremes and ask students to identify where they think they want to put the peg. In the middle? 50/50? 60/40? 70/30? They can then use the sides of the line to annotate and identify the key points they want to make in support of one side (or the counter arguments to the other). Socratic questioning – why that? Why not a 70%? Why do you think it might be? – helps to scaffold the students who aren't sure into defending their thinking. You can 'pair' the ends if you want to provoke a more direct discussion: ask the person at each extreme to justify to each other, or people close to the middle to debate.

This doesn't tend to work so easily for questions like our deserts example, though. There are three parts – how are students to identify where on the washing line model that might go? In this example – and ones with multiple factors – a pie chart might work better. We provide (or quickly sketch) a circle, and ask students to fill up the pie chart with different factors – most important first. As before, the students can fill up (or annotate around) the pie chart with the key factors that they want to use in their paragraphs to explain and justify those factors as important.

The critical follow up conversation is 'explain why you put the lines where you did'. This requires students to evaluate why they ranked one thing first, or allocated this proportion of 'extent' to one factor rather than another. Their judgements and evidence for this conversation are exactly the kind of critical discussion that pushes them towards those highest marks; and this approach can replace essay planning as a concept of bullet point lists or paragraphs – students can quickly assign the lines, and use them in exam conditions!

CASE STUDY 6: CERI BOYLE (ASSISTANT PRINCIPAL, @CBOYLIO)

Scaffolding: KS5 English

The significant transition step from GCSE to A level English Literature essay writing can be a barrier for many students to overcome when they embark upon Year 12. A large part of this is due to the nature and high grade criteria demands of the A Level papers, compared to the demands of the GCSE papers. When A Level students begin their studies, they are expected to be able to develop thesis statements supported by confident arguments, with debates woven through. They are also expected to explore patterns of evidence across the text to build developed and nuanced analysis, as well as integrate the evaluation of different viewpoints. Therefore, for students to meet these demands and reach their full potential, it is essential that teachers effectively scaffold evaluative essay writing from the outset of the course. Alongside this, teachers must make sure that students are supported to activate their metacognitive skills so that they are able to apply the strategies and advice given to different aspects of the specification which have different assessment criteria. It is imperative that students are supported to develop their academic writing style and that they can calibrate accurately so that they know they are producing high level analysis in exam conditions. An important starting point is to embed a confident understanding of the assessment objectives to scaffold the essay writing.

A key strategy I utilise to scaffold this work is reverse planning. In order to scaffold excellence, reverse essay planning is used to demystify the success criteria and to exemplify academic writing style. The template is designed to support students to be reflective about how the exemplar is addressing the criteria. To design the resource, the teacher needs to unpick the ingredients needed for a strong paragraph including the specific assessment objectives needed for the essay type (Boyle, unpublished).

Purpose of Paragraph (in this I will prove):	Topic Sentence:
Relationship to essay question:	Points of Support (evidence):
AO1 included	**AO2 analysis**
Links to context?	
Are improvements needed?	

When reverse essay planning is introduced, I use a metacognitive modelling approach to ensure I am demonstrating the thinking of an experienced examiner (which I am fortunate to be). For example:

- This section feels clear – it has a focus on the question, and I understand the point being made. It is also linked to evidence. My next decision is whether it feels confident. What might suggest confidence? Does this phrase sound convincing? Is the analysis developed?

- This modelling and transference of 'expert' thinking is reinforced by a simple tick system which links to the levels being awarded at each stage of the essay, so I will explain why I am giving one tick, two tick etc and draw students into discussion about why.

Regular modelling of this approach takes place in class with students becoming increasingly involved in the evaluation. This is supported by home learning tasks:

- Booklets with worked examples of reverse essay plans and a range of exemplar essays and reverse planning templates are used to build in plenty of practice as well as the acknowledgement that there are different ways to meet the criteria. These will be discussed and evaluated in lessons too.

- Students using the same tick system and annotations which have been modelled by the class work described above scaffolds meaningful student self-assessment and builds effective calibration when producing developed analysis and full essays. This also scaffolds meaningful feedback after assessments as students can be directed to add comments based on the teacher's ticks to show that they understand why their work has met a certain level at each point in the essay (and then improve if needed).

- The reverse planning template can also be used as a forward planning resource to support students to ensure all aspects of the marking objectives and criteria are met and to scaffold detailed essay planning.

Detailed evaluation of exemplar essays using this reverse engineering approach can then be complemented by retrieval of the different essay criteria and approaches to build schema. Students can be involved in developing summary scaffolds to retrieve the key advice (Boyle, unpublished).

A STREETCAR NAMED DESIRE	PROSE	POETRY: SECTION A (UNSEEN COMPARISON)
\multicolumn{3}{c}{**PARAGRAPH ONE:**}
\multicolumn{3}{l}{**Thesis statement:** set out a confident argument with focus on the question being asked and introduce a possible debate or different interpretations}
Include links to context – the text and characters as microcosms E.g. Williams perhaps presents the relationship between Stanley and Blanche as a microcosm of the emergence of New American values in defeat of the Old South.	Set up comparison/contrast and make links to potential authorial intent with possible links to context E.g. Both Atwood and Shelley appear to be presenting warnings to the reader to be mindful of the potential harmful consequences of science where developments happen in the name of progress without full consideration of ethical considerations.	Set up comparison and introduce a confident/sophisticated argument with different possible interpretations. Introduce allegorical meanings tentatively E.g. It would appear that 'Unseen' and 'named poem' are both approaching the idea of ageing through the concept of liminality. A key difference, however, is the narrative perspective with an omniscient voice in . . . compared to the first-person perspective of.
\multicolumn{3}{c}{**PARAGRAPH TWO**}
Topic sentence – mini thesis statement for this paragraph drawing out an element from your introduction	Topic sentence should be comparative	Topic sentence should be comparative

(Continued)

(Continued)

A STREETCAR NAMED DESIRE	PROSE	POETRY: SECTION A (UNSEEN COMPARISON)
E.g. A key factor to explore in Williams' construction of this relationship is the ambiguity around who is seen as the antagonistic force.		
WHAT?- key idea/meaning/point to develop **HOW?** Explore methods used to develop this idea-link to a range of methods/evidence for each point and explore patterns/changes across the text/s **WHY?** Explore different possible interpretations, links to context and critical interpretations where relevant		
	LINK BACK TO SECOND TEXT **WHAT?** **HOW?** **WHY?**	**LINK BACK TO SECOND TEXT** **WHAT?** **HOW?** **WHY?**
END WITH A MINI CONCLUSION TO YOUR PARAGRAPH – THIS SHOULD COME BACK TO COMPARISON WHERE AO4 IS ASSESSED		
REPEAT PROCESS FOR FURTHER PARAGRAPHS – PROBABLY 2 FURTHER SECTIONS IN A TYPICAL A LEVEL TIMED ESSAY		
CONCLUSION – COME BACK TO YOUR INITIAL THESIS STATEMENT AND PROVIDE A CONCLUDING STATEMENT/THOUGHT/EVALUATION LINKING CLOSELY BACK TO THE QUESTION FOCUS		

What have we learnt about how to produce a top grade essay?

Poems of the decade	A Streetcar Named Desire	Prose

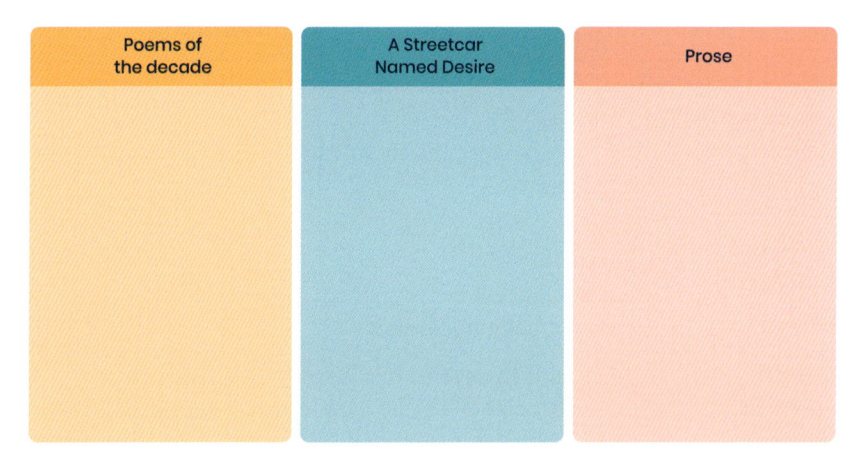

FIGURE 9.1 Regular reverse essay planning also allows for retrieval activities which encourage schema building (Boyle, unpublished)

This can be made more challenging by using a Venn diagram or comparison alley approach to ensure students are confident about the different essay requirements, drawing on the detailed way they have analysed example essays throughout the course and then applying their learning to their own essay planning.

Using this approach requires repeated incidences of teacher modelling to build student confidence, but the investment of time leads to much greater student understanding of marking criteria and how to build academic evaluative analysis. Since adopting this approach, I have seen a significant shift in the confidence and sophistication of students' writing as well as their ability to produce work which meets the highest level criteria in timed conditions. There has been a very positive improvement in the proportion of students reaching the highest grades at A level and students going to university to study English who feel confident in their ability to produce sophisticated essays.

CASE STUDY 7: RICHARD WHEADON (ASSISTANT HEADTEACHER, @RICHARDWH84)

Scaffolding: KS5 Environmental Science

At KS5 Environmental Science, students are tasked with crafting two substantial essays, each carrying a weight of 25 marks, alongside multiple shorter mark essays. This represents a significant shift from the KS4 Science curriculum, where the most detailed written response questions typically consist of concise inquiries, necessitating approximately six sentence, bullet-point responses.

Given this change in both breadth and depth, it becomes important to provide the necessary scaffolding to equip students for this transition. Students will have more practice with extended disciplinary writing in other subjects. For instance, in English Literature, considerations of tone and style in relation to the audience are paramount, whereas in History, students are tasked with interpreting extracts. Both of these require the students to then articulate their knowledge through extended written responses. Scientific essay and extended writing is more limited at KS3-4, and it presents with subtle distinctions from the writing conventions they encountered in other subjects. This creates the necessity for students to engage in frequent deliberate practice and the strategic implementation of scaffolds to ensure the development of a consistent writing style in this domain.

In scientific essay writing, the consistent and accurate use of relevant tier 2-3 terminology is paramount, ensuring that all information presented is directly pertinent to the essay title. To facilitate this, the scaffold we provide students with is the specification points essential for inclusion in the essay. We ask students to mind-map, initially focusing solely on key terminology associated with these specification points. We then use a visualiser to demonstrate how the specification points can be incorporated into the mind map, highlighting that both the specification points and the mind map itself are temporary aids that will eventually be phased out. The timing of this removal is contingent upon the prior attainment and evolving proficiency in essay writing of individual students throughout the course. Typically, collective mind mapping persists for the initial months of the A Level program. Some pupils require continued scaffolding, which is identified through comparative marking which allows me to check for understanding in a timely manner. Support is then provided in small group settings, while others work independently. This support is primarily verbal with the goal to develop students' independence. Similarly, students must learn to identify the prerequisite specification points independently, as these will not be provided in an exam. Thus, we prioritise developing students' ability to discern core knowledge pertinent to essay questions through active recall exercises conducted throughout the course. At the start of lessons, students are provided with an essay question and have to produce the mind map in five minutes. Over time this helps to build up students' schemas and will help in the removal of the scaffold of both the specification points and mind mapping.

To attain top marks in essay writing, pupils must demonstrate both depth and breadth in their responses. While the scaffolds implemented thus far ensure that pupils can achieve the necessary breadth, the subsequent focus lies on enhancing the depth of their essays. A primary scaffold employed for this purpose is the modelling of the 'PEE' approach - Point, Evidence, Explain. Different schools and different subjects will use different models for their essay writing, however PEE is the one we have found most useful for scientific writing. The initial step involves utilising PEE to elaborate on the mind map, ensuring that each aspect of the identified key terminology is explored to the appropriate depth. This process is demonstrated using a visualiser, supplemented by a writing frame providing tier 2 vocabulary designed to elaborate on the mind map. Just as with the modelling of mind mapping, the writing frame serves as a temporary scaffold, gradually phased out for individual students at varying points in their progression. Assessment for learning approaches including peer assessment is used to identify when pupils are ready to remove their writing frames. Peer assessment is a challenging task for some pupils and therefore a clearly defined tier 2 vocabulary list is an excellent starting point for this. With pupils required to skim read each other's work and identify how many tier 2 words their peer has used, peer assessment is very controlled and reduces the risk of poor peer feedback. If a student regularly uses the tier 2 vocabulary list, then a peer can suggest they stop using the writing frame, something which we consolidate by modelling. One aspect to note about the PEE structure is that it is a scaffold to initially identify a core structure for writing, but it should not be used as a straightjacket approach in which students do not extend their phrasing and structure beyond this initial base point.

Once pupils have acquired confidence in both the depth and breadth of knowledge essential for essay writing, our attention shifts to refining their introduction and conclusion paragraphs. Initially, these components are withheld to prevent students from cognitive overload, allowing them to concentrate on constructing schemas of the necessary knowledge. Introducing an introduction paragraph serves as an effective means of practising active recall, prompting pupils to articulate key points for their essays without specific examples. To reinforce this skill, months into the course, we provide students with a writing frame for crafting introductions and task them with drafting them from memory based on previously created mind maps. Model examples are provided to the pupils, and they are required to self-assess their introductions against the model, allowing them to decide when they feel the writing frame is no longer required. This may initially be an 'I do' approach with pre-prepared model examples used, but soon moves to co-constructed answers alongside the class.

A similar approach is adopted for conclusions, wherein pupils are tasked with emphasising key points. We use think, pair, share to list these key points and arrange them hierarchically in a diamond nine, justifying their selections. This method aims to transform inflexible knowledge into flexible knowledge, culminating in the final step of preparing pupils to write essays that encompass the requisite breadth and depth. This approach ensures that key terminology is consistently and accurately utilised throughout, maintaining a sustained focus on the essay's objectives.

In conclusion, the use of key specification point checklists followed by retrieval practice, mind mapping, tier 2 vocabulary lists and the withholding of introductions and conclusions are all temporary scaffolds designed to maximise pupils' performance in essay writing. It is important that pupils know that these tools will eventually be removed prior to their end of Year 13 examinations, and they should not become reliant on them. This is very much a 'try it and see' approach where we ensure we regularly check for understanding and remove scaffolds wherever we can see student confidence and independence is building.

Chapter 9 Self-Reflection Questions

Take a few minutes to reflect on the questions below and jot down your answers...

1. What effective scaffolds do you currently use for the specific ages/stages you teach?

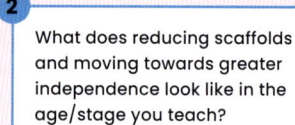

2. What does reducing scaffolds and moving towards greater independence look like in the age/stage you teach?

3. If you are a primary teacher or a secondary teacher that teaches more than one subject, where could you find out more about disciplinary scaffolding practice for your age/stage?

References

Cambridge International A Level Geography (9696) (2018) *Paper 31* (Online). Available at https://www.cambridgeinternational.org/programmes-and-qualifications/cambridge-international-as-and-a-level-geography-9696/past-papers/

Clements, D. H. (2000) 'Concrete' Manipulatives, Concrete Ideas. *Contemporary Issues in Early Childhood*, 1(1), 45–60

Kirschner, P. A. & Hendrick, C. (2024) *How Learning Happens: Seminal Works in Educational Psychology and What They Mean in Practice* (Second edition). New York: Routledge

Meyer, J. & Land, R. (2003) *Threshold Concepts and Troublesome Knowledge: Linkages to Ways of Thinking and Practising Within the Disciplines*. Oxford Brookes University

NAEYC (2009) *Developmentally Appropriate Practice in Early Childhood Programs Serving Children from Birth through Age* (Online). Available at https://www.naeyc.org/sites/default/files/globally-shared/downloads/PDFs/resources/position-statements/PSDAP.pdf. Accessed 17th July 2024

Ofsted (2024) *Deep and Meaningful? The Religious Education Subject Report*. Ofsted (Online). Available at https://www.gov.uk/government/publications/subject-report-series-religious-education/deep-and-meaningful-the-religious-education-subject-report. Accessed 26th July 2024

10 Scaffolding of homework

> Most homework teachers set is crap.
>
> *(William, 2014)*

There is no doubt that homework is one of the most divisive topics discussed in education, and it generates some strong opinions. Whilst many parents communicate that regular homework at secondary school is the mark of a good school, some parents are vocal about homework, especially for younger students, being a bad thing. Many would agree with Kirstie Allsop: 'Homework is an absurd hangover from another time. Much, much better to focus on reading, reading, reading and more reading' (2017). Teachers likewise disagree about homework, exemplified by the recent TeacherTapp (2023) poll (see Figure 10.1).

Boxer (2022) summarises, 'When it comes to teacher experience, the picture is a bit less rosy, and from our many conversations we have learnt the following:

- Lots of teachers set homework
- Lots of teachers don't think that homework in general is helpful to students
- Lots of teachers don't think the homework *they themselves* set is helpful to students. There is, therefore, a tension at play. On the one hand, research indicates that homework is helpful. On the other hand, teachers tell us it isn't.'

I think the students at my school are given too much homework

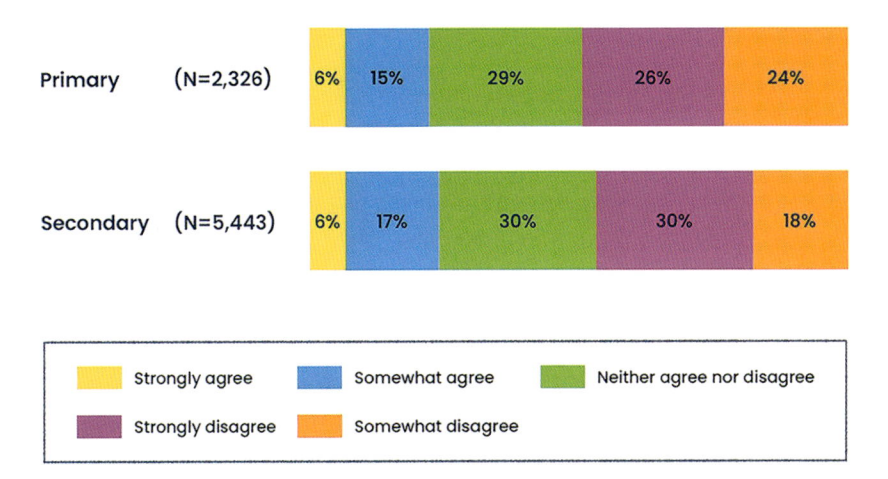

Primary (N=2,326)	6%	15%	29%	26%	24%
Secondary (N=5,443)	6%	17%	30%	30%	18%

Legend: Strongly agree | Somewhat agree | Neither agree nor disagree | Strongly disagree | Somewhat disagree

FIGURE 10.1 Graph showing whether students are receiving too much homework

Part of what makes this topic so divisive is that the evidence around homework is weak. In the recent EEF evidence review of homework, four key findings were explained:

1. 'Homework has a positive impact on average (+5 months) particularly with pupils in secondary schools
2. Some pupils may not have a quiet space for home learning so it is important for schools to consider how home learning can be supported.
3. Homework that is linked to classroom work tends to be more effective. In particular, studies that included feedback on homework had higher impacts on learning.
4. It is important to make the purpose of homework clear to pupils' (EEF, 2021).

However, it is important to note that the security of the evidence is rated low by the EEF due to the fact many of the studies used were not randomised control trials or had not been independently evaluated. In addition, the +5 months figure above is specifically linked to secondary age students; the research for younger students is that it is much less beneficial.

We can, however, make some conclusions about homework from the research (Inner Drive, 2019). One research study showed that regular rather than infrequent homework was beneficial to performance, although there was a sweet spot in terms of timing, with anything over an hour a day leading to minimal gains. High expectation of homework completion by parents also seems to improve performance, although the actual homework led to greater benefits when it was completed independently. Homework is also cited as bringing other perhaps less obvious benefits, though. By encouraging independence, it helps students learn to organise themselves and their workloads and to get into good routines and study habits. Certainly by the time students reach GCSEs, there is an expectation that students will not be able to perform well in exams if they are not in the routine of working independently on revision.

If homework in some form is here to stay then, we need to ensure that the homework we do set is really worthwhile and carefully scaffolded so that it helps remove attainment gaps, rather than increasing them.

One key mistake often made is to not scaffold the process of homework itself. Quigley (2024) outlines how

> we can all fall for the 'planning fallacy' – assuming we have more time and capacity than we have, but pupils are particularly prone to poor planning. Youngsters and teens alike simply don't plan in the ways we'd hope without ample scaffolding. . . . Planning strategies, checklists, and more than can help when supported with cumulative practice to scaffold independence . . . whether it is working on an online maths app, or practising a musical instrument, independent learning needs substantial teaching to happen.

We can 'name', 'frame' and 'sustain'; independent learning strategies and craft a timely shift of responsibility to learners.

Therefore, we must consider how we support students in being able to plan out their homework timetable for the week (this works well as part of a tutor/pastoral curriculum, then subsequently explicitly supported by subject teachers when they set homework) giving effective scaffolding so that they can map out their time and then study effectively. Moreover, we must avoid the error of thinking that students will blindly know how to focus their time (the distraction of mobile phones, being the main scourge), know how to use an online homework platform (of which multiple may be being used across a student's suite of subjects), and know how to create revision tools as well as use them. Therefore supporting students with building these homework and independent learning habits, rather than assuming that they have somehow picked them up via osmosis, is vital. As mentioned, first ensuring that there is a whole school focus on memory and independent learning through structured pastoral or tutor time curriculums is important in laying effective foundations. Students will then require additional scaffolding through subjects as well so that students know what homework and revision/independent learning looks like in that particular subject.

A further thing to consider is the importance of transition points. How does homework in KS1 differ from KS2 for example? Are there additional types of homework now being set, and if so, how are students prepared for that transition? Similarly the same consideration needs to be given at the KS2 into KS3 point, KS3 into KS4 and KS4 into KS5. This is particularly the case at KS3-4 'as students progress through an increasingly specialised secondary curriculum, we need to ensure that students are trained to access academic language and conventions of different subjects' (EEF, 2018). Whilst the EEF were focusing on the importance of disciplinary literacy when they wrote this, it can easily be applied to thinking about how we plan for students to be able to successfully access and complete effective disciplinary specific homework at the various transition points where content and skills became increasingly challenging, and rely more on independent learning particularly at KS5.

Mistakes to avoid

I would assert that there is quite a lot of homework being set on a daily basis which probably is not helping students to learn very much at all and possibly is, as Dylan asserts, 'crap' (William, 2014). So what kind of homework should we be avoiding?

1. Avoid open-ended projects

The first piece of advice to ensure homework is completed successfully is to avoid open-ended projects or tasks. When I first started teaching, this kind of homework was really popular – in History, students might spend a whole half term researching and completing a presentation on a figure from history completely unrelated to the schemes of learning we were working through in the classroom. While on the one hand this allowed for independent study, used students' research skills and perhaps built a little historical understanding, this kind of homework only served to increase attainment gaps. Some students struggled with time management and left the half term project until the night before it was due. (Later we tried to counteract this by chunking into weekly tasks but inevitably the same students still struggled.) Some students struggled with access to the library or to the internet while other students produced pages and pages of beautiful work copied from Wikipedia. Additionally, some students struggled to filter information they found online and just produced incorrect work, and of course on the flip side teachers now have the extra challenge of students using AI tools like ChatGPT.

Aside from the inevitable gaps between students which this task produced, the marking workload was unbearable, and I spent many a half term holiday trailing through hundreds of projects giving pointless feedback which many students would never look at. Some students had clearly spent many hours on these projects, and yet I wondered how much actual learning had taken place.

This kind of homework presents some significant problems, particularly around the filtering of information:

> One issue is that without guidance, pupils simply learn and embed misconceptions. I remember one occasion after my pupils were asked to complete a report on London, when I received a number of pieces in which they had mixed up information about London, UK and London, Canada. On another occasion, pupils completed work on climate change in which many of them had discussed, at length, how global warming was caused by a hole in the ozone layer.
> (Enser, 2019)

Ultimately, we are the experts, and therefore without that expert input, modelling and help when they get stuck, we are limiting learning opportunities by setting students this kind of task: 'If students cannot get help when they are stuck and the homework is likely to create conditions where students struggle and flounder, it risks having a negative impact' (Sherrington, 2017).

2. Avoid differentiated or choice homework

Another type of homework which was popular for a while was that of the chilli challenge differentiated homework grid. This involved students opting into a homework task that they felt able to do based on its level of 'spice' or challenge. We have already explored in Chapter 1 the problems with differentiation in this way, where students choose their own level of difficulty for a task. Students often put a barrier on their own capabilities, or go for the easiest or quickest option. Just as we know extension tasks limit what students can achieve, homework tasks with similar choices (unless they are all of equal difficulty and time needed) provide students with an opt-out and therefore limit access to more challenging tasks and therefore may widen learning gaps. It is also possible that some students will pick the more challenging option, but may not have the knowledge or understanding to complete it effectively, and may then lose motivation.

3. Avoid homework for homework's sake

Finally, homework which should be avoided is that where it set with no clear purpose and especially so when it is only set because of the 'school homework timetable':

> The pressure to set homework just because the timetable says it should be set, add to set that type of homework just because it is the flavour of the month, creates a host of problems. It means that it is often an afterthought, rather than intrinsic to the lesson, or involves setting tasks that achieve very little in terms of what pupils have learnt from the process.
>
> (Enser, 2019)

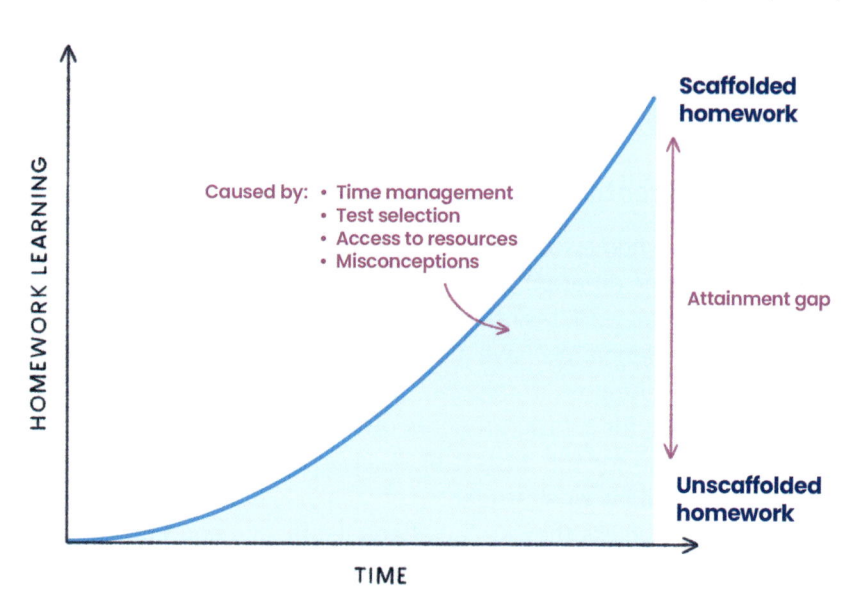

FIGURE 10.2 Graph showing the benefits of scaffolded homework

Purpose and feedback

It's important therefore to ensure that there is a clear purpose to the homework and, as per the EEF recommendation, that it is linked meaningfully to classwork. At Durrington Research School, departments are asked to write homework policies which mean that homework set meets one of these four aims:

- **Embed** – consolidate learning that has taken place in the classroom, for example, revision for assessment or learning key knowledge. Example: in Spanish, preparing for a speaking assessment by revisiting key vocabulary and phrases using flashcards or sentence builders.
- **Practice** – refine knowledge and procedures learnt in the classroom based on feedback from the teacher. Example: DIRT (Directed Improvement and Reflection Time) activities.
- **Extend** – move learning beyond what has been achieved in the classroom, for example, adding breadth to their existing knowledge. Example: 'Meanwhile, Elsewhere' where history students are asked to study a differing piece of world history that was happening at the same time as the topic studied within the classroom.
- **Apply** – use learning from the classroom to complete a specific task, for example, writing a practice exam question based on content covered in a lesson. For example, using past exam papers in Maths or Science (Runeckles, 2018).

This really helps teams to think strategically about what homework in their subjects should be set for and to ensure the homework set has a clear purpose. Teachers should also ensure they communicate explicitly how the homework will benefit students. For example, I might set my GCSE class a piece of retrieval practice homework that is clearly linked to knowledge from lessons and explain how this kind of self-quizzing is a well-researched way to help them retain and remember vital knowledge needed for their exams. This kind of homework can be set in the form of a simple written retrieval grid or a Google Form quiz. Many schools are now using retrieval platforms such as Carousel or Seneca and the results from homework quizzes set, then feed into future lessons. For example, a common error identified by the teacher from the homework quiz that several students have made can easily be addressed in the next lesson. A 'Do Now' might be amended to give another opportunity to test a misconception for example. 'I saw that several of you make a mistake with Q3 on your homework, this is a really easy area to mix up so let's have another go at it now and see where we went wrong.' Equally, opportunity could be taken to speak to a student who had really struggled to point them in the direction of more resources on a particular topic or invite them to a small group revision session after school which might be running.

Not only is this making the teacher responsive, it also communicates the importance of completing the homework in the first place – it has a clear purpose. Instead of a written comment on a piece of work which students are unlikely to engage with, it also ensures there is direct feedback. Alex Quigley (2018) summarises how we can approach exploring purpose:

- 'Has the purpose of the homework been made clear to students?
- Are the students in possession of all of the resources required to undertake the task independently?
- What are the existing beliefs about home learning (students and teachers) that we need to recognise/challenge?
- How can we best leverage parental support for home learning that is effectively communicated?
- How do you plan to provide specific and timely feedback to students on their home learning?'

Linked to content

Retrieval practice also hits one of the other suggested EEF requirements, in that it is linked to classroom content. Students are not investigating something they have no knowledge of, and in this way there is a much reduced risk of students encountering unfamiliar concepts or vocabulary. For example, once you move onto a new unit, important vocabulary, concepts and knowledge can be tested from the previous unit, to ensure students embed this into their long-term memory. Cues or other scaffolds mentioned in Chapter 2 can also be utilised here. It can also be helpful to encourage students to keep trying these quizzes repeatedly until the knowledge is fully secured.

I often instruct my students to complete a quiz, find out where there are gaps of knowledge and understanding and then repeat. If you are setting homework in the form of reading or an exam question, it must be explicitly linked to something students have studied in lessons, perhaps helping them to understand wider context or to complete an exam question which has been started in a lesson. In these cases though, even though the content is linked to the lesson, there must be much more thought about further scaffolding this work. If this kind of homework is chosen, can any reading be chunked? Can line numbers be used on texts which need to be read? Can there be questions next to each paragraph rather than all being at the end to help reduce split attention? Could a Cornell Note template be used to help them to summarise their notes? Can a glossary be added and is there a clear routine if students get stuck?

Routinised

Whatever style of homework you set, another key way of scaffolding it is to ensure it is as routinised and as familiar as possible to students. Make homework predictable by always setting it and collecting it on the same day of the week wherever possible. Make the style of homework really familiar so that you aren't having to issue new instructions each time. For example, for my Year 11 class, a retrieval quiz can always be found in the same place, for example, a Google Classroom or Teams link. It is always around 30 minutes of work, with the same style of questions, and always set on a Friday and checked the following Friday with feedback in the lesson that day.

We know that clear instructions, a chunked approach where the length of task is manageable and routines really benefit students and ensure accessibility for all. If I set an exam question one week followed by a quiz the next week and then a research task the following week, it adds barriers which reduces the chances of successful completion. Our instructions must be very clear, and many students benefit from having this logged on a specific app or a platform such as Google classroom.

Quickly flashing up homework instructions on a slide in the last two minutes of a lesson when students are not expecting it, or explaining it as students pack up will not ensure that homework is done meaningfully and carefully. In her brilliant blog on homework, Jo Castelino describes two classrooms:

Classroom A	Classroom B
Homework is set weekly in the classroom with the purpose of practice, retrieval and application. Homework usually takes 15 minutes to complete but as the routine builds, the tasks may take longer. The format used for the homework tasks is consistent as well.	Homework is only set if the topic demands it. If students have fully practised something in the lesson, then homework is not set. The purpose of homework is to consolidate and extend lesson learning. The format of the homework may be similar or different depending on the task set, which depends on the lesson it is linked to.

But when my classroom looked more like Classroom B, I found fewer students completing homework. I believe one of the main reasons for this is that students don't know *when* to expect homework and so they cannot organise themselves well. By having the homework as a well established routine, students can simply focus on the task rather than wondering if and when homework will be set. In fact, having a set schedule has been suggested to help students remember when to set aside time for homework but is also linked to increased student achievement (Paulu, 1998).

(Castelino, 2022)

Barriers

Finally, as mentioned earlier in the chapter, we must ensure that homework is carefully scaffolded by reducing any barriers which might make homework completion more difficult. For example, understanding which students might not have access to a device and ensuring they have accessibility in school or an alternative method is important. Some students might have reading ages below chronological age, and therefore may need support with vocabulary. We should not add to the parental load, as some students may have limited or no parental support and may therefore need help with somewhere quiet to work, a weekly homework club or a staffed library space. Some students may need scaffolding in the form of organisational help; support with prioritising work, constructing a revision timetable or general help with study skills such as using the pomodoro technique, or utilising flashcards. Other students may need physical resources such as a revision guide, a lesson booklet or stationery.

If homework is to remain an important part of our school curriculum, then in the same way as classwork, it needs to be scaffolded and supported. In fact, as students are by its nature independent when completing homework, the scaffolding needs to be even more carefully planned for.

Chapter 10 Self-Reflection Questions

Take a few minutes to reflect on the questions below and jot down your answers...

1. What problems with homework have you encountered in your context?

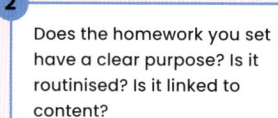

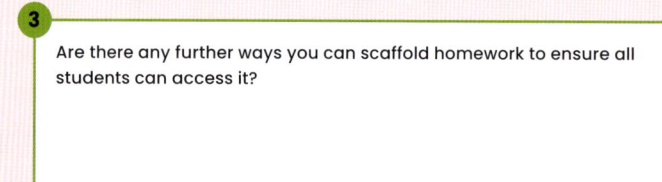

2. Does the homework you set have a clear purpose? Is it routinised? Is it linked to content?

3. Are there any further ways you can scaffold homework to ensure all students can access it?

References

Allsop, K. (2017) (Online). Available at https://twitter.com/KirstieMAllsopp/status/824749930577326080?t=-zGVr_zj3rJQkeJWtSOfyw&s=03

Boxer, A. (2022) *The Four Planks of an Effective Homework Policy* (Online). Available at https://carousel-learn.medium.com/the-four-planks-of-an-effective-homework-policy-bf38e48af732. Accessed 27th November 2023

Castelino, J. (2022) *Homework: Three Big Questions Plus One More* (Online). Available at https://drcastelino.wordpress.com/2022/09/30/homework-three-big-questions-plus-one-more/. Accessed 20th November 2023

EEF (2021) *Teaching and Learning Toolkit: Homework* (Online). Available at https://educationendowmentfoundation.org.uk/education-evidence/teaching-learning-toolkit/homework#:~:text=Homework%20that%20is%20linked%20to,fluency%20in%20a%20particular%20area). Accessed 21st January 2024

Education Endowment Foundation (EEF) (2018) *Improving Literacy in Secondary Schools* (Online). Available at https://educationendowmentfoundation.org.uk/education-evidence/guidance-reports/literacy-ks3-ks4. Accessed 16th April 2024

Enser, M. (2019) *Teach Like Nobody's Watching*. CrownHouse

Inner Drive (2019) *How Helpful Is Homework?* (Online). Available at https://blog.innerdrive.co.uk/how-helpful-is-homework?s=03. Accessed 16th November 2023

Paulu, N. (1998) *Helping your Students with Homework: A Guide for Teachers*. Office of Educational Research and Improvement

Quigley, A. (2018) *Huntington Research School Blog*: Homework: What Does the Research Say? (Online). Available at https://researchschool.org.uk/huntington/news/homework-what-does-the-evidence-say. Accessed 21st January 2025

Quigley, A. (2024) *8 Reasons Why Learning Fails, Alex Quigley* (Online). Available at https://alexquigley.co.uk/test-post/. Accessed 2nd August 2024

Runeckles, C. (2018) *Cracking Homework* (Online). Available at https://classteaching.wordpress.com/2018/10/04/cracking-homework/. Accessed 12th July 2024

Sherrington, T. (2017) *The Learning Rainforest*. John Catt Educational

TeacherTapp (2023) *Mayday! Mayday! The Demise of Flightpaths. Also, Feeling Rewarded at Work, and Who Loves Homework?* (Online). Available at https://teachertapp.co.uk/articles/mayday-mayday-the-demise-of-flightpaths-also-feeling-rewarded-at-work-and-who-loves-homework/. Accessed 16th November 2023

William, D. (2014) Quoted in Quigley, A. (2018) *The Truth About Homework* (Online). Available at https://www.theconfidentteacher.com/2018/01/the-truth-about-homework/. Accessed 15th November 2023

11 Potential pitfalls of scaffolding strategies

> Good ideas – even when they are well-rooted in evidence-based research – can be implemented in ways which render them no longer effective, or even counter-productive; becoming examples of what Dylan Wiliam (2011) and others have dubbed 'lethal mutations'.
>
> *(Rose, 2018)*

It would be remiss of us to presume that what we have written in this book so far is enough.

As with any Teaching and Learning strategies, it is easy to use them ineffectively, or for leaders to advise others to implement them in ways which lead to mutations of the strategy itself. Knowledge organisers, retrieval practice and even Rosenshine's Principles themselves have all become victims of this phenomena in the past; schools where teachers have to evidence all the principles each lesson, where every lesson must start with the same five retrieval questions (five questions, 5 minutes), or where knowledge organisers have become ineffective pretty posters of icons; 'Whenever a practice becomes mandated there seems to be a tendency for it to lethally mutate' (Didau, 2023). These lethal mutations happen 'when evidence-informed practice is modified beyond recognition from the original practice' (EEF, 2023) and unfortunately can be pretty common, as noted by Evidence Based Education's (2023) 'Retrieval Practice: Myths, Mutations and Mistakes'. That's not to say that these school leaders don't have the best intentions; often these

DOI: 10.4324/9781003467069-14

mutations 'creep up' due to the simplifying or misunderstanding of research; 'Consider a sound idea changing by only 1% every day. After a year, it will have changed by a huge 37%' (Inner Drive, 2023).

It is no surprise therefore that scaffolding would be vulnerable to the same poor implementation. In addition, as we outlined in Chapter 1, using scaffolding as part of adaptive teaching is something which many teachers find extremely difficult to do well. It's important for us to pause and consider the possible pitfalls around the use of scaffolding in schools in order that we can possibly pre-empt some of these errors.

School wide

Restrictive school-wide policies

The first possible pitfall is around the challenge of implementation. In the battle to ensure consistency, school leaders can impose a one-size-fits-all approach which can be extremely damaging. As an example of this, I have seen well-meaning school leaders misuse 'I do, We do, You' and insist on this for a lesson structure seen in every lesson rather than as a modelling process. Similarly, I have seen the prescription of 'I do, we do, you do' modelling to be seen in every lesson. The thought process here is commendable, the school wants teachers to prioritise the support of students through a really thorough modelling process, fading the support over time. However, this is just not appropriate for every lesson or every class. We have to remember that a class at the beginning of a unit for example may have different scaffolding needs to a class who are ready to sit an assessment and are practising independently. Indeed, this lesson by lesson approach has pitfalls in itself; 'the lesson is the wrong unit of time . . . thinking about an individual lesson leads us down the wrong path to the wrong solutions' (Isaksen, 2015). Learning does not fit into nice one hour units of time. An 'I do, we do, you do' could be used in each lesson in this way, but it would be artificial, unresponsive and probably waste vast amounts of learning time. It simply isn't true that a strategy like this is needed in every lesson in every subject.

Didau pursues this line of thought, considering how we plan:

> Dividing schemes of work into individual lessons distracts teachers from concentrating on what is to be learned over time. . . . I've come to understand that some concepts require extensive explanation and some skills need considerable modelling.
>
> (Didau, 2015).

We need to think of the curriculum journey over a series of lessons instead, thinking carefully about which tools we will use over that period of time, rather than a prescriptive idea of what every lesson must include.

For a leader to mandate something as complicated and adaptive as scaffolding strategies to look a certain way and be present in every lesson is for them to fail to understand the strategy itself. One way to change this is to start thinking about principles of great teaching rather than the actual strategies themselves. Rather than insisting on particular strategies being present every lesson (in this case an 'I do, we do, you do'), consider that modelling as a principle should be prioritised across a scheme of learning, with teachers gradually fading their support so that students are working independently, with ultimately the teacher left to decide what form that takes and how it is used. This is a vision for subject leadership Adam Robbins develops (2021), advocating 'Principles not Practices';

> Schools often crave consistency within all they do. This is built on the fundamental idea that there is a 'best' way of doing things – if only there was! . . . . In an aim to create a cookie cutter department to please our line managers, we often accidentally create several issues for our staff;
>
> - We try to make them all teach in the exact same way, which might not suit their personality or natural strengths
> - We prioritise resources over techniques. We look at *how* it is done instead of considering *why* in more detail

- We remove an aspect of intellectualism from the profession, which in the long run, reduces autonomy, agency and ultimately wellbeing.

A one-size-fits-all approach is ultimately likely to lead to mutations and poor implementation, with a knock on effect on teacher motivation and student success. It fails to take into account the responsive nature of scaffolding support as where 'pupils' background knowledge is uniquely strong, pupils may subtly slide along the continuum' (Quigley, 2022) of scaffolding. In addition, it makes the mistake mentioned in an earlier chapter in considering that scaffolding simply consists of writing frames or written support. It also ignores the scaffolding strategies that are age and stage appropriate, as well as the unique scaffolding strategies that practical subjects will use. We know scaffolding instead works best when it encompasses verbal support or visual diagrams. In summary then, a prescriptive top-down policy like this can lead to scaffolding being implemented in a restrictive and unhelpful manner.

Lack of subject autonomy

In a similar vein, one particular scaffolding approach is not going to suit all subjects or even all enquiries/units within a subject and therefore it would be a mistake for a leadership team to impose a particular style of scaffold across all subjects. There should be freedom for a teacher, with all the knowledge of the subject and the students, to decide which scaffold is needed at a particular time, who needs it and what it looks like. A structure strip which perfectly guides my History students through a source question on Paper 2 might need to look different for a Paper 1 question and again look different at A Level. And of course an extended writing scaffold which works for me in my History lessons might be extremely restraining for a Geography or English teacher. Subjects have different demands, and we need to respect this. For example, a 12 mark GCSE question can look very different across essay writing subjects: Geography students are expected to include case studies and cartography, in RE they're expected to use sources of wisdom and their own worldview, and in History to use substantive knowledge or extracts from sources and therefore one-size-fits-all scaffolding edicts can be dangerous;

Potential pitfalls of scaffolding strategies 307

One of my perennial frustrations as a teacher was when a strategy – apparently working successfully in one subject area – was identified as 'best practice' and imposed on different subjects. . . . It's vital that teachers are able to successfully adapt (them) to the context of their subject but still maintain fidelity to the central core of these ideas. Where the central ideas are not well understood or where the adaptation to subjects is not treated with care, even really great ideas can mutate into monsters.

(Rose, 2018)

It is for this reason that when exploring any professional development (PD) focus like this, or indeed bringing in any sort of whole school policy, it should be subject-led with time given to view them through the subject disciplinary lens. Instead, a PD leader might triangulate time in whole-school training to consider scaffolding principles, for example, scaffolding vocabulary support. Time could then be ring-fenced for subjects to discuss what that might look like for them (with middle leaders having training in advance of this so that they are empowered to drive it in their teams). This could be followed by line management conversations, piloting of scaffolds, sharing of good practice and critically thinking about what works well and what doesn't within each subject. Ideally, time needs to be given for subjects to collaborate within their subject communities and adapt so that either they can reject: 'No, this doesn't work within our subject', 'this works within a limited capacity' or 'we think this works and works for us like this'. Not only will this mean that teachers have the freedom to apply a principle in the way that works for that subject, it means that teacher motivation is likely to be higher, with changes not imposed on them.

Assuming one size fits all
Focus on ensuring that the principle is adhered to, but the strategy for doing so can vary.

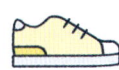

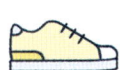

FIGURE 11.1 The problems that come with a one-size-fits-all approach

Teacher focused

Content first

One easy pitfall with scaffolding which it may be easy for a teacher to fall into is that of letting the strategy lead the planning, rather than considering the subject content first, something mentioned in the explanations chapter for example in relation to storytelling, where it is easy to let the pedagogical device drive the lesson plan rather than the content (Vallance, 2024).

It's an idea which has been written about before. 'Any debate about teaching methods needs to take place under the auspices of "what am I trying to teach?"' (Fordham, 2018). Lee Donaghy (2019) explains,

> I would argue strongly that what we teach (the subject content) is too often overshadowed by how we teach (pedagogy). Good pedagogy isn't necessarily generic, as the nature of the content of a subject has much bearing on how that content is taught.

There is therefore a danger that teachers let the technique or device lead the lesson plan or sequence.

Instead an appropriate thought process might be:

- What is the challenging knowledge that I need my students to know?
- How can I scaffold this knowledge delivery so that it is accessible for all?
- What principles of effective pedagogy would be best utilised to consolidate this knowledge?
- How can I scaffold the literacy elements of the content?
- What formative assessment methods can I use to check understanding by students?
- What scaffolding is needed to ensure that all students can be successful in embedding the knowledge?

Putting the technique before the content
The content should drive the focus, not the technique. Otherwise we are essentially putting the cart before the horse.

FIGURE 11.2 Putting content first, not the technique

Removing scaffolding too soon

Knowing when to remove scaffolding takes a lot of thought, gathering of data from students and also a lot of trial and error! A second error that teachers may make is that of removing scaffolding too quickly. As a parent eager to get the stabilisers off the bike in the common analogy of scaffolding, a teacher may be so keen to get their students working independently that this process is rushed. This can lead to demotivation, as students quickly flounder when left with no support. Of course, when a teacher checks the work, the scaffolding and support can quickly be reactivated, but in the meantime students may become despondent and feel like they are not capable. In turn, this can lead to behaviour problems and long term lack of confidence; 'Remember, students should be challenged but not defeated' (Riches, 2022).

The answer? Go slow, frequently check for understanding and reduce the scaffolding gradually over time. Sherrington's relay baton handover analogy is again a really helpful one here. Although originally used to describe the handover when moving between I, we and you modelling, I think this could apply to scaffolding in general.

> Zoom right in on that baton hand-over. It's not instantaneous; a crucial time passes when both people are holding the baton together. In that brief moment, they are communicating through the touch: *Have you got it? No, not yet. Ok, I'm still with you. Grip harder. Have*

you got it now? Nearly, keeping holding, I'm nearly there. Ok. You're ready. Off you go. Yes, I'm ready, let go. I already have ... you're away.
(Sherrington, 2020)

We need to be really careful and considered when deciding whether students are ready to move to an independent phase. We need to regularly check for understanding and be prepared to move back to more scaffolding if the indicators in student written and verbal responses tell us that they are not yet ready for full independence. In his blog *Why might I/We/You not be working for you?* Pete Foster explores the dangers of this kind of modelling in a microscopic way with one pitfall being a lack of this kind of adaptation by the teacher. He advises, 'Perhaps the easiest option when students are struggling is to turn our *You* into an extended *We*' (Foster, 2024). This aligns with the aforementioned 'continuum' that Quigley (2022) discusses – that we should not see 'I do, we do, you do' as three static stages to move through in a block format, but instead a scaffolding strategy where we may move the support backwards and forwards using our checks for understanding calibrate and direct us.

Leaving scaffolding in place for too long

Conversely, perhaps a more common pitfall with scaffolding is for teachers to become reluctant to remove it over time. It's important to remember that in the same way that the stabilisers should be removed from the bike, scaffolding should not be in place permanently. 'My feeling is that, too often, we leave the support structure in place for too long and students develop a dependency; an over-reliance on the support and a mutually reinforcing fear of failure' (Sherrington, 2015).

More than this, Sherrington warns that it is dangerous to leave scaffolding in place too long as it 'creates the illusion of learning' something we need to guard against. Ultimately, we need to give students the opportunity to struggle and even to fail. 'Scaffolding also requires that the teacher give up some of the control and allow the students to make errors. This may be difficult for teachers to do' (Van Der Stuyf, 2002). Learning from mistakes is a crucial part of the process, and good teachers will build this into a 'culture of error'.

Potential pitfalls of scaffolding strategies 311

> From the moment students arrive, they work to shape their perception of what it means to make a mistake, pushing them to think of 'wrong' as a first, positive, and often critical step toward getting it 'right', socialising them to acknowledge and share mistakes without defensiveness, with interest or fascination even, or possibly relief – help is on the way!
>
> (Lemov, 2021)

Scaffolding is as much about building confidence and encouraging students to try as it is about supporting the consolidation of knowledge, and we would be wrong to not give students the opportunity to practise this independence. We must be careful that scaffolds don't become a crutch which students rely on to their detriment.

It's important therefore to ensure we remove any scaffolding in stages.

> Teachers should remove all support when the student is fully confident they can successfully complete a task on their own and have demonstrated as much. However, if students get stuck on a more challenging version of the task, they still need help. This style of support helps students grasp concepts a lot more quickly and guide student practice. Rosenshine calls this process 'cognitive apprenticeship', as students learn effective strategies that enable them to become successful learners.
>
> (Inner Drive, 2021)

Release support too quickly or slowly

If we go too early, students may be overwhelmed. Delay too long and they can become dependent on the support.

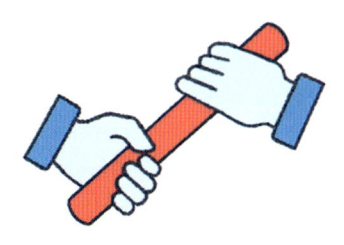

FIGURE 11.3 Scaffolding in stages

The drift into differentiation

The answer to the challenge of when to remove scaffolding comes back to knowing your students and being responsive to the needs of individuals. It can be easy for a teacher with the best of intentions to drift back into a differentiation mind-set (see Chapter 1), predetermining what support students need and what they are capable of, and in this way limiting them. Peps McCrea (2024a) outlines how our prior differentiation habits can be difficult to break. 'The unconscious, automatic nature of habits makes them notoriously resistant to change. The more established the habit, the more entrenched it becomes. This is "habit inertia" and it creates a challenge for teacher development.' It's important that teachers stay alert to this, and remember as we explored in Chapter 1 that 'support consists of the live conversations and additional unpacking of the material during the lesson' (Myatt, 2023). Rather than presuming which students will need scaffolding support and blindly handing them out, it is more effective to have any support pre-prepared and ready, and only distributed once checks for understanding have shown they are needed.

Be armed and prepared for how scaffolding might be needed and make checks for understanding a crucial part of your lesson, to guide how you should adapt as needed.

For example, whilst reading a piece of text in a History lesson, I may have pre-scaffolded with the definitions of difficult words provided for support. Each section of the reading asks students for a summary of the text in order for them to show understanding, and I model the first paragraph under the visualiser. However, whilst circulating when students are left to do this independently, I realise that some students are struggling with knowing what to summarise, so for the next section I again model, this time in more specific detail, sharing my thought process aloud. Whilst circulating again, only a couple of individual students then need my additional verbal support, which I can give easily. I might then give these students a checklist or sentence starter to guide them. In this example, some of the scaffolding is provided for all, I adapt to the responses of the class and give greater scaffolding support to those who need it, but crucially, all are reading the same challenging text, and I have not predetermined who will and won't be able to access the task.

Scaffolding drifts into differentiation
Predetermining what support students need and what they are capable of can limit their potential.

[Scaffolding] ------------→ [Differentiation]

FIGURE 11.4 Breaking differentiation habits

Language of scaffolding

In a similar vein, another potentially damaging approach related to scaffolding can be the language used by teachers when using scaffolding. An example of such language might be 'for those of you who can't do this like [insert names], here's some support' or grouping students together in such a way that the groupings clearly relate to ability. Often without meaning to, teachers can cause embarrassment to students who do need extra support, something Mark Roberts (2022) writes about with a specific focus on boys:

> Avoid saying things like 'Give me a shout if you're struggling' or 'hand up who needs some help'. Despite your good intentions, drawing attention to boys who might need extra support can cause embarrassment and resentment. . . . I find that phrasing it like this works much better:
> *If you're confident that you fully understand what you're doing, keep going. I'll be coming to give you some feedback shortly. If you're not certain about what you're doing, pause for a moment and look at the board. I'm going to give an example to help make it clear exactly what you need to do. While I'm doing this, if it suddenly clicks, you can get back to your work. If not, keep watching me until it makes sense.*

As mentioned earlier in this chapter, we need to foster a culture of error in our classrooms, where students are not afraid to try and make mistakes and our choice of language and way we scaffold can support this.

Relying on Teaching Assistants (TAs)

Finally, another potential pitfall of scaffolding is that it is left to TA support within a classroom setting and not led by the teacher. Current evidence tells us that TA impact on outcomes is inconsistent (EEF, 2021). One reason for this is that students can easily become dependent on the often intensive support from a TA, and therefore are not challenged to work independently. This often happens because TA deployment is with the students who often struggle the most. It is for this reason that the EEF (2021) goes on to recommend that schools think carefully about TA organisation. 'Schools should try and organise staff so that the pupils who struggle most have as much time with the teacher as others.'

One example of this might be a teacher explaining and modelling a task with the whole class then checking for understanding as usual. The teacher could then start working with the group of students who are struggling the most, whilst the TA circulates and assists the rest of the class. In addition, it's important that time is invested in training TAs to remove scaffolds in the same way as teachers, encouraging independence:

> TAs should aim to give pupils the least amount of help first. They should allow sufficient wait time, so pupils can respond to a question or attempt the stage of a task independently. TAs should intervene appropriately when pupils demonstrate they are unable to proceed.

In just the same way as a teacher would scaffold through models, cues and prompts, a TA can then support students who need more specific help to access the same curriculum as the rest of the class.

In summary, scaffolding is not easy to implement at school or teacher level. The primary focus is knowing your students well and responding to their needs as you move through and explore the curriculum together. It's also not a perfectly straightforward process, and you will naturally find yourself removing scaffolding, then adding some back in as you are responsive to what students can do and produce. In essence, it's one of the things which makes teaching so hard.

> Responsive teaching may be powerful, but it's not easy to implement. It requires:
>
> - Substantial mental bandwidth
> - A high degree of skill
> - A big dose of humility (because we'll often find that our teaching just doesn't work
>
> (Mccrea, 2024b)

The Pitfalls of Scaffolding

Assuming one size fits all
Focus on ensuring that the principle is adhered to, but the strategy for doing so can vary.

Putting the technique before the content
The content should drive the focus, not the technique. Otherwise we are essentially putting the cart before the horse.

Release support too quickly or slowly
If we go too early, students may be overwhelmed. Delay too long and they can become dependent on the support.

Scaffolding drifts into differentiation
Predetermining what support students need and what they are capable of can limit their potential.

Scaffolding ---------------> Differentiation

FIGURE 11.5 An overview of the pitfalls of scaffolding

Chapter 11 Self-Reflection Questions

Take a few minutes to reflect on the questions below and jot down your answers...

1. Are there any dangers of a scaffolding approach being mutated at a leadership level which resonate in your context?

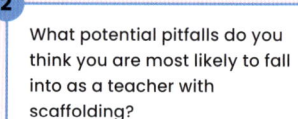

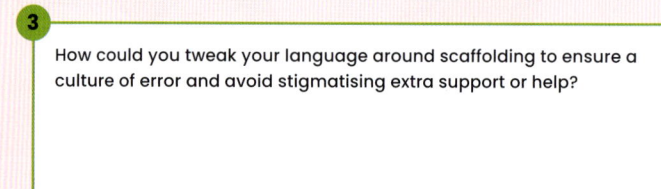

2. What potential pitfalls do you think you are most likely to fall into as a teacher with scaffolding?

3. How could you tweak your language around scaffolding to ensure a culture of error and avoid stigmatising extra support or help?

References

Didau, D. (2015) *The Problem with Lesson Planning* (Online). Available at https://learningspy.co.uk/leadership/problem-lessons/. Accessed 19th February 2024

Didau, D. (2023) *When Retrieval Practice Goes Wrong (and How to Get It Right)* (Online). Available at https://learningspy.co.uk/english-gcse/when-retrieval-practice-goes-wrong-and-how-to-get-it-right/. Accessed 17th May 2024

Donaghy, L. (2019) *Subject Knowledge – 10 Things Every Teacher Educator Should Know* (Online). Available at https://www.teachfirst.org.uk/blog/subject-knowledge-10-things-every-teacher-educator-should-know-series. Accessed 20th February 2024

EEF (2021) *Making Best Use of Teaching Assistants Guidance Report* (Online). Available at https://educationendowmentfoundation.org.uk/education-evidence/guidance-reports/teaching-assistants. Accessed 28th February 2024

EEF (2023) *What Are Lethal Mutations: TES Explains* (Online). Available at https://www.tes.com/magazine/tes-explains/what-are-lethal-mutations. Accessed 20th February 2024

Evidence Based Education (2023) *Retrieval Practice: Myths, Mutations and Mistakes* (Online). Available at https://2366135.fs1.hubspotusercontent-na1.net/hubfs/2366135/Retrieval%20Practice%20-%20Myths%2C%20Mutations%20&%20Mistakes.pdf. Accessed 1st August 2024

Fordham, M. (2018) *The Fundamental Weakness of Debate About Generic Pedagogy* (Online). Available at https://clioetcetera.com/2018/02/13/the-fundamental-weakness-of-debate-about-generic-pedagogy/. Accessed 20th February 2024

Foster, P. (2024) *Why Might I/We/You Not Be Working for You* (Online). Available at https://curriculumteamleader.wordpress.com/2024/03/21/why-might-i-we-you-not-be-working-for-you/. Accessed 28th Match 2024

Inner Drive (2021) *Rosenshine's Eighth Principle of Instruction: Provide Scaffolding and Support* (Online). Available at https://blog.innerdrive.co.uk/rosenshine-eighth-principle-of-instruction. Accessed 21st February 2024

Inner Drive (2023) *Lethal Mutations in Education* (Online). Available at https://blog.innerdrive.co.uk/lethal-mutations-in-education. Accessed 20th February 2024

Isaksen, B. (2015) *A Lesson Is the Wrong Unit of Time* (Online). Available at https://redorgreenpen.wordpress.com/2015/01/29/a-lesson-is-the-wrong-unit-of-time/. Accessed 30th September 2024

Lemov, D. (2021) *Building a Culture of Error: A TLAC 3.0 Excerpt* (Online). Available at https://teachlikeachampion.org/blog/building-a-culture-of-error-a-tlac-3-0-excerpt/. Accessed 21st February 2024

Mccrea, P. (2024a) *Habit Inertia: Evidence Snacks* (Online). Available at https://snacks.pepsmccrea.com/p/habit-inertia. Accessed 1st August 2024

Mccrea, P. (2024b) *What Exactly Is Responsive Teaching? Twitter Thread* (Online). Available at https://twitter.com/PepsMccrea/status/1744071412472598820. Accessed 29th February 2024

Myatt, M. (2023) *Death by Differentiation* (Online). Available at https://www.marymyatt.com/blog/death-by-differentiation. Accessed 21st February 2024

Quigley, A. (2022) *Closing the Writing Gap*. Abingdon, Oxon: Routledge

Riches, A. (2022) *Modelling and Scaffolding in the Classroom* (Online). Available at https://www.sec-ed.co.uk/content/best-practice/modelling-and-scaffolding-in-the-classroom. Accessed 12th July 2024

Robbins, A. (2021) *Middle Leadership Mastery; A Toolkit for Subject and Pastoral Leaders*. Wales: Crown House Publishing Ltd

Roberts, M. (2022) *The Boy Question*. Abingdon, Oxon: Routledge

Rose, N. (2018) *Avoiding Lethal Mutations* (Online). Available at https://www.ambition.org.uk/blog/avoiding-lethal-mutations/. Accessed 19th February 2024

Sherrington, T. (2015) *Beyond Dependency Learning; Scaffolding, Crutches and Stabilisers* (Online). Available at https://teacherhead.com/2015/02/07/beyond-dependency-learning-scaffolding-crutches-and-stabilisers/. Accessed 21st February 2024

Sherrington, T. (2020) *The Art of Modelling; It's All in the Handover* (Online). Available at https://teacherhead.com/2020/11/28/the-art-of-modelling-its-all-in-the-handover/. Accessed 21st February 2024

Vallance, J. (2024) *Ark Soane History Conference 2024*, 3rd February (Online). Available at https://www.eventbrite.com/e/ark-soane-history-conference-2024-tickets-768466432787

Van Der Stuyf, R. (2002) Scaffolding as a Teaching Strategy. *Adolescent Learning and Development*, Section 0500A, Fall (Online). Available at https://pileidou.files.wordpress.com/2013/11/scaffolding-as-a-teaching-strategy.pdf. Accessed 3rd March 2024

12 Professional development and scaffolding strategies

> A good leader creates the circumstances for teachers and students to flourish through intelligent accountability.
>
> *(Didau, 2018)*

So what if you are a school leader and you want to help teachers in your setting to understand how they can use scaffolding more effectively as part of their teaching armoury? How do we help others to practise using scaffolding, whilst resisting the pitfalls set out in the last chapter? And how do we ensure that disciplinary nuances of scaffolding within subjects are central to PD? There are a number of conditions which will help scaffolding practices to be adopted and used more successfully.

Recently, there have been some excellent publications which help us to understand what good professional development (PD) looks like based on the best research we have. The EEF Guide to Professional Development (2021) set out 14 mechanisms; 'Ensuring that mechanisms are incorporated into professional development makes it more likely that the PD will positively impact pupil outcomes'. They include focusing on managing the cognitive load of teachers, setting and agreeing of goals and modelling and deliberate practice. In his recent book *Exploring Expert Teaching* (2023) Peps Mccrea explains six essential ingredients of effective Professional Development, critical for improving teaching:

'Get it: Helping teachers to develop an understanding of the causal mechanics of teaching and learning.
See it: Helping teachers to develop a bank of strategies around what these mechanics look like in practice.
Try it: Engaging in rehearsal to help teachers contextualise these strategies for their subject(s), student and self.
Keep it: Helping teachers to build fluency in these strategies and embed them in the routines of their work.
Fit it: Tailoring development to the tasks and needs of teachers and, where possible their teams and schools.
Own it: Motivating teachers invest effort in these two processes and follow through with any commitments they make.'

Therefore, in the following recommendations we make for the effective implementation of scaffolding across a subject or school, we will take into account what we know works for effective PD and use this as a foundation.

Create a low stakes culture of continual improvement

Firstly, we know that adaptive teaching and the use of scaffolding is an aspect of teaching which teachers really struggle with. No teacher is going to master the art of effectively scaffolding overnight (even after reading this book, sadly!). And therefore it's important that leaders first create a supportive and safe environment for teachers to engage in deliberate practice (with modelling and feedback), in much the same way as they would for students. Teachers need to feel secure that if modelling goes wrong, or they need to add more scaffolding back in when they realise that they've let the stabilisers off too early, that a leader is not going to chastise them or place them on a support plan. There are many ways leaders can do this: through coaching, modelling of leaders' mistakes, through curriculum conversations or through low stakes lesson drop ins with nudges of improvement.

Expose teachers to one strategy at a time

The overwhelm for a teacher is immense. It's easy to feel as though you will never get better, or that you don't have time to put into practice everything you need to be doing to be an effective teacher. If leaders organise a PD session on scaffolding and go through all of the strategies mentioned in even just one chapter of this book, it's highly unlikely any of your teachers will master any of them. Make a commitment as a school to focus on scaffolding for an extended period of time. Plan out a programme of sessions focusing on different strategies, giving time for practice, feedback and refinement before adding more on to the teacher's already full plates. Think carefully about the order of your sessions so that they are logical and take into account the different levels of expertise you may have in the room.

Just as we would scaffold student learning, we must remember to apply the same principles to teacher learning. It may be that some teachers need more support to embed strategies than others, so it's important to link this to the low stakes drop ins mentioned above so that you can see where this support is needed (and this won't always be teachers earlier in their career!).

Let the content lead

As mentioned in the last chapter, it's important to plan backwards, starting with the content which is required to be learnt first and letting subject teams determine what works best for their subjects in terms of scaffolding approaches. As we have already established, the most effective scaffolding is when it is applied in response to data received, such as through questioning or circulation. Giving each subject and indeed each teacher the autonomy to decide which scaffolding techniques would be most effective in each of their contexts is important to ensure fidelity to the content first.

Within this, develop the expertise of and create capacity for Middle Leaders to truly pinpoint and understand what scaffolding means in their subject. Middle Leaders are the engine drivers of their department. Support must be given to upskill Middle Leaders so that they can realise the scaffolding vision of the school through a disciplinary lens.

Think carefully about quality assurance

Of course leaders want to and should monitor whether the professional development around scaffolding is having an impact in lessons and in books. However, we would advise hesitancy in terms of directly looking for evidence of scaffolding of books. In the days where differentiated worksheets were all the rage, it would be common for leaders to look for 'evidence of differentiation' in books. Not only is this problematic because of the issue of predetermining what content or challenge a student should be exposed to, it wasted hours of teachers' lives worrying more about what to evidence for a book look than what would actually make a difference to student learning. We would suggest that as leaders we shouldn't actually be looking for evidence of scaffolding if and when we do 'book looks'. Instead, book looks are part of a picture the teacher uses to see whether practice shows understanding of the content. However, books which show students are not making good progress through the curriculum (where perhaps answers are incomplete, there are misconceptions, or there is poor structuring of work) may suggest more or better scaffolding is needed. Equally, if students are spoken to during a lesson drop in and don't understand the work, the key terms or even why they are doing the task again it suggests extra scaffolding is needed. Surely if students are able to access the work and show good understanding, the message is that any scaffolding has worked. The point should not be to provide evidence of the scaffolding itself.

Devote time to modelling and rehearsal

The classroom is so cognitively demanding for teachers that it is easy for teachers to fall into habits and for certain aspects of teaching to become automated (Hobbiss et al., 2020). Although, on the one hand this means teachers can build up their skill level over time, it also means that 'if new research comes along showing that a certain teaching technique or move isn't the best way of doing things, this makes it harder to change that in line with what evidence suggests' (Sims, 2021). Therefore, instead of a one-size-fits-all approach to PD where teachers sit in a hall for an hour listening to what they need to do to improve, the evidence suggests investing time in modelling, and rehearsal is more effective in changing these habits and ensuring teachers make long-term changes to their practice.

Consequently, in a school where scaffolding is a key PD focus, leaders might use group rehearsal for specific strategies and give time for teachers to script and practise specific changes to their teaching. For example, a school focusing on the scaffolding of texts for reading might invest time in training and supporting Middle Leaders who then prepare and select models for their different subjects. They might then work with Middle Leaders to guide teachers to choose upcoming texts and work together to see how they could prepare them through the use of guided reading proformas, summaries, images or glossaries. This might be followed by feedback and further time to adjust scaffolds. Leaders might also do some group rehearsal of the questions which teachers could pose to the class to check for understanding and diagnose whether further scaffolding is needed, providing feedback as part of this process. In this way, leaders are ensuring the time and opportunity for modelling and rehearsal is given, and long term embedding of scaffolding strategies is more likely to occur.

Moreover, we must remember that PD must be sequential and sustained over a period of time. Time should be allocated in the subsequent weeks/months for practitioners to continue to carry out deliberate practice of these scaffolds, with drop-ins, feedback and peer support. This is because 'When experienced teachers try to change, they must devote extra mental effort to both execute the new practice *and* suppress any old habits they are trying to replace' (McCrea, 2024).

A school case study: Rachel Ball

In 2022, I started to further explore how we could ensure teachers were using scaffolding effectively. Lesson visits and book looks showed that scaffolding in some subjects was lacking, and in others scaffolding was left in place for far too long, with students given rare opportunities for completely independent practice. I started to consider how I could support teachers in seeing scaffolding as a temporary support and considered thinking of the support in terms of levels or a gradient. Our year-long project was then launched where we took several steps:

- Each subject identified their main teaching activities, whether that was reading a text in History, painting in Art or using coordinates in map work in Geography.

- Next each subject thought carefully about what heavy scaffolding would look like in that strategy and made a list of suggestions. For example, reading a piece of scholarship in History could be scaffolded by providing definitions for words in the text which students might struggle with, or were key to their understanding. Students might be questioned at the end of each paragraph and asked to write a summary or a title to summarise. There could be comprehension questions or prompts down the margin and the teacher would read aloud, perhaps modelling under the visualiser each section in turn. Students could even be guided as to in which paragraph they would find the answer.

- Then each subject thought about what it would look like when some of this scaffolding was removed. Perhaps some of the paragraph titles could be added independently after the first few had been modelled, or students given comprehension questions without the extra guidance. Teams did this one more time, until the scaffolding support left could be described as 'light', for example with only key words given as support in order for students to make independent summaries, or students receiving only very light modelling, perhaps for the first paragraph only, with just verbal prompts given when needed and to those students who needed it.

Heavy	Medium	Light
Essay questions or longer exam question: Sentence starters for every sentence in the paragraphs, allowing students to add their own sentences on top of these. A summary of what should be included in each paragraph. Examples of supporting quotes and evidence which could be used. Students could match up examples to specific paragraphs. A list of key words to be used in each paragraph with definitions. Share detailed success criteria, perhaps as a tick list. A structure strip used to focus each part of the essay. Detailed shared planning for example a 'we write'	A choice of sentence starters to choose from for each paragraph. A title for each paragraph is given. Page numbers where supporting quotes/evidence can be found. A list of key words to be used. Share shortened success criteria. Shared planning used first, for example a table with evidence which should be used. A 'we write' question followed by a similar 'you write'. Annotation of a model answer followed by a 'you write' of a similar answer. Live marking to demonstrate good parts	A sentence starter to begin each paragraph. Number of paragraphs needed. Names of books or websites where quotes/evidence can be found. Supply a dictionary/glossary to look up key terms. Share marks available and get the students to work out what they might get marks for before sharing the structure. Live marking to reinforce good answers.

FIGURE 12.1 An example of how to teach exam questions in History

Professional development and scaffolding strategies 327

The result was a scaffolding handbook for each subject where all of their main teaching activities were split into suggested 'heavy', 'medium' and 'light' approaches. Figure 12.1 show strategies that could be used when teaching exam questions in History.

It's important to note that this was in no way a rigid, fixed approach. No teacher was expected to decide in advance who should have which support and there was certainly no prescribed paperwork which went alongside this such as levels of support on a lesson plan! No teacher ever spoke about scaffolding levels of support with students, and it was expected that the vast majority of these scaffolding strategies were adaptations the teacher could make live in the lesson. No leader had a tick list of scaffolding they expected to see within a lesson drop in, and as already explained, nobody was looking for levels of scaffolding within books.

But the process of trying to define what different levels of scaffolding could look like was immensely powerful. Teachers commented that they had never thought about the different ways that they could provide scaffolding in so much detail before. Others reflected that this had made them consider whether they were providing enough opportunities for students to be independent by beginning to release scaffolding over time as students gained confidence. Another huge benefit was that this conversation and resulting handbook was subject specific, collated by the team themselves, and therefore provided a huge opportunity for subject development and autonomy.

The final stage was for each subject to gather examples of some of this scaffolding so that teachers both present and future could see what this could look like in the classroom. Some of this was collated through book looks and lesson visits. Some were written as verbal models, for example the prompts and cues which could be given to individual students. Video models would also be a brilliant addition here. This process not only led to some fantastic teaching and learning discussions and a great use of subject meeting time, but a handbook of subject-specific examples which teachers could then draw on when planning lessons and in team PD sessions. This was reinforced by our whole school drop in and coaching programme.

Importantly, each subject handbook was very much a living document and could be added to or changed over time depending on teaching techniques being tweaked, or feedback from staff. The main benefit simply was that it made scaffolding a priority, with everyone thinking about the level of support they were offering whole groups or individual students, whilst having the very highest of expectations of all.

In summary, professional development at school, phase, subject and teacher level is crucial, if schools are to get scaffolding right. Leaders must carefully consider their approach, guarding against the common pitfalls written about in Chapter 11. However, the pursuit is worth the payoff. In an educational landscape which is consistently in a state of flux and with the needs of our students broadening year on year, scaffolding is, and shall remain, a central tenet of effective teaching that ensures that all students are able to access the curriculum in meaningful ways.

Chapter 12 Self-Reflection Questions

Take a few minutes to reflect on the questions below and jot down your answers...

1. How could you structure your PD programme or sessions to ensure that scaffolding strategies will 'stick'?

2. What are the benefits to producing something like a subject handbook for scaffolding strategies?

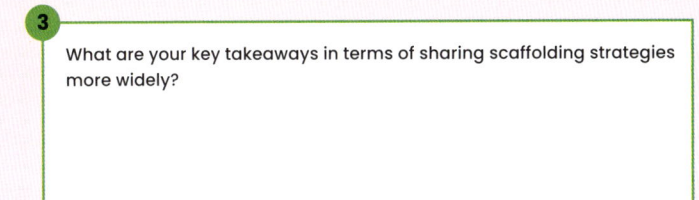

3. What are your key takeaways in terms of sharing scaffolding strategies more widely?

References

Didau, D. (2018) *The Illusion of Leadership* (Online). Available at https://learningspy.co.uk/featured/the-illusion-of-leadership/. Accessed 4th March 2024

EEF (2021) *Effective Professional Development* (Online). Available at https://d2tic4wvo1iusb.cloudfront.net/production/eef-guidance-reports/effective-professional-development/EEF-Effective-Professional-Development-Guidance-Report.pdf?v=1709500006. Accessed 4th March 2024

Hobbiss, M., Sims, S. & Allen, R. (2020) Habit Formation Limits Growth in Teacher Effectiveness: A Review of Converging Evidence from Neuroscience and Social Science. *Review of Education*, 9, 1

McCrea, P. (2023) Developing Expert Teaching. *Pepsmccrea.com* (Online). Available at https://www.ambition.org.uk/blog/extract-developing-expert-teaching-by-peps-mccrea/

McCrea, P. (2024) *Habit Inertia: Evidence Snacks* (Online). Available at https://snacks.pepsmccrea.com/p/habit-inertia. Accessed 1st August 2024

Sims, S. (2021) Quoted by Mahnken, K. (2021) *Force of Habit: New Study Finds That Routines Could Be Blocking Teacher Improvement* (Online). Available at https://www.the74million.org/force-of-habit-new-study-finds-that-routines-could-be-blocking-teacher-improvement/. Accessed 7th March 2024

Index

Note: Numbers in **bold** indicate a table. Numbers in *italics* indicate a figure on the corresponding page

Abedin, M. 170-171
adaptive scaffolding 119, 124, 175
adaptive teaching 13-15, 107; checking for understanding, importance of 21, 88; "I, we, you" process in 54; modelling in 54, 81, 88; scaffolding and 5-22; why it is so difficult to get right 18-20
Afflerbach, P. 99
Alexander, R. 174
Allison, S. 42, 50
analogies, use in explanation of 60-61
appositives 139, 140; adding *139*
Art: KS3 Art Curriculum Map *246*; scaffolding in art (Leadbeater) (case study) 243-245; scaffolding in art (Solly) (case study) 245-250
Art History 245, 247
Atherton, A. 50

backwards fading 46, *46*, 143
Bandura, A. 42

Barnes, D. 175, 183
Barton, C. 31, 34
bell curve 17, 216
Bjork, R. 9
'Bloomers' 10
Boxer, A. 58, 61, 227, 229, 288; *see also* Slow Practical Method
breaking down: of art 245; of calculations in math 267, 270; of music 220, 222; of tasks 148, 247; of texts 87, 92, 100, 103, 107, 110, 163; of types of talk 182
Bruner, J. 16, 254

case studies: dialect and standard English 206-210; mastering independent and fluent writing in KS2 160-166; oracy and student agency 199-206; reading in primary 109-113; scaffolding in art (Leadbeater) 243-245; scaffolding in art (Solly) 245-250; scaffolding in dance 213-218; scaffolding

332 *Index*

early number counting 255-258; scaffolding early writing 258-261; scaffolding in DT 229-233; scaffolding through graphic organizers 66-70; scaffolding KS5 English 277-282; scaffolding KS5 Environmental Science 283-286; scaffolding in music 218-222; scaffolding in music competition 222-226; scaffolding and oracy 199-210; scaffolding religion and worldviews 261-265; scaffolding in PE (Keary) 238-243; scaffolding in PE (Walker) 233-238; scaffolding science practicals 226-229; scaffolding supporting students with maths in KS5 psychology 265-270; scaffolding teaching synopticity in A†Level Geography 270-276; scaffolding writing in KS2 157-160; scaffolding before the writing task in KS1 147-154; using scaffolds in writing at Upper Key Stage 2 (UKS2) 166-169; using writing packs as scaffolds for Year One 154-157
Caviglioli, O. 67, **129**
chronology connection *35*
Clark, J. 28, 177
Coe, R. 9
cognitive apprenticeship 311
cognitive challenge 7
cognitive development 171
cognitive engagement 29
cognitive instruction 131

cognitive load 29, 30, 58, 70, 118; managing 127; reducing 176, 221; of writing process 135, 142, 157
Cognitive Load Theory 28, 44
cognitive overload 124, 126, 157, 218
cognitive science 1, 27, 41
comfort blanket 49
comfort zone 8-9, 33
comparative modelling *48*
concept map 34, 63, 66-67, **130**
content and question format 128
Corbett, P. 167
Counsell, C. 123-124; 'Language of Discourse' 137-141
COVID-19 pandemic 171, 244
CPD 173, 212
culture of error 310

dance: scaffolding in dance (case study) 213-218
DARE mnemonic (Develop your topic sentences, Add supporting details, Reject arguments from the other side, End with a strong conclusion) 136
DEAR (Drop Everything and Read) approach 81, 83-84, 104
desired behaviors 17, 179
Desirable Difficulties 9, 33
DfE 131, 171
DfE Reading Framework 104
Didau, D. 13, 305, 320
differentiated worksheets 323
differentiation 1-2, *6*; adaptive teaching and 5-22; avoiding differentiated and choice homework 293-294; breaking differentiation habits 312, *313*; the

drift into 321-313; what's wrong with 5-8
DIRT activities 295
Donaghy, L. 308
DT 2, 36, 47; chunking of tasks in 231; 'DT teacher' training 78; scaffolding in DT (case study) 229-233

Early Career Framework 13; new 77
early number counting: scaffolding early number counting (case study) 255-258
early writing: scaffolding early writing (case study) 258-261; *see also* writing
Eaton, J. 213
Ebbinghaus' Forgetting Curve 27
EEF *see* Education Endowment Foundation
Education Endowment Foundation (EEF): diagram demonstrating 'a process from transferring responsibility from an adult to a child' 105; on disciplinary literacy 186, 291; *EEF Guide to Professional Development* 320; on effective diagnosis of reading difficulties 86; five a day tool 36; on homework 289, 295; Improving Literacy in KS2 guidance report 99; PEER framework 100; 'Reader's Theatre' 101; recommendations on reciprocal reading 91-2; report 2020 18; report 2021 91; retrieval practices and requirements of 296; review in cognitive science 44; on scaffolding 18; simple view of writing *118*; writing process in five adaptive chunks *119*
English: dialect and standard English (case study) 206-210; scaffolding KS5 English (case study) 277-282
Enser, M. 293-294
Environmental Science: scaffolding KS5 Environmental Science (case study) 283-286
Evidence Based Education 303
exam questions 106-108
explanations: analogies 60-61; chunking 58-60, *60*; pre-teaching of vocabulary 62; storytelling as form of 70-72, 308; scaffolding of 58-72; visual scaffolds as 63, *64*; *see also* FAME approach; graphic organizers

FAME approach (Fading, Alternating, Mistakes, Explanation) 44-45
Fisher, D. 16, 43, 49
flight paths 1, 13; removing target grades and 12-13
Foster, P. 212, 310
Frayer models 62, 186-187
Frey, N. 16, 43, 49

Gaunt, A. 174, 180, 186-190; Talk Tokens or Thumbs in 192-193
Geography 270-271; effective visual scaffold for students in *64*; exploratory talk in 189; scaffolding teaching synopticity in A†Level Geography (case study) 270-276

Giovanelli, M. 142
Gjerdingen, R. 223
Goldenberg, G. 91
Goodwin, D. 67
Govier, J. 191
grammar expectations 165
Grant, A. 11
graphic organizers 62-3, 65; scaffolding through graphic organizers (case study) 66-70
GSCE 61, 250, 290, 295, 306; English Literature 277; Geography 270-271; History 124, 126, 202; Music 222-223; PE 201
Gudmundsdatter Magnusson, C. 79
guided reading 89, 90

habits: bad 237; differentiation 312, 313; independent learning 291; study 290; teachers' 323-324
habits of discussion 192
Harford, Sean 13
History 52; GSCE 124, 126, 202; homework in 292; KS4 222; 'Meanwhile, Elsewhere' 295; modelling in 41, 47, 52; reading in 81; storytelling in 71-72; structure strip in 306; writing in 123-124, 137, 273, 283; Year 7 (seven) 79; Year 9 (nine) 120
Hochman, J. C. 128, 131; fragments 140; Kernel sentences 134; Revise and Edit 141; *Writing Revolution* 134
Hodgkinson, S. 179
homework: barriers to 299-300; graph showing the benefits of scaffolded homework 294; graph showing whether students are receiving too much 289; linking to content of 296-297; mistakes to avoid 292-295; purpose and feedback 295-296; routinisation of 297-299; scaffolding of 288-299
Hoskins, Bob 170, 194
Hough, J. 123, **129**
Howe, C. 170-171

independent silent reading 103-106
Inner Drive 21, 311
interthinking 171, 185, 201
I, We, You approach 51-54; diagram of 53; example of 53; Novice vs. Expert 52

Kaboom! 219-220, 252n1
Kernel sentences 134, 182
King, Martin Luther, Jr. 194
Kirschner, P. A. 19, 63
Knight, R. 170, 185
Kod·ly method 218, 252n1
Kod·ly, Z. 218
Koskinen, P. 91
KS1/KS5: scaffolding at 255-285; scaffolding early number counting 255-258; scaffolding early writing 258-261; scaffolding KS5 English (case study) 277-282; scaffolding KS5 Environmental Science 283-286; scaffolding religion and worldviews (case study) 261-265; scaffolding supporting students with maths in KS5 psychology (case study) 265-270; scaffolding teaching

Index   335

synopticity in A†Level Geography 270-276

Land, R. 255
Lemov, D. 81, 91, 311; on habits of discussion 192; SLANT and STAR 177
Littleton, K. 185; see also interthinking
Lovell, O. 58, 68

Mansworth, M. 8-9
Mary Queen of Scots 48, 65; guided reading of story of 89, 90
McCrea, P. 80. 82, 178, 191, 312, 314, 320
memory model 28
Mercer, N. 179, 185; see also interthinking
metacognitive modelling 213, 278
metacognitive oracy 43, 45, 81, 86-88, 247; innovation in writing and use of 163; reciprocal reading and 91; seeing the big picture using modelling and 131-133
metacognitive skills 180, 194, 232
metacognitive thinking 18, 159, 168
Meyer, J. 255
Middle Leaders 123, 173, 307, 322-324
mind map 66-69, 283-285
modelled reading, teacher-led 87, 101
modelling: comparative 47, 48; I-We-You 51-54; live 47-50; seeing the big picture using metacognition and 131-133; scaffolding through 41-54; student models 51; visualisers 43-44, **133**, 222; worked examples 44-47

Mulholland, M. 8
music: scaffolding in music (case study) 218-222
music competition: scaffolding in music competition (case study) 222-226
Myatt, M. 5, 71, 82, 101

NAEYC 254
Needham, T. 54, 143
Newmark, B. 12
Novice vs. Expert in I, We, You Do 52
novice vs expert teacher 20

Ofsted 13; Religious Education research report 262
Olinghouse, N. G. 131
one-size-fits all approach 305, 306-307, 324; problems of 307
oracy: dialect and standard English (case study) 206-210; scaffolding and 170-194; scaffolding and oracy (case study) 199-210; oracy and student agency (case study) 199-206; see also talk

paired reading 100-103
PD see Professional Development
PE see Physical Education
Pearson Edexcel 126
Physical Education (PE): scaffolding in PE (Keary) (case study) 238-243; scaffolding in PE (Walker) (case study) 233-238
practical subjects: scaffolding and 212-250; scaffolding in art (Leadbeater) (case study) 243-245; scaffolding in art (Solly) (case study) 245-250;

scaffolding in dance (case study) 213-218; scaffolding in DT 229-233; scaffolding in music (case study) 218-222; scaffolding in music competition (case study) 222-226; scaffolding in PE (Keary) (case study) 238-243; scaffolding in PE (Walker) (case study) 233-238; scaffolding science practicals (case study) 226-229
Principles not Practices 305
Pinkett, M. 11
Pritchard, B. 44-45
Professional Development (PD) 27, 78-81, 112, 307, 320-322; sustaining 324; team sessions in 328
psychology: scaffolding supporting students with maths in KS5 psychology (case study) 265-270
Pygmalion effect

Quigley, A. 54, 62

Raichura, P. 32-33
Rasinski, T. 106
'Reader's Theatre' 101
reading: detailed data for 85-86; exam questions 106-108; getting ready for 83-85; know-what to know-how for teachers of 77-81; literacy and 76-77; literacy as bedrock of curriculum for 81-83; paired and paired peer 101-102; in primary (case study) 109-112; scaffolding and 76-112; teacher-led modelled reading 86-91; template and concept in **94-97**; whole class/round robin 98-99; *see also* guided reading; reciprocal reading; repeated reading; silent reading
reading in primary (case study) 109-112
reciprocal comprehension strategies 93
reciprocal reading 88, 91-4, 100-1, 103, 105, 199; recommendations on 91-2; strategies 93
religion and worldviews: scaffolding religion and worldviews (case study) 261-265; suitcases of religious tools and stories 263-264, 265
repeated modelling 282
repeated reading 97, 99-103, 106; scaffolding 99-101
retrieval 124-125; exploratory or dialogic 183-184; talk process area 1 (one) 189
retrieval approaches 63
retrieval exercises 232
retrieval practices 30-31, 62, 148, 296; scaffolding of 31-36
retrieval practices and verbal prompts: scaffolding of 27-36, 68; retrieval questions 32; use of verbal prompts 36
reverse essay planning *282*
Robbins, A. 305
Roberts, M. 7, 11, 313
Rose, N. 303, 307
Rosenshine, B. 18, 59, 303, 311
Rosenshine's Principles of Instruction 27, 42, 303

Rosenthal effect 10
routinised homework 297-299
RUSS the question (Read, Underline, Summarize, Solve) 107, *108*, 126

Santangelo, T. 131
Say it Again but Say it Better 188
scaffolding: heavy, medium, and light **94-97**; language of 313; overview of pitfalls of *315*; potential pitfalls of strategies of 303-315; scaffolding in stages *311*; as term 15; what it is 15-18; why it is so difficult to get right 18-20; why it is important 15; *see also* case studies; [subject area]; Wood, D.
Scarborough, H. 109
Scheherazade 70
science practicals: chunked explanation of *60*; scaffolding science practicals (case study) 226-229
Sealy, C. 30
SEEC model (Select, Explain, Explore, Consolidate) 62
SEND 30, 34, 78
Shanahan, T. 94, 98, 102-106
Sherrington, T. 81, 217, 310; relay baton handover analogy 309-310, *311*; on scaffolding through modeling 41, 47, 50, 52-53; on Teach to the Top 16-17
Shires, L. 19
silence 33, 118
silent reading 84, 102; independent 103-106
Simple Model of the Mind 27

simple view of writing *118*
single paragraph outlines (SPO) 135-135
SLANT (Sit up, Listen, Ask and Answer, Nod, Track the Speaker) 177
Slow Practical Method 227, 229
SPO *see* single paragraph outlines
spoken language development, types of 174, *174*; in the classroom 174-175; *see also* talk
STAR (Sit up, Track the Speaker, Ask Questions, Respect Those Around You) 177
stories: benefit of 70; 'stickiness' of 71
storytelling 70-72, 308
Stott, A. 180, 186-190; Talk Tokens or Thumbs in 192-193
subject autonomy 306-307, 327
subject teams 322
Such, C. 105
subtitles 87-88, 91,
suitcases of religious tools and stories 263-264, 265
Sumeracki, M. 27, 34
'summary bullseye' 188
Sweller's Cognitive Load Theory 27, 28-29

talk: aide-memoires for 184; dialogic 167, 175, 181, 183, 185; different types of 173-175; classroom culture of and rules for 171, 176-194; cognitive development and 171; contracts for 177-179; effective 175; exploratory 175, 176, 183, 185; Frayer models 186-187; habits of

discussion in 192; metacognitive 43; mini-whiteboards for 185; mutual scaffolding for 185-186; paired 185; partner 151; peer 171; presentational 175, 181, 183, 184; purposeful 178; retrieval of 183-184, 189; scaffolded teacher talk 159; scaffolding of 172-173; scaffolding the content of what is being discussed 182-183; scaffolding the process of 189-190; scaffolding students' ability to understand the type of 179-182; scaffolding the vocabulary being used 186; scaffolding voice 193; scaffolds to create an environment for 175-177; 'summary bullseye' 188; talk-task 180-181; three stages of children understanding the process and types of 180-181; as tool for learning and literacy 170; 'turn and talk' 127, 128; Voice 21 talk tactics 192-193; word banks 187-188
talk-task 180-181
talk tokens 192-193
Talk for Writing (talk4writing.com) 120, 161, 167
target grades 6; removing flight paths and 12-13
Tarrant, C. 223-224
TAs *see* Teaching Assistants
Taylor, P. 142
teacher expectations and student outcomes 10, 12
TeacherTapp 288
'Teach to the Top' 8-11
Teaching Assistants (TAs): relying on 313-314

Tharby, A. 42, 50
Thornton, G. 135
'turn and talk' 127, 128

visualisers 43-44, **133**, 222
voice: scaffolding 193
Voice 21 talk tactics 192-193
Vygotsky, L. 16

Webb, J. 122, 142
Wexler, N. 128, 131; fragments 140; Kernel sentences 134; Revise and Edit 141; *Writing Revolution* 134
Wiliam, D. 5, 303
Wilkinson, S. 191
Willard 174
William, D. 177, 190, 288
Willingham, D. 70
Wood, D. 15, 151, 254
word banks 187-188
word recognition 109
word triplets 140
worked examples 44-47
writing: barriers presented by 117-121, 125; DARE mnemonic 136; drafting 131-133; EEF on 122; EEF simple view of writing *118*; EEF writing process in five adaptive chunks *119*; elevating written responses 137-141; independent and fluent writing in KS2 (case study) 160-166; planning 127-130; primary case studies 147-169; putting pen to paper 133-135; review and revision 141-143; scaffolding and 117-143; scaffolding writing in KS2 (case

study) 157–160; scaffolding of writing at primary 121; scaffolding of writing at secondary 122–123; simple view of *118*; single paragraph outlines (SPO) 135–135; using scaffolds in writing at Upper Key Stage 2 (UKS2) (case study) 166–169; *see also* case studies; writing frames

writing frames 136–137, *138*

writing packs: using writing packs as scaffolds for Year One (case study) 154–157

writing process *119*

writing task: scaffolding before the writing task in KS1 147–154

Yousafzai, Malala 194

Zone of Proximal Development 16

Zutell, J. 106

Did you love reading about the research on Scaffolding?

Want to get amazing online training for your staff that can take their understanding even further?

Then **The Teacher CPD Academy.** is for you!

Simply scan this QR code

Or head over to
teacherCPDacademy.com

Or email
info@innerdrive.co.uk

to request a free trial.

We **illuminate research** with **inspiring** and **interactive** modules, interviews and keynote talks.

So, do not hesitate. A **brilliant professional development platform** for all your colleagues is only a click away!